The Great Depression and the Americas

Access to History
for the IB Diploma

The Great Depression and the Americas

Peter Clements

HODDER
EDUCATION
AN HACHETTE UK COMPANY

The material in this title has been developed independently of the International Baccalaureate®, which in no way endorses it.

The Publishers would like to thank the following for permission to reproduce copyright material:

Photo credits: p18 Image courtesy of the Advertising Archives; **p22** Bettmann/CORBIS; **p37** Popperfoto/Getty Images; **p51** Bettmann/CORBIS; **p54** Bettmann/CORBIS; **p64** Bettmann/CORBIS; **p78** The Granger Collection/TopFoto; **p88** Tennessee Valley Authority; **p106** Bettmann/CORBIS; **p115** Corbis; **p117** Bettmann/CORBIS; **p129** Library of Congress, Prints & Photographs Division, FSA/OWI Collection, LC-USF33-002972-M3; **p136** Library of Congress, Prints & Photographs Division, FSA/OWI Collection, LC-DIG-ppmsca-23845; **p158** Canada. Dept. of National Defence/Library and Archives Canada/C-031058; **p172** The Granger Collection/TopFoto; **p194** Mary Evans Picture Library; **p219** Alinari/TopFoto.

The publishers would also like to thank the following for permission to reproduce material in this book: p135 'Brother, Can You Spare a Dime?' by E.Y. 'Yip' Harburg and Jay Gorney. Published by Glocca Morra Music (ASCAP) and Gorney Music (ASCAP). Administered by Next Decade Entertainment, Inc. All Rights Reserved. Used by Permission.

Acknowledgements: p23 Harper & Row for an extract from *Only Yesterday* by Frederick Lewis Allen, 1931; **p86** Penguin for an extract from *Hard Times: An Oral History of the Great Depression* by Studs Terkel, 1970; **p154** Harbour Publishing for an extract from *The Chuck Davis History of Metropolitan Vancouver* by Chuck Davis, 2011; **p169** CBC/Radio-Canada (www.cbc.ca/history) for an extract from a written account of life in the camps from Ron Liversedge; **p184** Cambridge University Press for an extract from *The Cambridge History of Latin America* by L. Bethell (editor), 1986; **p206** John Kraniauskas for the translated lyrics to *Cambalache* (Junkshop), written in 1935 by Enrique Santos Discépolo.

Every effort has been made to trace all copyright holders, but if any have been inadvertently overlooked the Publishers will be pleased to make the necessary arrangements at the first opportunity.

Although every effort has been made to ensure that website addresses are correct at time of going to press, Hodder Education cannot be held responsible for the content of any website mentioned in this book. It is sometimes possible to find a relocated web page by typing in the address of the home page for a website in the URL window of your browser.

Hachette UK's policy is to use papers that are natural, renewable and recyclable products and made from wood grown in sustainable forests. The logging and manufacturing processes are expected to conform to the environmental regulations of the country of origin.

Orders: please contact Bookpoint Ltd, 130 Milton Park, Abingdon, Oxon OX14 4SB. Telephone: (44) 01235 827827. Fax: (44) 01235 400401. Lines are open 9.00–5.00, Monday to Saturday, with a 24-hour message answering service. Visit our website at www.hoddereducation.com

© Peter Clements 2012

First published in 2012 by
Hodder Education,
An Hachette UK Company
Carmelite House, 50 Victoria Embankment
London EC4Y 0DZ

Reprinted with revisions 2015.

Impression number   5
Year   2017

Cover photo: © ACA Galleries, New York and the Estate of William Gropper/Photo © 2004. Smithsonian American Art Museum/Art Resource/Scala, Florence
Illustrations by Gray Publishing
Typeset in 10/13pt Palatino and produced by Gray Publishing, Tunbridge Wells
Printed in Dubai

A catalogue record for this title is available from the British Library

ISBN: 978 1444 156539

Contents

Dedication

Keith Randell (1943–2002)

The original *Access to History* series was conceived and developed by Keith, who created a series to 'cater for students as they are, not as we might wish them to be'. He leaves a living legacy of a series that for over 20 years has provided a trusted, stimulating and well-loved accompaniment to post-16 study. Our aim with these new editions for the IB is to continue to offer students the best possible support for their studies.

Introduction

This book has been written to support your study of HL option 2: History of the Americas, Topic 12: The Great Depression and the Americas, mid 1920s–39 of the IB History Diploma.

This introduction gives you an overview of:

⭐ the content you will study for The Great Depression and the Americas

⭐ how you will be assessed for Paper 3

⭐ the different features of this book and how these will aid your learning.

 # What you will study

In late October 1929, the New York Stock Exchange crashed. Thousands of people lost all the savings that they had invested in stocks and shares. Thousands of businesses collapsed. There are stories of businessmen throwing themselves in despair from the high ledges of the skyscrapers in which they worked. The collapse shocked many people because they believed the US economy was doing very well at the time. It was the era of the 'Roaring Twenties', a period of unparalleled prosperity in American history. It was the age of jazz, movies, motor cars and fast living. Now a terrible economic depression had set in, with millions out of work, optimism gone, hope forlorn.

In 1932, Americans voted Franklin Delano Roosevelt to be their president. He offered new hope with a 'New Deal'. For the first time, the government would make itself responsible for people's welfare; and it would create jobs, and offer old-age pensions and social security. To many, Roosevelt was a saviour; others saw him as a dictator who increased the role of government to an unacceptable level.

However, the Great Depression is not just the story of the USA. It ushered in a world-wide collapse, not least in the other countries of the American continent. In Canada, for example, gross national product (GNP) fell by 40 per cent and by 1933 as much as 27 per cent of the workforce was unemployed. In the countries of Latin America, which relied heavily on the USA and Western Europe for investment and trade, exports fell dramatically – by over 70 per cent in Bolivia and Peru, 65 per cent in Argentina and 60 per cent in Brazil. Prices collapsed. Many countries saw more authoritarian governments, some modelled on the Fascist dictatorships of Europe.

This book covers the history of the American continents in the 15-year period between the lead-up to the Great Depression in 1929 and the outbreak of war in Europe 10 years later, when the effects of the economic collapse were largely dissipated. It will:

- begin by examining the decade of the 1920s in the USA to consider how healthy its economy and political system was (Chapter 1)
- discuss the collapse of the US stock market and the part this and other factors played in causing the Depression (Chapter 2)
- explore life during the Depression and the efforts made to restore prosperity in the USA and elsewhere (Chapter 3)
- examine the New Deal in depth, what it was and what changes it brought about (Chapter 4)
- consider the causes and effects of the Depression and how effectively they were dealt with in Canada (Chapter 5)
- consider the causes and effects of the Depression and how effectively they were dealt with in the countries of Latin America, focusing on Argentina and Brazil (Chapter 6).

 # How you will be assessed

The IB History Diploma can be studied either to Standard or Higher Level. It has three papers in total: Papers 1 and 2 for Standard Level and a further Paper 3 for Higher Level. It also has an internal assessment which all students must do.

- For Paper 1 you need to answer four source-based questions on a prescribed subject. This counts for 20 per cent of your overall marks.
- For Paper 2 you need to answer two essay questions each from a different topic. This counts for 25 per cent of your overall marks.
- For Paper 3 you need to answer three essay questions from two or three sections. This counts for 35 per cent of your overall marks.

For the Internal Assessment you need to carry out a historical investigation. This counts for 20 per cent of your overall marks.

HL option 2: History of the Americas is assessed through Paper 3. You must study three sections out of a choice of 18, one of which could be The Great Depression and the Americas, mid 1920s–1939. These sections are assessed through Paper 3 of the IB History Diploma which has 36 essay questions – two for each of the 18 sections. In other words, there will be two specific questions that you can answer based on The Great Depression.

Examination questions

For Paper 3 you need to answer three of the 36 questions. You could either answer two from one of the sections you have studied and one from another section, or answer one from each of the three sections you have studied. So, assuming The Great Depression and the Americas is one of the sections you have studied, you may choose to answer one or two questions on it.

The questions are divided up by section and are usually arranged chronologically. In the case of the questions on The Great Depression, you should expect numbers 23 and 24 to be on this particular section. When the exam begins, you will have five minutes in which to read the questions. You are not allowed to use a pen or highlighter during the reading period.

Remember you are to write on the history of the Americas. If a question such as, 'Discuss the impact of the Great Depression on the society of one country of the region' is asked, do *not* write about Germany. You will receive no credit for this answer.

Command terms

When choosing the three questions, keep in mind that you must answer the question asked, not one you might have hoped for. A key to success is understanding the demands of the question. IB History Diploma questions use key terms and phrases known as command terms. Some common command terms are listed in the table below, with a brief definition of each. See the appendix of the IB History Guide for more detail. Examples of questions using some of the more common command terms and specific strategies to answer them are included at the end of Chapters 2–6.

Command term	Description	Where exemplified in this book
Compare and contrast	Discuss both similarities and differences of two events, people, and so on	Page 140
Discuss	Similar to 'examine.' Be sure to support your arguments with appropriate evidence. This would be a good opportunity to discuss different historical interpretations.	Page 228
Evaluate	Make a judgement while looking at two or more sides of an issue.	Page 178
Examine	Make careful and critical observations about a specific issue.	Page 73
To what extent	Discuss the various merits of a given argument or opinion	Page 44

Answering the questions

You have two-and-a-half hours to answer the three questions or 50 minutes each. Try to budget your time wisely. In other words, do not spend 75 minutes on one answer. Before you begin each essay, take five to seven minutes and compose an outline of the major points you will raise in your essay. You can check these off as you write the essay itself. This is not a waste of time and will bring organization and coherency to what you write.

Well-organized essays that include an introduction, several well-supported arguments and a concluding statement are much more likely to score highly than essays that jump from point to point without structure.

The three essays you write for Paper 3 will be read by a trained examiner. The examiner will read your essays and check what you write against the IB mark scheme. This mark scheme offers guidance to the examiner but is not comprehensive. You may well write an essay that includes analysis and evidence not included in the mark scheme and that is fine. It is also worth remembering that the examiner who will mark your essay is looking to reward well-defended and argued positions, not to deduct for misinformation.

Each of your essays will be marked on a 0–15 scale, for a total of 45 points. The total score will be weighted as 35 per cent of your final IB History. Do bear in mind that you are not expected to score 45/45 to earn a 7: 27–30/60 will equal a 7. Another way of putting this is that if you write three essays that each score 10, you will receive a 7.

Writing essays

In order to attain the highest mark band (13–15), your essays should:

- be clearly focused
- address all implications of the question
- demonstrate extensive and accurate historical knowledge which supports your thesis
- demonstrate knowledge of historical processes such as continuity and change
- integrate your analysis
- be well structured
- have well-developed synthesis
- evaluate different historical perspectives

Your essay should include an introduction in which you set out your main points. Do not waste time copying the question, but define the key terms stated in the question. Best essays probe the demands of the question. In other words, there are often different ways of interpreting the question.

Next, you should write an in-depth analysis of your main points in several paragraphs. Here you will provide evidence that supports your argument. Each paragraph should focus on one of your main points and relate directly to the question. More sophisticated responses include counter-arguments.

Finally, you should end with a concluding statement.

In the roughly 45 minutes you spend on one essay, you should be able to write 3–6 pages. While there is no set minimum, you do need explore the issues and provide sufficient evidence to support what you write.

At the end of Chapters 2–6, you will find IB-style questions with guidance on how best to answer them. Each question focuses on a different command term. It goes without saying that the more practice you have writing essays, the better your results will be.

The appearance of the examination paper

Cover

The cover of the examination paper states the date of the examination and the length of time you have to complete it: 2 hours 30 minutes. Instructions are limited and simply state that you should not open it until told to do so and that three questions must be answered.

Questions

You will have five minutes in which to read through the questions. It is very important to choose the three questions you can answer most fully. It is quite possible that two of the three questions may be on The Great Depression, especially after mastering the material in this book. That is certainly permissible. After the five minutes' reading time is over, you can take out your pen and mark up the exam booklet:

- Circle the three you have decided to answer.
- Identify the command terms and important points. For example, if a question asked, 'To what extent did Roosevelt's New Deal policies end the Great Depression?', underline To what extent and New Deal policies. This will help you to focus on the demands of the question.

For each essay take five to seven minutes to write an outline and approximately 43–45 minutes to write the essay.

 # About this book

Coverage of the course content

This book addresses the key areas listed in the IB History Guide for HL option 2: History of the Americas: The Great Depression and the Americas, mid 1920s–39. Chapters start with an introduction outlining key questions they address. They are then divided into a series of sections and topics covering the course content.

Throughout the chapters you will find the following features to aid your study of the course content.

Key and leading questions

Each section heading in the chapter has a related key question which gives a focus to your reading and understanding of the section. These are also listed in the chapter introduction. You should be able answer the questions after completing the relevant section.

Topics within the sections have leading questions which are designed to help you focus on the key points within a topic and give you more practice in answering questions.

Key terms

Key terms are the important terms you need to know to gain an understanding of the period. These are emboldened in the text the first time they appear in the book and are defined in the margin. They also appear in the glossary at the end of the book.

Sources

Throughout the book are several written and visual sources. Historical sources are important components in understanding more fully why specific decisions were taken or on what contemporary writers and politicians based their actions. The sources are accompanied by questions to help you dig deeper into the history of the Great Depression.

Key debates

Historians often disagree on historical events and this historical debate is referred to as historiography. Knowledge of historiography is helpful in reaching the upper mark bands when you take your IB History examinations. You should not merely drop the names of historians in your essay. You need to understand the different points of view for a given historiographical debate. These you can bring up in your essay. There are a number of debates throughout the book to develop your understanding of historiography.

Theory of Knowledge (TOK) questions

Understanding that different historians see history differently is an important element in understanding the connection between the IB History Diploma and Theory of Knowledge. Alongside some of the debates is a Theory of Knowledge style question which makes that link.

Summary diagrams

At the end of each section is a summary diagram which gives a visual summary of the content of the section. It is intended as an aid for revision.

Chapter summary

At the end of each chapter is a short summary of the content of that chapter. This is intended to help you revise and consolidate your knowledge and understanding of the content.

Skills development

At the end of Chapters 2–6 are:

- examination guidance on how to answer questions, accompanied by advice on what supporting evidence you might use, and sometimes sample answers designed to help you focus on specific details
- examination practice in the form of Paper 3 style questions.

Timeline

This gives a timeline of the major events covered in the book which is helpful for quick reference or as a revision tool.

Glossary

All key terms in the book are defined in the glossary.

Further reading

This contains a list of books and websites which may help you with further independent research and presentations. It may also be helpful when further information is required for internal assessments and extended essays in history. You may wish to share the contents of this area with your school or local librarian.

Internal assessment

All IB History diploma students are required to write a historical investigation that is internally assessed. The investigation is an opportunity for you to dig more deeply into a subject that interests you. This gives you a list of possible areas for research.

CHAPTER 1

The USA in the 1920s: prosperity?

In popular mythology, the 1920s in the USA saw a period of unparalleled economic prosperity that ended suddenly in October 1929 with the collapse of the New York Stock Exchange. This picture is far too simple. There certainly was a boom period and the New York Stock Exchange did indeed collapse. However, these two events are not necessarily directly connected; the relationship between them is complex. This chapter examines the USA during the 1920s. You need to consider the following questions throughout this chapter:

✪ How prosperous was the USA in the 1920s?
✪ How far did economic factors in the 1920s contribute to prosperity?

 ## The extent of prosperity

▶ *Key question: How prosperous was the USA in the 1920s?*

In the 1920s there was a real feeling of prosperity and optimism among many groups in the USA. It had emerged from the First World War as the most prosperous country on earth. Many believed that the USA would set an example to the world with its emphasis on technological developments, economic efficiency and minimal government interference in business.

The figures for prosperity appear to speak for themselves.

- Following a brief post-war **recession** in 1920 and 1921, average unemployment never rose above 3.7 per cent in the years 1922–9.
- Inflation never rose higher than one per cent.
- Employees were working fewer hours: an average of 44 per week in 1929 compared with 47 in 1920.
- Employees were paid more. The **real wages** of industrial workers rose by 14 per cent between 1914 and 1929, and on average they were two or three times higher than those in Europe.
- There was huge economic growth. Production of industrial goods rose by 50 per cent between 1922 and 1929. **Gross national product (GNP)** stood at $73 billion in 1920 and $104 billion in 1929. Consumption of electricity doubled, and in 1929 alone $852 million worth of radios were sold.

 **KEY TERM**

Recession Downturn in the economy.

Real wages The value of wages in terms of how much they will actually buy.

Gross national product (GNP) The total value of goods and services produced in a country.

Many Americans had more time for leisure and more money to spend on it. Electrical labour-saving devices, such as vacuum cleaners and washing machines, were introduced and became affordable by more and more people. Motor cars eased travel both to and from work and for leisure pursuits. It was the golden age of cinema: by 1929, 80 million tickets were sold weekly for the movies. Sport attracted vast crowds of paying spectators. When Gene Tunney defended his heavyweight boxing title against Jack Dempsey in September 1927, the attendance was 107,943 and receipts were a record $2,658,660.

Problems with evidence

Caution is needed when using figures, such as those quoted above, and the specific examples that support them. They might give us an overall picture, but they cannot tell us about individual circumstances. For example, the unemployment figure of 3.7 per cent does not tell us whether it applied to all sectors of the economy or whether some industries suffered high or seasonal unemployment. Were many employees just part-time? What could they buy with their wages? Was the overall prosperity spread throughout the nation or was it principally located in specific parts of the country? Did it apply to all ethnic groups? How did women fare? The statistics above answer none of these questions.

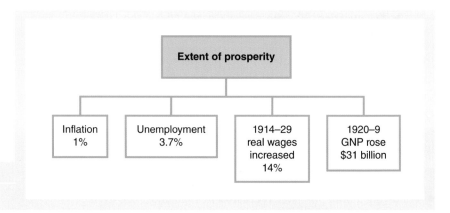

The extent of prosperity

② Reasons for prosperity

▶ *Key question: How far did economic factors in the 1920s contribute to prosperity?*

The prosperity of the 1920s was based on several factors such as:

- favourable government policies that included high **tariffs**, tax reductions and a benevolent foreign policy
- technological advances

- new business methods
- easy credit
- advantageous foreign markets.

In this section these factors will be considered in turn.

Government policies

Republican presidents of the 1920s believed in as little government involvement as possible in the running of the economy. According to President Calvin Coolidge (1923–8), 'The chief business of the American people is business.' It was the policy of his government to let business operate, as far as possible, free of regulation. Both he and his Treasury Secretary, Andrew Mellon, believed firmly in the **free market**. Mellon, a Pittsburgh banker and industrialist, was one of the richest men in the USA. He believed that wealth filtered down naturally to all classes in society and that therefore the best way to ensure increased living standards for all was to allow the rich to continue to make money to invest in industrial development.

There appeared to be much sense to this argument. Industrial expansion meant more job opportunities, which in turn meant more employment, more wage earners, more consumption, more industrial expansion and so on. During the 1920s this policy seemed to work and Mellon had few contemporary critics.

The basic government policy was *laissez-faire*. However, the picture was not quite as simple as that, and the government did intervene to support business with benevolent policies in four main ways.

High tariffs
The Fordney–McCumber Act, passed in 1922, raised tariffs to cover the difference between domestic and foreign production costs. In almost every case it became cheaper for American consumers to buy goods produced within the USA than from abroad. The tariff level made foreign goods more expensive than goods produced in the USA, even when they could be produced in their home countries more cheaply. In effect, this meant that for some products import duties were so high that domestic producers were given an almost guaranteed market.

Throughout the 1920s the general level of tariffs was upwards. The level of foreign trade was obviously reduced by this, while domestic demand for goods remained high. However, as we shall see in a later section (pages 19–20), the power and influence of USA businesses meant they still exported goods abroad while importing less. American industry stood to make huge profits from the high-tariff policy. It also meant of course that Americans bought comparatively few foreign goods. The USA's main trading partners responded to protectionist measures by raising their own tariffs.

← **How far did the governments of the 1920s intervene in the economy?**

 **KEY TERM**

Free market A system that allows the economy to run itself with minimal government interference.

Laissez-faire An approach where the government deliberately avoids getting involved in economic planning, thus allowing the free market to operate.

Tax reductions

The government reduced federal taxes significantly in 1924, 1926 and 1928. These reductions mainly benefited the wealthy. During his eight years in office, Mellon handed out tax reductions totalling $3.5 billion to large-scale industrialists and corporations. Despite this, Coolidge's government actually operated on a surplus; in 1925, this was $677 million and in 1927, $607 million. The avowed aim of the government was to reduce the **national debt**, and it seemed on course to do so. However, federal tax cuts meant little to people who were too poor to pay taxes in the first place.

Fewer regulations

Economies in government meant fewer regulations and fewer personnel to enforce them. The **Federal Trade Commission**, for example, was increasingly unable and unwilling to operate effectively. This trend meant that businesses were often left unhindered to carry on their affairs as they saw fit. Laws concerning sharp business practice, such as **price fixing**, were often ignored. Where the government did prosecute, the offenders usually won on appeal.

This lack of regulation could be an important contributor to a company's profits. Many people welcomed less government. However, it should also be remembered that there was, for example, no organization with the authority to stop child labour in the textile mills of the southern states, where, in the 1920s, a 56-hour week was common and wages rarely rose to more than 18 cents an hour.

Foreign policies

President Coolidge avoided intervention in foreign affairs wherever possible. This was in part due to budget cutting and a recognition that Americans did not want to see their troops getting caught up in foreign disputes. Outstanding disputes with Mexico over the rights of American businesses to own land there, for example, were solved by diplomacy. This policy of conciliation helped American investment abroad by removing any ill feeling towards the USA. However, there were exceptions to this; for example Coolidge continued the American occupation of Nicaragua and Haiti by US Marines.

→ # Technological advances

During this period, technological advances in industrial production made possible huge increases both in the quantity and in the variety of products on sale. The motor vehicle industry and electrical consumer goods are particularly striking examples of this.

The motor vehicle industry

The motor vehicle industry grew dramatically in the 1920s. By the end of the decade there were 23 million cars on the road and the industry was the biggest in the USA. It was the largest market for commodities, such as steel

KEY TERM

National debt The amount of money owed by the government.

Federal Trade Commission Body charged to ensure businesses were operating fairly.

Price fixing Where companies agree to fix prices between them, thereby preventing fair competition.

How far did developments in technology enable industrial expansion?

and rubber, and cars were one of the most desirable products among consumers. Asked about workers' aspirations, one official said that 65 per cent are working to pay for cars.

Henry Ford revolutionized the motor vehicle industry. He had begun to use methods of **mass production** long before the 1920s and his famous Model T car had first appeared in 1908. Previously, cars had been only for the wealthy, but Ford wanted ordinary Americans to be able to afford one.

Henry Ford and mass production
When Henry Ford introduced his moving line assembly in 1914, the cost of the Model T came down from $950 to $500. By 1920 Ford was producing 1,250,000 cars per year, or one every 60 seconds. By 1925, when the price had fallen to $290, the Ford factory could produce one every 10 seconds. Petrol, meanwhile, cost between 20 and 25 cents a gallon at a time when average wages in manufacturing industries were in the region of 50 cents an hour.

By this time, Ford was facing increasing competition from General Motors and Chrysler. These 'Big Three' firms dominated the American motor industry and it was very difficult for independent companies to survive unless they produced specialist vehicles for the wealthy. In 1930, 26.5 million cars were on American roads.

Despite the demand, the supply always exceeded it, and in this industry as in many others, it was increasingly obvious that demand had to be actively encouraged. Henry Ford was slow to learn this lesson. His Model T was renowned for durability and trustworthiness. However, there was no variety: only black ones were ever produced. The car came without frills. It was certainly adaptable; farmers could even attach a plough to it. However, his rivals, in their models, emphasized variety, comfort and style.

When, in 1927, Ford noticeably began to lose his share of the market, he closed down his factory for five months, laying off 60,000 workers. During this layoff, the factory was retooled for the new Model A vehicle. If the market was to remain buoyant, car design had to stay ahead of it and customers had to want to buy the new model rather than keep the old one.

Ford also introduced a minimum wage of $5.00 per day and acted as a benevolent dictator to his workforce. His factories were very clean, with excellent safety records, and nutrition experts ensured every employee's lunchbox contained 800 calories. He would not accept unions, however, and used strong-arm men to stop any union activity.

Ford is generally recognized as changing not only the motor industry but industrial organization in total. Few historians would disagree with their colleague Michael Parrish, who wrote that, 'Ford transformed industry by providing cheap reliable transportation options for the masses.'

Some historians, such as Hugh Brogan, also recognize that while Ford may have led the motor car industry in terms of technological developments he

KEY TERM

Mass production Making large numbers of the same item using machinery and conveyor belts.

was slow in terms of marketing and organization. By the late 1920s Ford was copying his competitors – and of course had to shut down the entire plant in 1927 to retool for the Model A.

The effects of the growth in car ownership

In economic terms, by 1929, the motor industry employed seven per cent of all workers and paid them nine per cent of all wages. By far the largest industry in the USA, it also stimulated many others, as shown in Source A. This shows the percentages of the total production of various items in the USA that were used by the car industry alone. The temporary closure of Ford was indeed a contributory factor to the recession of 1927. Not only were his workforce laid off, but the loss of business by companies providing components to Ford created real problems in the economy.

SOURCE A

? What can you learn from Source A about the importance of the car industry to the national economy?

Use of materials by the car industry.

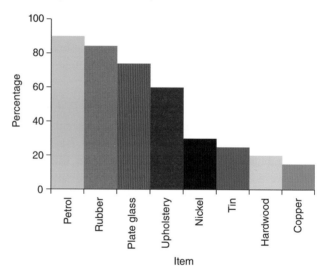

Road building

Breaking with the policy of *laissez-faire*, the federal government expended a great deal of energy on road building in the 1920s. Until 1921 this had largely been the responsibility of the individual states and many had made little progress since the previous century. Of three million miles of road in 1920, the vast majority were intended solely for the horse. Only about one per cent of roads were suitable to take the pounding of motor vehicles. The horse was by far the main form of road transport and the quantity of its dung on the highways was felt to be a national health hazard.

The Federal Highway Act of 1921 gave responsibility for road building to central government, and highways were being constructed at the rate of 10,000 miles per year by 1929. But this was not enough. New roads could not keep pace with the growth of traffic. Congestion was common, particularly in the approaches to large urban centres. In 1936 the Chief Designer in the Bureau of Public Roads reported that between 25 and 50 per cent of modern roads built over the previous 20 years were unfit for use because of the amount of traffic that was quite simply wearing them out.

Motor vehicles also created the growth of new service industries such as garages, motels, petrol stations and used-car salerooms. They gradually changed the landscape alongside the highways of the USA.

Improved transportation also afforded new opportunities for industry, for example, goods could be much more easily moved from factories to their markets. The number of truck registrations increased from less than one million in 1919 to 3.5 million by 1929, when 15 billion gallons of petrol were used and 4.5 million new cars were sold.

Electrical consumer goods

The development of new technologies such as mass production led to the large-scale development of labour-saving devices, for example vacuum cleaners and washing machines. This is because they were much cheaper to produce. In 1912, 2.4 million items of electrical goods were sold; in 1929 the figure was 160 million.

However, this trend should not be exaggerated. Much of rural America was still without electricity in the 1920s. Even where electrical power was available, many items we take for granted today were not widely in use. In 1925, for example, Clarence Birdseye patented his freezing process but in 1928 there were only 20,000 refrigerators in the whole country. While there was an industrial capacity to produce millions of electrical goods, by the end of the decade nearly everyone who could afford them or who had access to electricity already had them. This meant there was serious overproduction. As we shall see in the next chapter (page 35), this was to lead to problems in the economy by the late 1920s.

New business methods

This was a period that saw the growth of huge corporations, of **management science** and of advertising, which through the exploitation of the new mass media, gained an influence previously unimagined. The effect was to make business more efficient and well run, which in turn helped profits to grow.

Growth of huge corporations

Most large corporations, such as Firestone which produced rubber, were manufacturing businesses. They could invest in and exploit the plentiful raw materials of the USA on a vast scale. By 1929 the largest 200 corporations possessed 20 per cent of the nation's wealth and 40 per cent of the wealth generated by business activities. Mergers in manufacturing and mining enterprises trebled to over 1200 during the decade, leading to even larger business concerns. Many became **Trusts**.

🔑 KEY TERM

Management science The application of technological and scientific ideas to running a company successfully – such as time and motion, where the amount of time it should take to complete a process in manufacturing is timed and subsequently monitored. The aim is to use scientifically proven methods to run the company.

Trusts Companies that collude to control manufacture, supplies and prices to ensure that other firms cannot compete, thereby guaranteeing profits for themselves.

How far did new business methods contribute to economic growth?

Large corporations could dominate an industry in various ways:

- They could operate a **cartel** to fix prices. Although this was technically illegal, the government tended to turn a blind eye. They could, as in the case of the petroleum companies, control the entire industrial process. This involved the exploitation of the raw materials, the manufacture of the product, its distribution to wholesale and retail outlets, and its sale to the consumer.
- Some organizations, for example US Steel, were so huge that they could dictate output and price levels throughout the industry. They could create **holding companies**. For example, Samuel Insull built up a vast empire based on electrical supply. Eventually he controlled 111 different companies with as many as 24 layers between him and the company actually distributing the electricity. The chain became so complex that even he lost an overall understanding of it. Many businessmen turned up on the boards of directors of numerous companies. The result was that firms supposedly competing with each other were in effect one and the same, with the power to fix output and prices.

It is important to remember that government policies made these developments possible and that they acted against the interests of small businesses. However, at the time many people saw businessmen as heroes who had made possible the great boom period they were enjoying. There was even a prayer especially for businessmen.

SOURCE B

What are the values and limitations of Source B as evidence of how businessmen viewed themselves?

'A Man's Thanksgiving', *American Mercury* 16 (April 1929): 427–8.

God of businessmen, I thank Thee for the fellowship
of red blooded men with songs in their
hearts and handclasps that are sincere; […]
I thank Thee for telephones.and telegrams that link
me with home and office, no matter where I am. […]
I thank Thee for competition and its spur to greater achievement.
I thank Thee for the joy and battle of the business arena, the thrill of victory and the courage to
take defeat like a good sport; […]
I thank Thee for hard, relentless toil and the inspiration of creating something worthwhile;
I thank Thee for children, friendships, books, fishing,
The game of golf, my pipe and the open
Fire on a chilly evening.
AMEN

Advertising and salesmanship

The new mass media, principally cinema and radio, brought about a revolution in advertising.

Cinema

By 1928 there were 17,000 cinemas in the USA. Few areas were out of the reach of the 'movies'. A 10-cent ticket could buy admission to a fantasy world far beyond the previous experience of the vast majority of the audience. The darkened auditorium enabled people to forget their troubles for a few hours and to enter into a world of beauty and glamour where seemingly no one had to work or pay the mortgage.

With millions of cinema-goers aching to copy the appearances and lifestyles of the movie stars, the potential for advertising was enormous. The big producers were not slow to exploit this, and the time between the features was soon filled with commercials.

Radio

The radio business effectively began when the KDKA station in Pittsburgh announced the results of the 1920 presidential election. As other stations started to broadcast, a demand for radio sets was created. These began to be mass produced in 1920.

By 1929 there were 618 radio stations throughout the USA, some of them broadcasting from coast to coast. The vast majority of them were controlled by two companies, the National Broadcasting Company and Columbia Broadcasting System. The potential audience was vast. An estimated 50 million people listened to live commentary on the 1927 Dempsey–Tunney heavyweight fight referred to earlier on page 10. In 1922 the radio station WEAF in New York began the most important trend when it broadcast the first sponsored programme, advertising the delights of Jackson Heights, a housing development.

As more advertisers began to sponsor programmes, radio networks began to poll listeners to see what sort of programmes they wanted. With more and more programmes catering to mass appeal, which was based firmly in the areas of light music and humour, there was considerable criticism from those who felt radio should be educational and enlightening. However, these critics were firmly in the minority. By the end of the decade, radio costs were generally covered by advertising and many programmes were firmly linked in people's minds with the name of the sponsor.

The constant need to create demand

The growth in industrial production needed a continuous market. It was no longer enough, as Ford had done with his Model T, to sell a durable unchanging product that might last the purchaser for life. Now, to fuel the boom, it was necessary for people to buy new things frequently. They had to be convinced that they could not do without the latest model of an electrical appliance or the new design in clothing.

This necessitated far-reaching developments in advertising and salesmanship. Indeed, with most products virtually the same in quality, these often became the deciding factors in the market. A successful advertising campaign might well be the only difference between huge profit and huge loss. Possibly the most important aspect of a campaign was to find some way to differentiate between one's product and that of one's competitors: to promote a unique selling point.

For many consumers advertising techniques worked. Not only did they associate products with a slogan, but they also believed they could not manage without the advertised product. The *Kansas City Journal-Post* was hardly exaggerating when it wrote, 'Advertising and mass production are the twin cylinders that keep the motor of modern business in motion.'

SOURCE C

? How effective is the advertisement in Source C in making you want to buy the Jordan car? Examine the sales techniques used and content in your answer.

'I am the Playboy.' A classic 1920s' advertisement which connected Jordan cars with adventure and excitement. It was one of the first adverts to concentrate on image rather than give information about the product.

JORDAN

I am the Playboy

I am the companion of people who know where they are going.

It is a great satisfaction to associate with those who possess good judgment and good taste—those who know what it means to own a wonderful horse—those fortunate ones who can have whatever they want.

Independence—freedom—the enjoyment of something besides mere transportation —speed—dash—the smooth flow of power from a wonderful Line Eight—the thrill of really going somewhere. That's living.

JORDAN MOTOR CAR COMPANY, *Inc.*, CLEVELAND, OHIO

A wonderful horse—a gorgeous day—and all the world in tune—a tang in the air—exhilaration—life in its ecstasy.

Easy credit

The massive consumer boom was financed largely by easy credit facilities. By 1929 almost $7 billion worth of goods were sold on credit; this included 75 per cent of cars and half of major household appliances. One study showed that men earning $35 a week were paying the same amount per month for the family car.

Unfortunately, while the ready availability of credit enabled consumers to buy goods they otherwise could not have afforded, it often led to problems if the borrowers took on debts they could not repay. Companies, as well as individuals, used easy-credit facilities to finance many of their operations. It seemed that almost everyone was in debt, but there was little concern over this. It was assumed that everyone's credit must be good. Banks and loan companies seemed to be falling over backwards to lend money, often with few questions asked.

> **How important was the availability of credit in facilitating consumption?**

SOURCE D

A popular joke in the 1920s.

Husband: 'I just paid the doctor ten dollars on his bill.'

Wife: 'Oh, goody, two more payments and the baby's ours.'

What point is being made in the joke in Source D?

Advantageous foreign markets

Reference has already been made to high tariffs that protected US markets. However, the government also encouraged businessmen to develop extensive interests abroad, particularly in terms of raw materials that fuelled technological developments. Business corporations bought **oil concessions** in many countries, including Canada, Venezuela, Iraq and the Dutch East Indies. The Firestone Corporation developed a rubber industry in Liberia, while the Guggenheims invested in South America for nitrates, copper and lead. The United Fruit Company had a larger budget in Costa Rica than the government of that country. Often US investment saw the development of public health schemes and schools in developing countries to provide and maintain a healthy and adequately educated workforce.

> **How far was the USA involved in international trade and investment?**

 **KEY TERM**

Oil concessions Involvement in foreign oil industries on favourable terms.

Five-Year Plan Where the government plans the economy, setting targets to be achieved over a five-year period.

The USA also exported vast amounts of manufactured products. The USA dominated Canadian markets; indeed, US automobile firms effectively destroyed the native Canadian industry, which simply could not compete with them (see page 149). Similarly, the Canadian electrical industry was dominated by US firms in terms of both supply of power and manufacture of products.

Of particular interest is the economic relationship between the USA and Soviet Russia. While Coolidge's government refused to recognize the Soviet state, American businessmen were nevertheless encouraged to develop commercial ties. The First **Five-Year Plan** for Soviet economic growth was so dependent on its success for exports from the USA that the Soviet Amtorg Trading Corporation set up offices in New York City. By 1928, 25 per cent of all foreign investment in Soviet Russia emanated from the USA and, astonishingly, 33 per cent of all exported Ford tractors went to Soviet Russia; indeed, by 1927, 85 per cent of all tractors in Soviet Russia were manufactured by Ford.

In all, private investment by the USA in foreign countries rose from $7 billion in 1919 to $17.2 billion by 1930. As we will see in the next chapter, this international reliance on American investment would have devastating effects on the global economy when the Great Depression arrived.

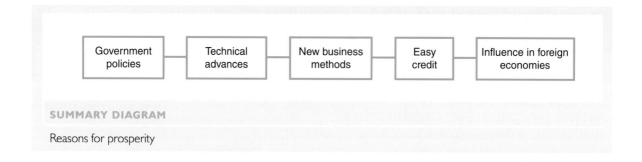

SUMMARY DIAGRAM

Reasons for prosperity

Chapter summary

The USA in the 1920s: prosperity?

We have seen that during the 1920s the USA seemed to be enjoying a boom period, particularly in the development and marketing of consumer goods. Unemployment remained low and industry seemed efficient, often through the introduction of new technological, marketing and management techniques.

Low inflation, high tariffs keeping foreign goods out of the USA and benevolent government policies were other factors that fuelled the consumer boom. The USA was enjoying the greatest 'boom' period in its history and for those working in the new industries such as the motor industry and appliance manufacturing, the prosperity seemed real and never-ending. The period wore a happy face. However, as we will see in the next chapter, one did not have to delve very far beneath the surface to discover real problems within the system.

CHAPTER 2

The Wall Street Crash and the causes of the Great Depression in the USA

This chapter has three aims: to give an account of the Wall Street Crash; to examine the causes of the Great Depression; and to consider the effects of the Crash. It considers the events leading to the Crash and examines how healthy the US economy actually was before it by looking at some of the underlying causes of the Great Depression. Finally, it discusses the relationship of the Wall Street Crash to the onset of the Great Depression.

You need to consider the following questions throughout this chapter:

✪ What chain of events led to the Wall Street Crash?

✪ How widespread were the signs that the economy was faltering?

✪ What was the relationship between the Wall Street Crash and the onset of the Great Depression?

✪ How strong was the American economy in the 1920s and how real was the prosperity?

① The Wall Street Crash

▶ *Key question: What chain of events led to the Wall Street Crash?*

In October 1929, the New York Stock Exchange crashed. It handled about 61 per cent of stocks and shares transactions in the USA. Crashes in other stock exchanges throughout the country and abroad soon followed. While the collapse in Wall Street had been forecast by many financial experts, their warnings had gone largely unheeded. The event was to affect millions of people, most of whom did not own stocks and shares.

The stampede to sell

On Thursday 24 October 1929, a massive amount of selling began in the New York Stock Exchange. This forced prices down and led to more selling still as **brokers** feared they would be left with worthless stock. By 11a.m., a mad panic had set in. US Steel, which had opened that morning at 205.5 points, was down to 193.5, General Electric had fallen from 315 points to 283 and Radio Corporation of America had collapsed from 68.75 points to 44.5. No one appeared to understand what was going on.

← What happened between 24 and 29 October 1929?

 **KEY TERM**

Broker A person who buys and sells stocks and shares.

People are afraid of the unknown, of things they cannot control, and what was going on here was certainly out of control. On one wall of the Stock Exchange was a large board recording transactions; this was called the **ticker**. Unfortunately, as the volume of sales mushroomed, it could no longer keep pace with them and began to fall badly behind. At 10-minute intervals, a separate bond ticker in the corner would punch out a list of selected up-to-date prices. As brokers hushed to hear these read out, they realized with horror that stocks bought possibly just moments earlier were now worth considerably less than they had agreed to pay for them.

As more and more brokers rushed to sell, the scenes became so wild that the police had to be called in to restore order. As news of the panic spread, an excited crowd gathered outside the building. A workman repairing a high building was believed to be a broker contemplating suicide. He was possibly inadvertently responsible for the myth that bankrupted brokers were throwing themselves from the rooftops. Comparatively few brokers did, in fact, go **bankrupt**. It was largely their clients' wealth that was being lost.

SOURCE A

The original 1929 caption reads: 'Photograph shows the street scene on Black Thursday, the day the New York stock market crashed, and the day that led to the Great Depression.'

Look closely at the photograph in Source A. Are there any indications of actual panic? Explain your answer carefully.

SOURCE B

Extract from *Only Yesterday* by Frederick Lewis Allen, published in 1931. This is a classic account of the 1920s in the USA by a leading journalist of the period and has been republished many times.

As the price structure crumbled, there was a sudden stampede to get out from under. By eleven of clock traders on the floor of the Stock Exchange were in a wild scramble to 'sell at the market'. Long before the lagging ticker could tell what was happening, word had gone out by telephone and telegraph that the bottom was dropping out of things and the selling orders redoubled in volume . . . Down, down, down . . Where were the bargain hunters who were supposed to come to their rescue at times like this? . . . There seemed to be no support whatsoever. Down, down, down. The roar of voices which rose from the floor of the Exchange had become a roar of panic.

What are the advantages and disadvantages of using descriptive sources like Source B in understanding what happened during the Wall Street Crash?

Efforts to protect the market

A meeting of six important bankers took place in the offices of J.P. Morgan Ltd in the afternoon of 24 October. Each of them agreed to put up $40 million to shore up the market by buying stocks and shares. Thomas W. Lamont, senior partner at J.P. Morgan Ltd, held a press conference. 'There has been a little distress on the stock market', he said, with a masterly sense of understatement. He went on to explain that this was due entirely to a technical difficulty, and the situation was 'susceptible to betterment', by which he meant things would improve.

Meanwhile, the vice-president of the Stock Exchange, Richard Whitney, a floor broker for J.P. Morgan Ltd, was buying stock above current prices in lots of 10,000 in an attempt to restore confidence in the market. The bankers having come to the rescue, confidence returned and the situation improved. At the close of the day, the market had fallen by 33 points to 299.5, or nine per cent of its value.

The ticker, however, did not record the final transactions until eight minutes past seven in the evening – dealing closed at 3p.m. – and clerks worked long into the night on the accounts resulting from all this business.

Altogether nearly 13 million shares had changed hands. By comparison, a normal day's transactions would be about three million. Stock market employees caused the police to be called to Wall Street again because of their boisterous behaviour in letting off steam after such a frenzied day.

For the next few days calm was restored in the market. Everyone who had weathered the storm breathed a sigh of relief. A Boston investment trust placed an advertisement in the *Wall Street Journal*: 'S-T-E-A-D-Y Everybody! Calm thinking is in order. Heed the words of America's greatest bankers.'

On Sunday, churchgoers heard that a divine warning had been sent concerning the dangers of financial greed and speculation. However, there was little evidence that many would heed the warning. Most newspapers appeared confident that the stock market was healthy and the days ahead would see a rush to buy at the new lower prices.

The Crash

While the volume of trading on Monday was less than that of the previous Thursday, the fall in prices was far more severe. The **Dow Jones Industrial Average** showed a drop of 38 points on the day's trading, down to 260. This time no Richard Whitney had appeared with orders to buy. It was not their business, the bankers explained, to protect stock-market prices, but simply to ensure the market was orderly.

Next day, confidence collapsed completely. This was Tuesday 29 October, the day that the stock market on Wall Street crashed. Altogether, 16,410,030 shares were sold and the Dow Jones Industrial Index fell a further 30 points to 230, a fall of 11.73 per cent. In the chaos of frenzied selling, there was talk of closing the exchange at noon, but it was felt this would simply increase the panic. Prices continued to fall, and despite occasional rallies the overall trend was downward. In a few weeks, as much as $30 billion had been lost out of over $100 billion. This represented a sum almost as great as that which the USA had spent on its involvement in the First World War. Source C gives some indication of the level of losses.

SOURCE C

The fall in share prices.

Company	Share price on 3 September 1929	Share price on 13 November 1929
American Can	181.87	86.00
Anaconda Copper	131.50	70.00
General Motors	72.50	36.00
Montgomery Ward	137.87	49.25
Radio	101.00	28.00
Woolworth	100.37	52.25
Electric Share and Bond	186.75	50.25

? Look at Source C. Which company saw the biggest fall? What might be the effect of share price falls such as this?

How far reaching was the Wall Street Crash?

→ Extent of the Wall Street Crash

Even after October 1929, prices still stood higher than they had done at any time during the previous year. What had been wiped out were the spectacular gains of the first nine months of 1929. After the Crash, experts did not believe that lasting damage had been done. On 26 October, for example, the Harvard Economic Society felt that the fall in prices would be temporary and would not cause any economic depression. Prices did not really plunge until 1932, when it was clear that the Great Depression was going to continue into the long term and recovery was not, as President

Hoover (see Chapter 3) had continued to insist, just around the corner. On 8 June 1932, for example, the *New York Times* Index closed at 58.46. By contrast it had stood at 164.43 in November 1929, less than a month after the Wall Street Crash.

It is often popularly believed that the Wall Street Crash led to the Great Depression. However, many historians have argued that it was simply one sign of a depression already well on the way. Moreover, stock markets had crashed before and have done since without any ensuing economic depression. In order to analyse the part played in this history by the Wall Street Crash, it is necessary to examine its impact within the context of an economy whose growth was, as we shall see in the next section, already slowing.

SUMMARY DIAGRAM

The Wall Street Crash

2 Problems in the economy

▶ *Key question: How widespread were the signs that the economy was faltering?*

While it appeared on the surface that the economy was booming during the 1920s, there were many warning signs that things were not so healthy. These included:

- uneven distribution of wealth
- rural poverty
- the instability of 'get-rich-quick' schemes
- problems with the banking system
- the cycle of international debt
- a slowdown in the economy.

In this section these will be dealt with in turn.

How were income and
industry distributed
within the USA?

Uneven distribution of wealth

Industry and income were all distributed unevenly within the USA, which
meant that some regions were much more prosperous than others. In
addition, patterns of employment could be unstable, for example with
short-time working. Different sections of society were better off than
others. Many women, for example, did not share in the prosperity of the
1920s, nor did ethnic groups such as Native Americans and African-
Americans.

Distribution of income

Income was distributed very unevenly throughout the country. The north-
east and far west enjoyed the highest **per capita incomes**; in 1929 these
were $921 and $881, respectively. In comparison, the figure for the south-
east was $365. To paint an even gloomier picture, within the region of the
south-east, in South Carolina, while the per capita income for the non-
agricultural sectors of the economy averaged $412, that of farmers was
only $129.

In 1929, the Brookings Institute, a research organization, found that income
distribution was actually becoming more unequal. Its survey discovered that
60 per cent of American families had annual incomes of less than $2000. Two
sociologists, Robert S. Lynd and Helen Lynd, conducted major surveys about
how people lived in the town of Muncie, Indiana, which they identified as
'Middletown'. As part of their investigations, they sampled 100 families and
discovered that 75 per cent earned less than the amount the Federal Bureau
of Labor recommended as the minimum income needed to support an
acceptable standard of living. Nevertheless, they found that most residents,
whatever their social class, shared conservative values that people should
fend for themselves and problems could be overcome by hard work.

Women

Women did not, on the whole, enjoy improved career opportunities during
this period. By 1930, for example, there were only 150 women dentists and
fewer than 100 female accountants in the whole of the USA. In 1928, the
League of Women Voters reported that while 145 women held seats in state
legislatures, there were only two women among the 435 delegates in the
House of Representatives.

There were more jobs for women as clerical workers and salespeople, but
overall they tended to remain in comparatively low-paid and often menial
jobs; 700,000 women were domestic servants. There were few female
industrialists or managing directors. The number of women receiving a
college education actually fell by five per cent during the decade. Even when
women worked in the same job as men, they normally received less money.
Despite the image of fun-loving young women known as 'flappers', women
were generally expected to concentrate on marriage and homemaking. It is

largely a myth that the 1920s saw more opportunities for women to get to the top in terms of employment opportunities. Fewer than two per cent of judges or lawyers were female.

Legislation did little to help women, although the Sheppard–Towner Act of 1921 funded healthcare for pregnant women and gave women some control over the clinics it set up. However, some **feminists** feared this measure simply reinforced the stereotypical view of women's main role as having children and drew attention away from the need for birth control. Legislation to protect women in the workplace such as the banning of night shift work was similarly attacked. This was because it often meant women simply lost their jobs when they were no longer allowed to work such shifts. Therefore they became more economically dependent on men. Despite the efforts of the Women's Party set up by former **suffragist** Alice Paul, women never voted as a block and women's movements remained fragmented throughout this period.

Native Americans and African-Americans
Native Americans and African-Americans did not share in the prosperity.

Native Americans
Policy towards Native Americans was based on the Dawes Severalty Act of 1887. This had as its lynchpin the twin notions of **assimilation** and **allotment**. Native American children, for example, were taught in Christian schools and forced to adopt 'Western' dress.

More significantly, the policy of allotment meant that the old tribal units were broken up and the reservations divided into family-sized farms of 160 acres. Surplus land was to be sold off.

The destruction of Native American culture had often left the people listless and apathetic. Allotment had been a failure particularly for those Native Americans who were not farmers by tradition. Moreover, much of the land allocated to them was unsuitable for productive farming. In fact, of 138 million acres owned by Native Americans at the time of the Dawes Severalty Act, 90 million acres had fallen out of their hands by 1932.

Many Native Americans lived in squalor and idleness. Often unscrupulous whites had swindled them out of their land or had acquired it below market prices. By 1926 a Department of the Interior inquiry found that the Act had been a disaster for Native Americans and that the policy of allotment in particular should be reversed.

African-Americans
African-Americans made up 10 per cent of the total population, but 85 per cent still lived in the south, itself the poorest region in the USA. There was considerable migration north in search of better opportunities, particularly to the large cities, but here too African-Americans faced discrimination in housing and employment. Often they were concentrated in 'ghetto' areas

KEY TERM

Feminists Those who sought to improve women's opportunities.

Suffragists Those who sought the vote for women.

Assimilation The idea that Native Americans should adopt American lifestyles and values; their traditional way of life should disappear.

Allotment Each Native American family was given a plot of 160 acres to farm. This went against the traditional idea of common land ownership.

such as Harlem in New York, whose African-American population had swelled from 50,000 in 1914 to 165,000 in 1930. Here overcrowding and poor living conditions added to the problems in the mainstream economy.

A study showed that, in Pittsburgh, African-Americans remained unskilled through lack of employment opportunities and were forced to operate in the casual labour market such as working in hotel kitchens. This left them more exposed to joblessness and fears of destitution than before they had begun their migration north. The **Ku Klux Klan** still terrorized much of the midwest and south, although the number of **lynchings** was falling. Comparatively few African-Americans were allowed to share in any prosperity; 14 per cent of farmers were African-Americans.

Rural poverty

The **census** showed in 1920 that for the first time the USA was essentially an urban nation. The total population was 106,466,000; of these 31,614,000 lived on the land, but the rest lived in towns. As the majority of Americans had hitherto lived in rural areas, the **farm lobby** had been very powerful in influencing the government. However, it now felt that its influence was under threat from other groups such as those representing urban interests.

Economic problems facing farmers

The years preceding the 1920s had been relatively good ones for farmers. During the war years prices had risen over 25 per cent, and more land had been taken into cultivation. However, after the war, falling demand led to falling prices. For example, wheat fell from $2.50 to $1 per bushel. There were several reasons for this:

- **Prohibition** cut the demand for grain previously used in the manufacture of alcohol. In addition, higher living standards meant Americans ate more meat and comparatively fewer cereals.
- The development of synthetic fibres lessened the market for natural ones, such as cotton.
- At the same time, technical advances meant that more crops could be produced on the same or even a reduced acreage. During the 1920s, 13 million acres were taken out of production. Farm population fell by five per cent yet production increased by nine per cent.
- Greater use of tractors meant fewer horses were necessary and this in turn meant less demand for animal food.
- Ironically, because many farmers became more efficient through mechanization and new techniques, such as the use of improved fertilizers and better animal husbandry, they simply produced too much.

As a result of these factors, possibly as many as 66 per cent of farms operated at a loss. **Wage labourers**, **tenant farmers** and **share-croppers** – in the south, these were mainly African-Americans – fared particularly badly. Some

---

🔑 KEY TERM

Ku Klux Klan Racist group advocating white supremacy. It adopted methods of terror to intimidate other groups such as African-Americans and Jews. During the 1920s it was particularly prevalent in the southern and midwestern states.

What were economic conditions like in farming communities?

🔑 KEY TERM

Lynchings Illegal hangings, often used by the Ku Klux Klan as a means of terror.

Census Survey undertaken every 10 years to enumerate everyone in the country.

Farm lobby Politicians and interest groups who put forward the farmers' case to the federal government and Congress.

Prohibition The banning of the manufacture, transportation and sale of alcohol for consumption.

Wage labourers People who worked for wages.

Tenant farmers People who rented the land they farmed.

Share-croppers Farmers who rented land and were paid by the landowners a percentage of what they produced.

farmers grew rich by selling their land for housing and industrial development, but most appeared not to share in any prosperity in the 1920s.

Overproduction

The biggest problem for farmers was overproduction. Too much food meant prices were too low. Farmers were reluctant to underproduce voluntarily because they could not trust their neighbours to do the same. Ideally, they sought guaranteed prices, with the state possibly selling their surplus abroad for whatever price it could get. American farmers produced so much that there were surpluses despite the rising population. However, prices had fallen to below those of 1914. Farmers considered the 1914 price to be the 'parity' price, by which they meant the price that enabled them to break even on the costs of production.

President Coolidge did little to relieve farmers from their distress. More and more farmers saw their mortgages foreclosed and lost the land their families had farmed for generations. Many farmers naturally became very bitter.

'Agricultural businesses'

The days of the small-scale, self-reliant farmer had already largely passed. In order to survive in the long term, farmers needed to make a profit. The 1920s saw the growth of '**agricultural businesses**' – large-scale, well-financed cereal cultivation, ranching and fruit production enterprises – using the techniques of mass production. They required comparatively little labour, except possibly in the case of fruit gathering at harvest time.

It was mainly the small-scale farmers who went bankrupt. These often asked the state for help, as they thought of big business and the banks as being in league against them.

Role of the government

Many farmers blamed the government for their plight. During the war, it had urged them to produce more but now it did little to compensate them for their losses. Many farmers were particularly angered by the fact that tariffs protected industry but not agriculture.

Government policy was to encourage farms to co-operate to market their produce. To this end the Agricultural Credits Act of 1923 funded 12 Intermediate Credit Banks to offer loans to co-operatives. However, the measure was of little benefit to small farmers. The last thing they needed was more debt. But large agricultural businesses could afford to take loans to market their produce more effectively, thus squeezing the small farmers even more.

Two measures of the early 1920s did, in theory, protect farmers from foreign competition: the 1921 Emergency Tariff Act and the 1922 Fordney–McCumber Act (see page 11) placed high tariffs on food imports. However, because foreigners retaliated by placing similar tariffs on American foodstuffs, farmers could not export their surpluses.

 **KEY TERM**

Agricultural businesses
Large-scale farms using machinery and techniques of mass production.

Although the farm lobby was reluctant to accept it, if the USA continued to develop as an industrial nation, manpower and resources would have to be shifted away from farming. Agriculture would have to change, and change eventually it did.

Distribution of industry

The older industries of the USA had been centred in the north-east and midwest, especially in the states of Illinois, Michigan and Pennsylvania. They had grown originally on the basis of nineteenth-century technology, powered by coal and steam. Old industries were generally experiencing hard times. Coal, for example, suffered from competition from newly discovered energy sources, notably oil. The introduction of synthetic fibres lessened the demand for cotton. Moreover, changes, particularly in young women's fashions, such as shorter skirts, reduced the quantity of material required. The textile mills of the south employed cheap labour, including children, and many northern mills, whose workforce enjoyed higher wages and shorter hours of work, simply could not compete in a shrinking market. Railways faced competition from motor transport, although it must be said that, because of the expansion of the economy, rail-freight traffic increased by 10 per cent during the decade. As we have seen, farmers fared particularly badly during this period.

The new industries, such as those of motor vehicles and appliances, were also drawn to the regions of the north-east and midwest. This was due to the availability of minerals such as coal, the well-established transport network, a mobile, often immigrant labour force, and proximity to centres of large population, such as Boston, Philadelphia and New York. As a result, other regions of the USA, notably the west and the south, had only sparse industrial development, with comparatively small towns still acting as commercial centres for wide rural areas. In other words, things had not altered in much of the USA since the previous century, and for much of the country the major occupation was still agriculture.

Stability of employment

Employment was often unstable owing to fluctuating demand for goods. Robert and Helen Lynd found that, during the first nine months of 1924, of 165 families they surveyed, 72 per cent of the workers had been unemployed at *some stage* in their working lives. Of these, 43 per cent had been jobless for over a month. This was at a time when there was very little welfare or unemployment benefit and most relief was supplied by charitable organizations.

Labour Unions

Workers could not, on the whole, look to labour unions for help. The government did nothing to protect them, and indeed the Supreme Court had blocked attempts by unions to ban child labour and impose a minimum wage for women as being unconstitutional. Many employers operated **'yellow dog' clauses** by which their employees were not allowed to join a

union. During the 1920s union membership, which in the early 1920s stood at four million, declined overall by one million. In 1910, 8.5 per cent of the industrialized workforce was unionized; in 1930 this figure had fallen to 7.1 per cent.

Interestingly, the employers in the new industries tended to be most anti-union, which explains why during this period unions failed to get more than a toehold in these. The older industries tended, as we have seen, to be in trouble during the decade. The government successfully sought injunctions against union activities earlier in the 1920s and by the close of the decade, employees generally were more anxious to keep their jobs than embark on union agitation.

The instability of 'get-rich-quick' schemes

While many people saw easy credit as a strength in the economy, there were also considerable drawbacks. 'Get rich quick' was the aim of many Americans in the 1920s; they invested in hugely speculative ventures and inevitably many lost their money. Moreover, this situation provided golden opportunities for confidence tricksters and crooks. In the early 1920s, for example, Charles Ponzi, a former vegetable seller, conned thousands of gullible people into investing in his ventures. He promised a 50 per cent profit within 90 days. Few, of course, ever saw a cent of their money again. When sentencing him to prison, the judge criticized his victims for their greed. Ponzi had not forced people to part with their money.

The period saw other more large-scale speculations, notably during the Florida land boom and on the stock exchange in the latter part of the decade.

The Florida land boom

While on bail awaiting trial, Ponzi found employment selling land in Florida. This was a venture well suited to his talents. Until this time, Florida was a relatively undeveloped state with a small population. In 1910, Miami was by far the biggest city but with a population of only 54,000. Then wealthy industrialists such as Henry M. Flagler of Standard Oil built elegant hotels in the state for the rich to enjoy holidays there. With the coming of the motor car, Florida's all-year-round sunshine became accessible to the nation's middle classes and massive interest grew in the state as a paradise for vacations and retirement.

This led to a land boom. Between 1920 and 1925, the population of the state increased from 968,000 to 1.2 million. There were large-scale coastal developments. Parcels of land began to be sold to wealthy northerners on the basis of glossy brochures and salesmen's patter. People began to invest their money in unseen developments, hoping to sell and make a quick profit. Often they paid on credit, with a 10 per cent deposit known as a 'binder'. Success stories abounded to fuel the boom. It was said that

> **What problems were caused by 'get-rich-quick' schemes?**

someone who had bought a parcel of land for $25 in 1900 had sold it for $150,000 25 years later.

The land boom could be sustained only as long as there were more buyers than sellers. But demand tailed off in 1926. There were scandals of land advertised as within easy access of the sea that was really many miles inland or in the middle of swamps. One company, Manhattan Estates, advertised land as being three-quarters of a mile from the 'prosperous and fast growing' town of Nettie, a place that did not exist. Then nature played its part, with hurricanes in 1926 killing 400 people and leaving 50,000 homeless. With thousands of people bankrupted, the Florida land boom collapsed, leaving a coastline strewn with half-finished and storm-battered developments. With a Mediterranean fruit-fly epidemic devastating the state's citrus industry in the 1930s, recovery did not begin until the Second World War when Florida became a major military training centre.

SOURCE D

Building taking place on the Miami seafront during the Florida land boom.

? What impression does the photograph in Source D give about the extent of new building in Florida?

Stock market speculation

It seemed that few people were prepared to learn the lessons of Florida. As one way to get rich quickly closed so another seemed to open up. In the period from 1927 to 1929 many Americans went 'Wall Street crazy'. Easy credit meant many were able to invest in stocks and shares. They could be bought 'on the margin' – on credit with loans from their broker.

Increasingly, people purchased stocks and shares not to invest in a company but as a speculation. If the price rose shares were sold, so making a quick and easy profit. For a time this seemed to work. Share prices seemed constantly to rise, some spectacularly so. According to the Wall Street Index, stock in the Radio Corporation of America rose from 85 to 420 points in the course of 1928. There were stories of ordinary people making immense profits.

Of course, in reality relatively few ordinary people ever dealt in shares; the figure was probably never higher than 1.5 million. What was more significant was that large concerns were investing their profits in the stock of others. For example, Bethlehem Steel Corporation and Electric Bond and Share each had invested $157 million in the market by late 1929. If prices should fall, these firms might lose their investments and go bankrupt.

Problems with the banking system

The banking system of the USA was out of date by the 1920s even though the central banking system had only been created in 1913. Twelve regulatory reserve banks were headed by the Federal Reserve Board – usually known as 'the Fed'– with seven members appointed by the president. The system, it was felt, allowed banks to regulate themselves without the government having to interfere. However, there was a significant potential problem. The reserve banks represented the interests of the bankers and so could not be completely relied on to act in the best interests of the nation if there was a conflict of interests. As we shall see (page 58), the reserve banks limited the amount of money in circulation during the Great Depression. This meant high interest rates for the banks as less money was available for borrowing.

> **How did the banking system lead to problems in the economy?**

However, critics argued that more money in circulation would encourage more economic activity, which might help to cure the Depression.

While national banks had to join the centralized system, local state banks did not. Most ordinary people's money, particularly in rural and semi-rural areas, was invested in the latter. In the 1920s, there were almost 30,000 banks in the USA. Most were very small and therefore unable to cope with financial problems. If they collapsed their depositors would probably lose virtually all their savings.

The Federal Reserve Board wanted to keep the market buoyant so it favoured low interest rates. This fuelled the easy credit discussed above. The Fed also wanted to see a flow of gold from the USA to Europe, so Europeans could afford to pay back their debts.

The cycle of international debt

The cycle of international debt was at the heart of the economic problems of the USA. America's priority was for Europeans to repay the loans they had taken out to finance the First World War. When the problem of European countries' ability to repay came up, Coolidge is reported to have said, 'They hired the money, didn't they?' Although the quotation is possibly fictitious, it did accurately express the sentiment of many Americans that the countries should repay their loans. However, most European countries, still suffering

> **What was the cycle of international debt and how did it lead to problems in the US economy?**

from depressed economic conditions arising from the war, could not afford to repay them.

In February 1922, Congress created the Debt Funding Commission. It suggested that the maximum deadline for repayment should be 1947 at an interest rate of 4.25 per cent. However, the simple truth was that Europeans just could not afford to repay the loans. The prohibitive tariffs made matters worse. European countries could not export their manufactured goods to the USA in great quantities; therefore they found it impossible to earn the money to repay the loans. Much of their gold reserves went to the USA as loan repayments.

However, an agreement was made with Britain in January 1923 for it to repay its $4.6 billion debt within 62 years at an interest rate of 3.3 per cent. Following this, agreements were made within the next five years with 15 countries under which interest rates were to be scaled down and more generous repayment time limits allowed.

The problems caused by Germany

Repayment of debts was only part of the problem. Germany had, by the terms of the Treaty of Versailles, been forced to pay **reparations** of $33 billion to the victorious nations of Europe. Under the **Dawes** and **Young Plans**, the USA lent it the money to do so. With this money, the European victors repaid the USA what they could of the loans. The USA was thus effectively paying itself back with its own money. Indeed, the $250 million it lent to Germany under the Dawes Plan corresponded to the amount Germany actually paid the Allies in reparations, which in turn corresponded to the amount the USA received from the Allies in debt repayments.

This situation became even more confused through the Dawes and Young Plans scaling down German reparations. With Germany paying the European victors less, this meant that they in turn could repay less of their own debts to the USA. All in all, no one gained from an incredibly complex situation that, according to one commentator, would have made more sense if 'the US had taken the money out of one Treasury building and put it in another'.

The banks hoped the movement of American funds to Europe would help the victors to repay the loans. American investors did increasingly put their money in European ventures. However, this investment took place particularly in Germany where $39 billion was invested after the Dawes Plan. Wall Street brokers earned fat commissions for putting investors in touch with businesses requiring investment. Massive overinvestment took place. Once again it was often a case of investors hoping to make a quick profit without going too carefully into the actual details of the transaction. As a result, there were absurd examples such as the Bavarian village that asked for $125,000 to build a swimming pool, and received $3 million.

However, with reparations reduced, investment in Germany hardly helped the European victors to repay their American loans. Its main effect was to make the tangle of international debt even more complex.

A slowdown in the economy

← What were the signs that the economic boom of the 1920s was slowing down?

The boom was dependent on continuing domestic consumption. High tariffs and generally depressed economies in Europe meant that American producers could sell comparatively little abroad. There were, by the late 1920s, three indicators that the boom was slowing down.

Problems in small businesses

The decade witnessed the growth of huge corporations with considerable marketing power. As a result, smaller businesses often faced hard times. During the course of the 1920s, for every four businesses that succeeded, three failed. The number of motor vehicle companies, for example, fell from 108 in 1920 to 44 by the end of the decade in part because of the growth of the larger companies which absorbed many of the smaller ones, but also because many of the smaller ones could not compete in a diminishing market. Tariffs notwithstanding (see page 11), the government was in reality no more prepared to help out failing industrial concerns than it was to help the farmers.

The construction industry

Economic historians tend to agree that the state of the construction industry is generally a good indicator of the overall health of the economy. The mid-1920s saw a great boom in construction, particularly in housing, office building and highways. However, after 1926 demand began to tail off. This led to a fall in demand for building materials, skills such as plumbing and the transportation of building materials. This, in turn, led to higher unemployment in construction-related businesses and had serious knock-on effects on concerns dependent on the construction industry.

Falling domestic demand

By the late 1920s, production was outstripping demand. The domestic market was becoming flooded with goods that could not be sold. More and more people were in no position to spend on non-essential items. In April 1929, for example, it was estimated that 10 per cent of Philadelphia's labour force was unemployed. Even though the national unemployment statistics remained low, Irving Fisher, a University of Yale economist, estimated that in 1929 as many as 80 per cent of the American people were living close to subsistence, even when they were in work.

Downward spiral

With growth in the new industries beginning to slow, full-time employment fell and the economy entered into a downward spiral. A fall in income led to a fall in demand, which in turn led to a fall in production that added to unemployment and underemployment (short-time working). However, the fact that the economy was experiencing problems was concealed by superficial optimism and the frenzy of stock market speculation.

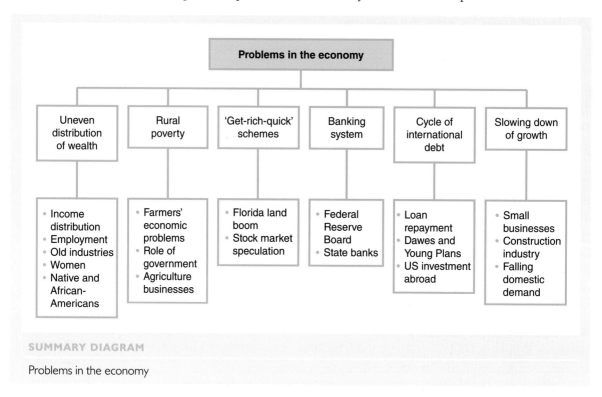

Problems in the economy

 Effects of the Wall Street Crash

▶ *Key question: What was the relationship between the Wall Street Crash and the onset of the Great Depression?*

Despite the myth, the Crash did not actually cause the Great Depression. This was widely recognized at the time and has been largely accepted by historians ever since. American business was too big and too diversified to be influenced to a significant extent by the stock market alone. There is little doubt that by the time of the Crash, the Depression was well on the way.

As well as overspeculation, living on credit and get-rich-quick schemes, there were the great inequalities of wealth and prosperity; problems with international trade; depression in staple industries, such as agriculture; overproduction and falling domestic demand, which had already resulted in serious problems in the building and, to a certain extent, the car industries.

The Crash was essentially a financial issue, while the Depression had much deeper causes, of which financial problems were only one.

However, although there is little doubt that the Crash was more of an effect than a cause of the Depression, we have to recognize that effects can worsen the problems they have resulted from. In this respect the Crash was an important trigger in worsening the Depression.

Effects of the Crash on the economy

There is some disagreement about the relative significance of the effects of the Wall Street Crash on the economy, although most commentators are in broad agreement about what they actually were.

> **How significant were the effects of the Wall Street Crash on the US economy?**

SOURCE E

Bankrupt investor Walter Thornton tries to sell his luxury roadster for $100 cash on the streets of New York City following the 1929 stock market crash.

$100 WILL BUY THIS CAR MUST HAVE CASH LOST ALL ON THE STOCK MARKET

Collapse of businesses

Individuals and business concerns lost billions. Thousands were bankrupted and even those who remained solvent were often hard hit. Clarence Mitchell's bank lost half its assets; the President of Union Cigar plunged to his death from the ledge of a New York hotel when stock in his company fell from $113.50 to $4 in a single day. Even the very wealthy financial family, the Rockefellers lost over $50 million in a vain effort to shore up the market.

> How well does this photograph in Source E reflect the human despair engendered by the Wall Street Crash?

Consumer durables
Goods that can last a long time, for example, motor cars and electrical appliances.

Credit squeeze When it is difficult to obtain credit.

The point is, of course, that people who had lost heavily could no longer afford to consume or invest further. So much of the prosperity of the 1920s had been based on continuing demand for **consumer durables**, and these tend not to be replaced when times are hard. Therefore, the industries that supplied these products in the USA found demand slipping further. The power of advertising, for example, had little influence on a people who increasingly had nothing to spend. All this was eventually to lead to a massive level of company cutbacks and often bankruptcy. As workforces were laid off, there was even less money within the economy for spending. This led in turn to a further slowing of the economy as it ground its inexorable way into a depression.

Collapse of credit

The stock market crash led to the collapse of credit. Loans were called in and new ones refused. Although stock might now have little value, it was nevertheless accepted by banks as repayments from brokers who could not otherwise repay their debts. With their own assets thereby reduced, banks were even less likely to make further loans. This led to a **credit squeeze** and to an accompanying fall in demand and business activity. No one, it seemed, was prepared to take a financial risk.

How significant was the loss of confidence in the US economy?

Effects of the Crash on confidence in the USA

The Crash signified an end of confidence. To many people, Wall Street had symbolized the prosperity of the 1920s. The stock market had seemed invulnerable. The influential economic historian J.K. Galbraith has argued that even though the number of stock market players was comparatively few, the idea of stock market speculation had become central to how confident society felt. In other words, belief in the continuing success of the stock market had become almost a certainty, like a belief in the ideas behind the Declaration of Independence.

The warning voices had been ignored. People had chosen to listen instead to the soothing tones coming from the White House and big business. When those same voices continued in the wake of the Crash, they were no longer believed. Their credibility was fatally undermined; but more, they were despised as belonging to those who had let the nation down by destroying its fundamental beliefs. In this situation, national confidence sank to rock bottom. This in turn deepened the Depression to whose onset people had for too long been oblivious.

With the country increasingly in the grip of the Depression, with confidence shattered and new uncertainties pervading society, attention now began to focus on the president in the White House, Herbert Hoover.

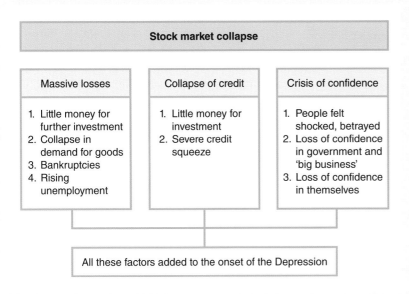

Effects of the Wall Street Crash

 # Key debate

▶ **Key question:** *How strong was the American economy in the 1920s and how real was the prosperity?*

How strong was the American economy?

It is easy with hindsight to see the problems in the American economy. At the time, however, detailed understanding of how a developed economy works was far less sophisticated than it is today. While there was concern among experts, some even forecasting accurately the coming collapse, they had little influence. Many historians would agree with Hugh Brogan, who wrote in 1985 that, 'At every stage the story displays the devastating consequences of a bland unawareness of economic and political essentials.' J.K. Galbraith was particularly scathing about the role of the banking system, with too many small, weak banks with the possibility of collapse at the first sign of trouble.

Other economic historians, however, have been less critical. The American economy seemed to be doing well especially when compared to others, notably those in Europe. After all, the figures denoting growth seem to speak for themselves. It is also important to note that the capitalist system survived the coming financial collapse almost intact. Many of the manufacturing and marketing companies of the 1920s have continued to operate to the present day, as have the banking and investment houses.

President Hoover had no doubts as to the strength of the economy; at the end of the 1928 presidential election campaign he made a speech as reported in Source F.

How reliable is the account in Source F? Explain your answer with particular reference to the provenance of the source.

SOURCE F

An extract from a speech made by President Hoover in 1928.

We have ... in the 1920s ... decreased the fear of poverty, fear of unemployment, the fear of old age ... Prosperity is no idle expression. It is a job for every worker, it is the safety and safeguard of every business and home ... We are nearer today to the ideal of the abolition of poverty and fear from the lives of men and women than ever before in any land.

How real was the 1920s' prosperity?

Commentators at the time and historians since have spent much time debating how real the prosperity was in the 1920s. Some, like Paul Johnson, believe it was sound enough for the economy to correct itself in response to the Wall Street Crash, while others feel it was flawed and the collapse was bound to happen. Some historians feel those in charge of the economy did not understand how market forces actually worked.

Lewis Frederick Allen

Allen was a journalist who wrote one of the most significant accounts of the USA in the 1920s, *Only Yesterday*, published in 1931. In arguing that the economy was fundamentally unsound, he gave seven reasons in support:

- Overproduction of capital and goods – too much was being produced which not enough people could afford to buy, while eventually all those who could afford stock had it.
- Pools of shady financiers operated to keep prices of goods artificially high.
- Asian markets paid largely in silver. There was a collapse in the price of silver, making it harder for them to buy American goods as prices rose accordingly.
- There was a shift in gold from other countries to the USA, making it harder for countries such as Britain to buy US goods (see page 34).
- International unrest meant unstable market conditions.
- Once the slowdown occurred it had a cumulative effect – as demand fell, more people lost their jobs so could afford to buy less.
- The lack of confidence resulting from the downturn meant people would no longer take financial risks.

Allen returned to this theme in 1952 in his book *The Great Change: America Transforms Itself.* Here he argued that the prosperity was unsound because business was preoccupied with paper, or artificial rather than real financial values. There was a willingness to speculate and propensity to shady financial practices such as the following:

- Developing holding companies which benefited a few but had a harmful effect on the many.

- Banks speculating and inflating corporation profits by selling them back and forth among themselves.
- Stock market **bull pools** which bought stock to increase the price, and then flooded the market with it, reducing the value for the majority who had held onto the stock – and often bankrupting the companies in the process.

The government meanwhile did not get involved or intervene to prevent such occurrences.

Thurman Arnold

Thurman Arnold was Dean of the Law College at the University of West Virginia. He later became an enthusiastic supporter of Roosevelt and the New Deal (see Chapter 4). He wrote an article on the 1920s' economy in 'The Aspirin Age', a series of essays published in 1949.

While Arnold agreed that the government had too limited a role, he felt that business – which did have the responsibility of regulating the economy – was entangled in a web it did not understand. Large-scale production and mass consumption had changed the economy but many of the structures were locked in the nineteenth century:

- The banking system regulated the economy, for example by withdrawing access to funding for those in whose success they had no faith.
- Overall the system was based on faith in institutions such as the banks, but in 1929, the collapse did not respond to their attempts to restore confidence.
- The solutions were based on beliefs held in the past. It was thought imperative for example to maintain prices. This meant people whose incomes were reduced, could no longer afford to buy, which led to greater unemployment and the massive downturn.

Hugh Brogan

In his history of the USA, Brogan entitles his chapter on the 1920s, 'Irresponsibility', making his feelings plain in arguing that the prosperity was not real. He noted that there were clear signs the prosperity was slackening as early as 1926, for example in the fall in the housing market. He goes on to say that the government was powerless to act even had it so wished. It had already lowered taxes as far as was possible. Neither of its other two alternatives was possible:

- The government could lower tariffs. The introduction of cheaper foreign imports would have stimulated their economies and forced US manufacturers to reduce their prices. American business would not tolerate this.
- The government could have intervened, for example with public works. This was the opposite of what they intended, that the federal government should do less not more. National debt shrank from $24 billion to $16 billion between 1921 and 1929.

🔑 **KEY TERM**

Bull pools Method by which unscrupulous brokers bought and sold stocks to and from each other to keep prices high.

- In arguing that, 'At every stage the story displays the devastating consequences of a bland unawareness of economic and political essentials', he would have agreed that business and bankers did not understand the way the economy worked. Even in the years of prosperity, 600 banks a year failed, while $3.9 billion was invested in German concerns, irrespective of whether they could ever make a profit, by US financiers using investors' money.

Paul Johnson

Paul Johnson is a British historian, who, writing in the 1990s, disagreed with Brogan by arguing that the 1920s' economy was sound and the prosperity was real. He argued that it was wrong to judge it by subsequent events (the Depression, which he later argued that federal governments made worse through their interventions – see page 61). Johnson felt that wealth was distributed more evenly than at any time in history so far, and people felt real economic security. He gives the example that 11 million families acquired houses in 1924. He also suggests that it was people such as clerks and factory workers who were buying shares in the biggest public utility companies. He argued that in the 1920s the USA was well on the way to becoming a property-owning democracy, and the Wall Street Crash would have righted itself, with prosperity returning by 1930.

Liaquat Ahamed

Ahamed, a financier himself, wrote a very influential book entitled *The Lords of Finance* in 2009. In arguing that even in the 1920s the economy was global and interrelated, he focused on the careers of four major central bankers in the USA, Britain, France and Germany. Ahamed argued that these men were prisoners of the orthodox belief that sound monetary policy had to revolve around the **Gold Standard**. This meant that the central bank of each country had to keep enough gold to support the amount of its paper currency. This meant borrowing was expensive because interest rates had to remain high to maintain the value of the currency which had to match the amount of gold. This limited trade and economic activities.

The big problem was there simply was not enough gold to finance world trade. Stocks of gold moreover tended to be concentrated in the USA and France – so countries such as Britain had to borrow heavily to buy it. This meant there was less money to invest in their own economies.

Overall, Ahamed argued that the strength of any individual economy was in a way irrelevant because of their interconnectedness, and the Depression was caused by economic mismanagement.

 **KEY TERM**

Gold Standard Where the value of money is based on the amount of gold in the nation's reserves.

Year	1922	1923	1924	1925	1926	1927	1928
Political	Fordney–McCumber Act	Dawes Plan	McNary–Haugen bill Tax cuts		Tax cuts		End of Coolidge's presidency
Social/economic				Florida land boom	Collapse of Florida land boom Peak of construction boom	Speculation on Stock Exchange Ford closure until introduction of Model A	

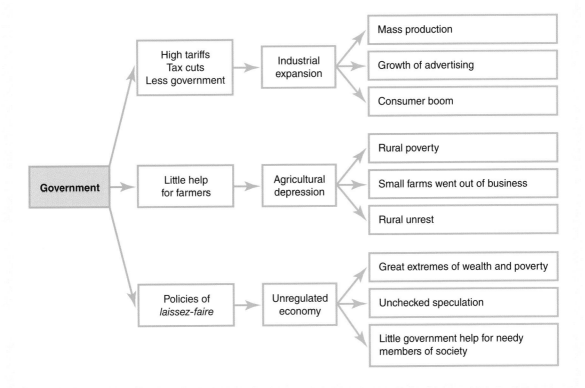

SUMMARY DIAGRAM

Prosperity?

The Wall Street Crash and the causes of the Great Depression in the USA

The prosperity of the 1920s was based on shaky foundations, although that prosperity seemed real to people at the time. However, it was uneven and some sectors of the economy, such as agriculture, appeared never to share in it. There were indicators that problems in the economy pre-dated the Wall Street Crash. These included slowdowns in the crucial construction sector, the cycle of international debt limiting trade, and overproduction leading to unemployment and a downturn in demand.

The Crash itself reflected weaknesses in the structure of the stock market that prompted unwise practices such as buying on the margin and exploitation by 'streetwise' dealers such as operating the bull pool. Also much of the prosperity was fuelled by a boom in credit which saw comparatively little real wealth actually being created.

The Wall Street Crash did not cause the Depression but was rather an indicator of its onset.

 Examination advice

How to answer 'to what extent' questions

The command term <u>to what extent</u> is a popular one on IB exams. You are asked to evaluate one argument or idea over another. Stronger essays will also address more than one interpretation. This is often a good question in which to discuss how different historians have viewed the issue.

Example

> <u>To what extent</u> was the prosperity of the USA in the 1920s based on solid foundations?

1 Beyond stating the degree to which you agree with the premise, you must focus on the words <u>prosperity</u> and <u>solid foundations</u> in the question. You should define these terms in your introduction.

2 First take at least five minutes to write a short outline. One strategy in your outline might be to consider the elements you think comprise solid foundations. Once you have listed these, then you can judge the degree to which these were present in the USA in the 1920s. Also be sure to write down evidence of prosperity. An example of an outline for an answer to this question might be as given opposite (page 45).

Solid foundations	Evidence
Fair distribution of wealth	Uneven. Women, African-Americans and Native Americans had fewer opportunities. Non-unionized labour
Low poverty levels	Especially bleak in rural areas
Sound banking system	Few financial safeguards. Stock market speculation
Strong manufacturing production	Overproduction and falling domestic demand
International trade/finances	Protective tariffs. Inability for Europeans to pay back war loans. Overinvestment

Prosperity

Some historians believe that the 'roaring twenties' marked a high point of home ownership and distribution of wealth, especially in comparison with other nations. They thought that the economy would have corrected itself without government intervention. However, most historians take a counter view: there were many danger signals prior to the stock market crash in 1929 and government involvement in the economy was necessary.

3 In your introduction, state what the key foundations should be for a prosperous nation. Include your thesis, which might be something like: 'In several fundamental areas, the seeming US prosperity was based on very shaky foundations.' An example of a good introductory paragraph for this question is given below.

On the surface, it appeared as though the USA was very prosperous during the 1920s. In comparison to European nations which were still suffering economic difficulties after the First World War, the USA was doing well. Factories were booming, people were buying homes in great numbers, and the stock market flourishing. However, there were other more important signs that all was not well. In several key areas, the foundations for a prosperous USA were shaky. Significant sectors of the population lived in poverty, particularly African-Americans and Native Americans. By the middle of the decade, the factories were producing more than could be consumed. The banking system had insufficient safeguards and rampant speculation led to financial weaknesses. Finally, trade relations with the country's major foreign partners were uneasy.

4   In the body of the essay, you need to discuss each of the points you raised in the introduction. Devote at least a paragraph to each one. It would be a good idea to order these in terms of which ones you think are most important. Be sure to make the connection between the points you raise with the major thrust of your argument. An example of how one of the points could be addressed is given below.

Prosperity can often be seen as how equitably wealth is distributed. In the USA in the 1920s, Native Americans lived in dire poverty. As a result of the Dawes Severalty Act of 1887, Native American families were given 160 acres of often unsuitable land to farm. The desire of the US government to assimilate the Native Americans was an enormous failure and resulted in a culturally corrupted ethnic group that did not share in the riches of the nation. In 1926, a government study detailed how the Act had harmed the original Americans. African-Americans also suffered. They made up roughly 10 per cent of the population and 85% lived in the poorest region of the USA, the south. There, they were usually dirt-poor farmers or sharecroppers who were prohibited from participating in the political process. The ones who migrated north in search of work often faced discrimination and poor living conditions. In many northern cities, they were forced to live in ghettos. These became increasingly overcrowded with the influx of migrants. In Harlem, for example, the population soared from 50,000 in 1914 to 165,000 by 1930. Those who found work usually worked in the casual labour market, which meant that they could be easily fired. Furthermore, the Ku Klux Klan, a white supremacist group, terrorized African Americans in particular and created a climate of fear for them. It is clear that the 1920s were not a prosperous time for the Native Americans and African-Americans. Without including them, it is difficult to state that the foundations of prosperity were broad and solid.

5 In the conclusion, be sure to offer final remarks on the extent to which prosperity was based on solid foundations. An example of a good concluding paragraph is given below.

> *In conclusion, it is clear that the prosperity of the USA during the 1920s was based on weak not strong foundations. In almost every sector of the society and economy, there were significant weaknesses that led to the Great Depression in 1929. In the former, women, African-Americans and Native Americans faced few opportunities to share in the nation's wealth. In the latter, while some areas exhibited industrial growth, much of the country was in a precarious state. Furthermore, wild speculation and the lack of financial oversight helped undermine the underpinnings of a strong nation.*

6 Now try writing a complete answer to the question following the advice above.

 # Examination practice

Below are three exam-style questions for you to practise on this topic.

1 To what extent was it true that the Wall Street Crash did not cause the Depression?

2 Discuss the main causes of the Depression.
(For guidance on how to answer 'discuss' questions, see page 228.)

3 Examine the reasons why farmers didn't share in the prosperity of the 1920s.
(For guidance on how to answer 'examine' questions, see page 73.)

CHAPTER 3

President Hoover and the Great Depression

This chapter examines the presidency of Herbert Hoover and how he tackled the Great Depression. It begins with an analysis of Hoover's beliefs, showing how he was ill equipped to deal with the scale of the Depression, and goes on to consider the extent of the Depression in human and economic terms. Hoover's policies will be evaluated in depth. Finally, the 1932 election will be discussed and the incoming president Roosevelt introduced. You need to consider the following questions throughout this chapter:

✪ What impact did the Great Depression have on the reputation of Herbert Hoover?

✪ How devastating were the economic and social effects of the Great Depression?

✪ Why was the Depression so extensive and long lasting?

✪ How successfully did President Hoover's administration tackle the Great Depression?

✪ Why was the 1932 presidential election so significant?

 The impact of the Great Depression on the presidency of Herbert Hoover

▶ *Key question: What impact did the Great Depression have on the reputation of Herbert Hoover?*

In the 1928 presidential election campaign, it is doubtful whether anyone could have beaten the Republican Herbert Hoover. In the 1932 campaign, he was generally criticized and had little chance of success. Hoover was a tragic figure, prematurely aged and the butt of cruel jokes throughout the country, such as the hitchhikers' placards that read, 'If you don't give me a ride, I'll vote for Hoover'.

In 1932, the economy dominated. However, while in 1928 Hoover received 21,392,190 popular votes to his Democratic opponent's 15,016,443, in 1932 Hoover's opponent, Franklin Delano Roosevelt, received 22,800,000 votes to his 15,750,000. This was actually a fairly respectable result for Hoover when one considers the attacks on him, his lacklustre campaign compared to Roosevelt's exciting one, and the fact that the election result seemed prejudged by most people. Hoover himself said, 'As we expected we were defeated in the election.'

SOURCE A

Popular slogan during the 1932 election campaign.

In Hoover we trusted
And now we are busted.

What impression does Source A give of people's feelings towards President Hoover?

Clearly, the issue that destroyed Hoover was the Depression and his inability to deal with it to any degree of success. In this chapter we will consider why he failed so completely. To aid our understanding it is important to consider Hoover's background and attitudes before going on to look at the depth of the problems that faced him and how he responded to them. We need also to examine the 1932 election campaign to see what, if anything, his opponent offered the American people that Hoover had not.

Journalist William Allen White called Hoover 'the last of the old presidents and the first of the new'. We need to investigate what is meant by this remark and consider how far it is justified by his response to the Depression. Finally, we shall consider the views of historians on the issues of why the Depression was so great and lasted so long.

Herbert Hoover: his background and beliefs

How did Herbert Hoover's background affect the beliefs he brought with him to the presidency?

If anyone deserved to be president then that person surely was Herbert Hoover. Rarely has anyone been so well qualified for the task or had so much confidence placed in his ability. Hoover encapsulated the **American dream**.

Herbert Hoover was shy and taciturn, uncomfortable with strangers and often shunned publicity. He was an administrator more than a politician, and avoided political tricks and infighting. Generally, however, Americans had very high expectations of his administration. After all, it seemed the economy was booming and, as Secretary of Commerce, he was widely believed to have been one of the architects of the prosperity of the 1920s.

 **KEY TERM**

American dream The belief that everyone can be successful through hard work and effort.

Hoover's beliefs
Hoover's tragedy was that he could not shift from his fundamental beliefs, which he acquired at an early age and never altered.

Self-reliance
Hoover believed people should be responsible for their own welfare. This attitude was to make him inflexible in his handling of the Depression. He simply did not believe the government should try to solve people's problems. It was up to the government to give people the ability to solve their problems by themselves.

'American individualism'
Hoover's political philosophy was spelt out in his book, *American Individualism*, published in 1922. He never moved away from its ideas

whatever the circumstances. He believed above all in equality of opportunity. He was a self-made man; he felt everyone else could be too. Everyone could, with hard work and initiative, become rich just as he had.

Having said this, he did not support strictly *laissez-faire* policies. He believed the government should co-ordinate the activities of capital and labour. He felt a balance should be struck between people's desire to do whatever they wanted themselves, and the needs of the wider community. The emphasis was always on the responsibility of the individual. Hoover saw the role of government as encouraging people to help themselves and others.

 # The USA during the Great Depression

▶ *Key question: How devastating were the economic and social effects of the Great Depression?*

The statistics of the Depression do not always illustrate the human cost. For this reason, the economic effects and the human dimension will be separated in the following account. It is also important to consider why this particular depression bit so deeply and lasted so long. The USA was, after all, quite used to depressions as part of the normal economic cycle, a cycle that Herbert Hoover was trying to break up so that prosperity would become the norm.

The economic effects

How extensive was the economic impact of the Great Depression?

There are no totally reliable unemployment figures for this period because the federal government did not keep centralized records until the mid-1930s. However, there is no doubt that unemployment soared. One historian wrote that the unemployment figures resembled the casualty figures in the battles of the First World War. An official government source suggests that unemployment rose from 3.2 per cent of the labour force in 1929 to 25.2 per cent by 1933; this meant that 12,830,000 were out of work. The Labor Research Association complained that these figures were underestimates and claimed that the real figure was nearer 17 million. Another source suggested that by 1933 one-third of the workforce was unemployed. It was estimated that the national wage bill in 1932 was only 40 per cent of the 1929 figure. However, the figures do not show the numbers in part-time and unregistered work, which were quite significant.

SOURCE B

Unemployed waiting for admission to the New York Municipal Lodging House, 1931.

What does the photograph in Source B suggest about the human impact of the Great Depression?

Uneven distribution of unemployment

Unemployment and underemployment were not evenly spread throughout the country. New York State alone had one million unemployed. In Ohio, the city of Cleveland had 50 per cent of its workforce unemployed and that of Toledo, a staggering 80 per cent. African-Americans and women were particular victims.

African-Americans

The magazine *The Nation* reported in April 1931 that the number of African-Americans out of work was four to six times higher than whites, and that poorly paid jobs traditionally reserved for African-Americans such as those of waiter and lift-attendant were now increasingly being offered to whites. African-American rural workers were used to depressed conditions. One black commentator from Georgia said, 'Most blacks did not even know the Great Depression had come. They always had been poor and only thought the whites were catching up.' However, employment opportunities in the northern cities, which had opened up in the 1920s, were now generally closed to them.

Women

Women, particularly those of the working classes, also did badly. Women in unskilled jobs were likely to be laid off before men, and those in domestic service suffered because families could no longer afford to keep them on. Married women often needed to work to keep the family solvent. However, because they had a job they were often accused of being responsible for male unemployment. It was quite common for them to be dismissed and their work given to men. In 1930 over 75 per cent of American school authorities refused to employ married women.

Effects on individual industries

There were some areas that survived the onset of the Depression. A local military base, state university or seat of state government could delay it because of the availability of employment on campus or base. Localized circumstances could also be significant, such as the temporary oil boom in Kilgore, Texas, which ironically led to a glut of oil and a collapse of prices in that industry. There were also 'depression-proof' industries, such as cigarette manufacture. This shielded Louisville and Richmond from the worst effects of the Depression until later. By 1933, however, nowhere in the USA could wholly escape its effects.

Having said this, business historians are keen to emphasize that the period of the Depression was also one of technical innovation – air-conditioning, airline travel, colour film and supermarkets were just some of the new ideas introduced in the 1930s. Not everyone suffered equally; some businesses did well at different times, and some were fortunate enough to avoid the Depression altogether.

Nevertheless, with fewer in productive work overall, the growth rate went into decline, from 6.7 per cent in 1929 to –14.7 per cent in 1932, representing a fall in gross national product (GNP) from $203.6 billion in 1929 to $144.2 billion in 1932. General price levels fell by 25 per cent during the period; farm prices fell by a half.

The separate statistics of decline indicate how individual industries fared. In the coal industry, production in 1932 was the lowest since 1904 and the workforce fell by 300,000; many of those in work were only part time and wages could be as low as $2.50 per day. Seventy-five per cent of textile firms were losing money, while iron and steel production fell by 59 per cent and US Steel Corporation's workforce was wholly part time by the end of 1932. Car sales fell from 4,455,178 in 1929 to 1,103,557 four years later.

The average number of people employed in the 'motor city' of Detroit fell by 21.5 per cent between 1928 and 1929. In Toledo, between May 1929 and spring 1932, Willis-Overland kept on only 3000 of their 25,000-strong workforce. In similar cases, the number employed by both General Electric and Westinghouse making electrical appliances was more than halved; the only electric goods not to suffer a significant decline in demand were lightbulbs, which needed to be replaced.

The construction industry, already in decline before 1929, saw the number of residential units built fall by 82 per cent between 1929 and 1932. Construction contracts were valued at $6.6 billion in 1929 but only $1.3 billion three years later.

SOURCE C

Index of total monthly manufacturing production from surveys of current business, where 100 represents the monthly average from 1923 to 1925.

September 1929	122
October 1929	117
November 1929	105
September 1930	91
October 1930	87
November 1930	85
September 1931	77
October 1931	75
November 1931	73
September 1932	68
October 1932	68
November 1932	65

What can you infer from Source C about manufacturing production between September 1929 and November 1932?

Problems with credit and banking

Credit had all but vanished. The stock market went into serious decline despite occasional rallies as in December 1929 and in April 1930.

Bank closures multiplied. There had been 5000 in the entire period 1921–9, but there were over 10,000 between 1929 and 1933. Most of these were small banks that had overextended lending in the times of prosperity and now could not meet their depositors' demands for their money. When farmers, for example, could not meet their mortgage repayments, the banks had to evict them and take the farms over. In doing so, the banks lost liquid assets in the form of mortgage repayments and gained bankrupt, often unsellable, farms in exchange.

Under these circumstances, depositors often lost confidence in their bank. This could lead to a 'run on the bank' to withdraw their money, which would force it to close down. Alternatively, many people simply needed to withdraw the money they had in their accounts; they may have lost their job, been on short-time working or needed to meet a debt. If enough people wanted their money at the same time, the result was the same: the collapse of the bank, with savings being lost for all those depositors who did not withdraw them quickly enough.

People often could not afford their loan repayments. This also led to banks not having enough money to pay to depositors, which in turn led to depositors losing confidence and rushing to withdraw all their money.

By 1933, the USA was a land of cash transactions, where those still in work fiercely protected their jobs, where credit was tight and no one was prepared to take a risk. It was also a land singularly unable to handle a major depression.

> **How did the Great Depression impact on people's lives?**

Social effects of the Great Depression

The human cost of the Depression was enormous. In this section we will consider how people's lives were affected and how the system of welfare was totally inadequate to deal with the scale of the problem.

Life for the unemployed

The USA was ill equipped to handle unemployment. Very little provision had been made for it. There was, for example, no federal unemployment benefit. The **work ethic** was very prevalent in America and unemployment among the able bodied was generally held to be their own fault. For this reason alone, the psychological effects of mass unemployment were devastating. There are many cases of people pretending still to be in work, to go out early each morning with a briefcase or tool bag, packed lunch and the like, to keep up appearances.

The strain on family life was intense. The number of marriages fell from 1.23 million in 1929 to 982,000 in 1932, with an accompanying fall in the birth rate from 21.2 per thousand in 1929 to 19.5 in 1932. Suicide rates increased from 14 per 10,000 in 1929 to 17.4 per 10,000 in 1932.

Hoboes

Many of the unemployed became **hoboes**. By 1932, it was estimated that there were between one million and two million of them, many of whom lived in shanty towns on the outskirts of settlements. Hoboes were usually given a hard time because people did not want to encourage transients

☞ KEY TERM

Work ethic The feeling that people should work hard and the unemployed should go out and find a job. It derived from the notion that how well one worked was a sign of one's worth, both personally and socially.

Hoboes People who wandered around the USA in search of work.

? What might be the dangers of travelling in the way shown in Source D?

SOURCE D

Hoboes aboard a freight train. Millions travelled around in search of work.

entering their areas. The Southern Pacific Railroad claimed to have thrown 68,300 of them from its trains. The state of California posted guards to turn hoboes away at its borders, and in Atlanta, Georgia, they were arrested and put into **chain gangs**.

The extent of relief

The nature of relief varied greatly because it was provided variously by states, local authorities or charities. Most came from charities. In fact, before 1932 no state had any system of recognized unemployment insurance and only 11 operated any kind of pension scheme, with a total outlay of only $220,000, aiding a mere 1000 people.

At a time when the population was ageing, the majority of elderly people lived below the poverty line. There were very few private pension schemes; in 1925, only 36,000 pensioners were in receipt of benefits from 500 pension plans. This meant old people traditionally had to keep working, live on their savings or rely on their children for support. The Depression meant that, in the main, these options were no longer viable.

To obtain any measure of relief, people often had to sell all their possessions, use up all their savings and become destitute. The stigma of receiving relief was deliberately intended to dissuade people from applying. Ten states, for example, removed the right to vote from relief applicants and some churches even banned those on relief from attending their services. *Fortune* magazine showed that only 25 per cent of those entitled to relief actually received any. Single people and childless couples were very unlikely to receive anything.

The strain on resources

For those who were entitled to relief, there was the added problem that the relief bodies were running out of funds. Charities naturally suffer a decline in revenue during a depression, at the very time when their funds are most needed. States, too, received less in taxes as unemployment rose. As a result, many had to cut rather than expand their services. In Arkansas, for example, schools were closed for 10 months in the year, while teachers in Chicago went unpaid during the winter of 1932–3. The simple truth was that charities could supply only six per cent of necessary funds in 1932, and states and local government agencies could not even begin to provide the shortfall of 94 per cent. In fact, in the years 1931 and 1932 when demand was greatest, most cut their relief appropriations. Michigan, for example, reduced funds from $2 million in 1931 to $832,000 in 1932.

The result was that many people went hungry or were starving. *Fortune* magazine estimated in September 1932 that as much as 28 per cent of the total population was receiving no income, and this estimate did not include the 11 million farm-workers, many of whom were in serious difficulties.

KEY TERM

Chain gangs Groups of convicts chained together while working outside the prison, for example in digging roadside drainage ditches.

Rural poverty

According to US Department of Agriculture statistics, 58 farms in every thousand changed hands in 1929, of which 19.5 were forced sales due to banks repossessing farms as a result of non-payment of mortgages. By 1936, this figure had risen to 76.6, of which 41.7 were forced. Often the auction of foreclosed farm property attracted violence. But there were other ways in which those repossessing property could be thwarted. Local farmers would agree only to bid a few cents and then return the farm to its former owner. Sometimes there was intimidation. In the face of this, two state governors said that payments on farm mortgages could be postponed until circumstances improved.

Poverty in the midst of plenty

The tragedy was that people went hungry in one of the richest food-producing countries in the world. Farm prices were so low that food could not be profitably harvested. In Montana, for example, wheat was rotting in the fields. Meat prices were not sufficient to warrant transporting animals to market. In Oregon, sheep were slaughtered and left to the buzzards. In Chicago, meanwhile, women scoured rubbish dumps for anything edible. Total relief funds in that city amounted to only $100,000 per day, which worked out at payments of only $2.40 per adult and $1.50 per child recipient per week. In 1931, there were 3.8 million one-parent families headed by a woman, with only 19,280 receiving any aid.

Why was it so difficult to end the Great Depression? →

The longevity of the Depression

Various explanations have been given for the duration of the Depression, which lasted from late 1929 until well into the mid-1930s, although they are usually closely interconnected.

- The USA needed to trade but foreign countries could not afford to buy American goods, which kept unemployment high.
- US business, including the banking sector, lacked the infrastructure to reform itself.
- The Depression eventually pervaded all parts of the country.
- Federal government intervention was inadequate.

As a result of these factors, confidence remained low.

Foreign economic crises

Herbert Hoover always blamed foreign economies for the Depression. It was their lack of purchasing power, he felt, that stifled trade and, as we shall see, many of his measures to combat the Depression were intended to strengthen foreign economies. Many historians would go along with his analysis up to a point. However, there is the counter-criticism that, although the USA was the richest country in the world, it had not, in the 1920s, assumed the role of world economic leader. American tariffs had restricted international trade, and were to do so even more ferociously after the

Hawley–Smoot Tariff in 1930 (see page 65). In particular, the USA may be criticized for not devaluing its currency when others were losing value, thus making American goods even more expensive for foreigners.

The nature of American business

The vast growth of the American economy came during the years following the Civil War after 1865, when the country rapidly settled the continent and underwent a major process of industrialization. However, government non-intervention meant that industries often came under the control of individuals or small groups who could control wages, prices and output to maximize their profits. While, on the surface, the system was highly competitive and dominated by market forces, in reality it was controlled by trusts and cartels. This meant that competition was limited.

By the late 1920s, the amount of goods produced was greater than demand even though the population was still growing. Therefore, the country was left with a problem of overproduction and excess capacity (or the ability to produce far more goods than were demanded by consumers). Relatively low wages and the unequal spread of prosperity meant that the population was consuming less than the economy produced. Unless new forms of demand could be found, the economy would continue to stagnate.

The extent of the Depression

Economic depressions are often unevenly distributed within a country. Some industries remain unscathed; others may even benefit. Some areas of the country escape. However, the extent of the Great Depression in the USA meant that no region or sector remained immune. This was to have two major effects that led to the Depression being prolonged.

The absence of alternative employment opportunities

Every country that has been through an industrial revolution finds that its old industries – coal, iron and steel, and textiles – lose their competitive edge in the face of competition from rivals whose more recent industrialization means that their methods of production are more modern and efficient. However, as the old industries contract accordingly, the workforce can normally expect to find employment in the newer industries, such as car assembly and the manufacture of electrical appliances. But, as we have seen, because of overproduction and underconsumption, these industries were hit particularly badly during the Depression in the USA. As a result, employment opportunities were no longer available in these either. Clearly, this prolonged the Depression.

The geographical extent of the Depression

The geographical extent of the Depression affected both rural and urban areas. Farmers, for example, had largely been depressed throughout the 1920s and so their purchasing power was poor. Because both rural and urban areas suffered neither could help the other.

Inadequate government intervention

A group of radical economists, including Rexford Tugwell and Adolph Berle, later to be important supporters of Franklin D. Roosevelt known as the 'Brains' Trust' (see page 80), argued that the Depression was caused by too many goods being produced and too few consumers being able to afford to buy them. A Brookings Institute Report of 1934, for example, showed that eight per cent of families had earned 42 per cent of the national wealth, while 60 per cent earned only 23 per cent. There was therefore a great inequality of wealth in the USA.

If the unregulated capitalist economy could not maintain a balance between the ability of people to buy goods and the level of earnings, then, it was argued, the government should intervene to do so. This clearly would mean making the rich pay more taxes to help make income more equal. With this increased revenue, the government could undertake public works to increase employment and 'kick start' the economy. In the USA, of course, the prevailing government policies had been the opposite of this, with economies in government spending and balancing the budget being seen as priorities.

Monetary policy

Associated in particular with the work of the economist Milton Friedman in the 1970s, **monetarist** theories argue that a decline in the amount of money in circulation often comes before a depression. Failure to increase this stock of money will prolong the depression as people have less money to spend. Altogether, the amount of money in circulation fell by about 33 per cent during the years 1929–33.

Monetarists argue that a three to five per cent annual increase in the amount of money in circulation is necessary to achieve a comparable rate of economic growth. Friedman argued, for example, that in October 1931 the rise in the **rediscount rate** from 1.5 to 3.5 per cent caused a 25 per cent fall in industrial production over the next year. According to monetarists, in other words, the tight monetary policy pursued by the Federal Reserve Board stifled recovery. This is because there was less money in circulation so people had less to spend, thus keeping the demand for goods low.

There is undoubtedly a large measure of truth in each of these explanations and they will be considered further in the key debate section below. Together they show that the Depression was a highly complex phenomenon with no easy solutions. However, increasingly, the federal government was expected to find the answers.

 **KEY TERM**

Monetarist Economic theory that governments can control the economy through regulation of the money supply.

Rediscount rate The interest rate at which banks borrow money from the federal reserve banks.

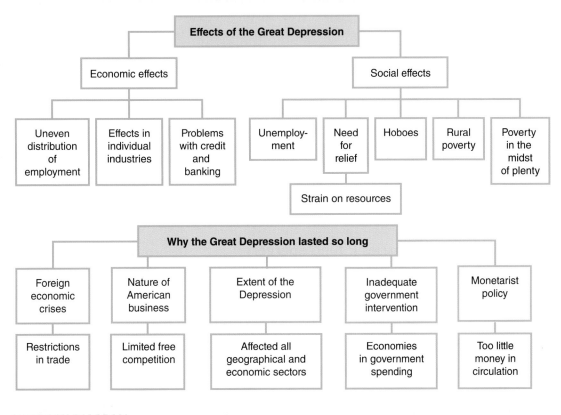

The USA during the Great Depression

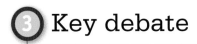 Key debate

▶ *Key question: Why was the Depression so extensive and long lasting?*

The economic cycle necessarily involves periods of depression in most industrial countries. However, the extent of the Great Depression, which coincided with the presidency of Herbert Hoover, was unprecedented. The reasons why it was so severe and why it lasted so long have been extensively debated both by historians and by those involved at the time. In this section we will consider the various interpretations.

Herbert Hoover

Hoover wrote extensively about the Depression in his memoirs. He called it the nightmare of his years in the White House. He insisted the Depression was European in its origin and was caused by the effects of the First World War, which led countries to continue to distrust each other.

T
O
K

In the practice of history, assigning causes and identifying effects is often a blame game. This is certainly true for those who have analysed the Great Depression. Identify an issue in your own time where the blaming and praising depend on the speaker's political views. (History, Language, Emotion, Reason.)

 KEY TERM

Customs Union
Agreement to abolish trade barriers between participating countries and raise those for other countries.

The **Customs Union** founded by Germany and Austria in 1931 angered Britain and France. They had continued to distrust their two former enemies who had been allies in the war. They now feared the Customs Union could be the start of some wider, possibly military union between Germany and Austria.

Britain and France retaliated to the Customs Union by demanding immediate repayment of bills owed to them by the banks of those two countries. This led to bank collapses that spread to other countries in Europe. The USA meanwhile could not continue to lend money to European countries because of the Wall Street Crash. The subsequent collapse of European banks in turn spread to banks in the USA to whom the European banks owed money that they could no longer repay.

Today there is some agreement, at least in part, with Hoover's analysis.

Charles P. Kindleberger

Other historians place more blame on Hoover himself, however. Writing in the 1980s, Charles P. Kindleberger argued that the Depression would have ended sooner if Hoover and the Federal Reserve Board had been more willing to lend money to the stricken banks. Hoover froze war debts and reparations payments, but the Hawley–Smoot Tariff reduced the levels of world trade and triggered retaliations. The Depression therefore lasted so long because trade was kept low.

Robert Sobel

Robert Sobel, an eminent historian of banking, argued that the Wall Street Crash did not in itself lead to any bank failures in the USA. Large-scale business collapse did not really begin until 1930–1. Sobel argued that Hoover could have done more to reform the financial system. It was effectively his inactivity that was in part responsible for the collapse.

J.K. Galbraith

Writing in the mid-twentieth century, J.K. Galbraith felt that if the economy had been sound, the effects of the Wall Street Crash would have been relatively minor. However, the Crash made deflation worse for two reasons.

First, a major problem was represented by the problems of financial pyramids that existed only to buy and sell stock. As the value of stock slumped these collapsed. Their collapse in turn led to the failure of the companies they controlled, which actually produced goods (generally at the bottom of the pyramid). This led to greater unemployment. The public lost confidence in the economy and were no longer prepared to get into debt to buy goods even if they could afford to.

Second, Galbraith also listed the evidence of too many small and weak banks, indebted foreigners and poor economic intelligence. The Fed, for example, believed the economy would right itself. If its members had loosened the money supply they could have stimulated the economy. In fact they made things worse by tightening the money supply by 33 per cent between 1929 and 1934.

Paul Johnson

Opposing the view that Hoover should have done more is British historian Paul Johnson, who felt that he should have done less. Johnson disagreed that the economy was weak and believed it would have righted itself. However, he argued that Hoover asked employers not to cut wages while he reduced taxes and increased government spending. This led to a huge government deficit and began, in Johnson's opinion, the **New Deal** that Roosevelt continued. Indeed, he argued that Hoover started more public works schemes in his four years of office than had been done in the previous 40. Hoover had earlier reduced taxes. Now he increased them to pay for the public works schemes. According to Johnson this simply showed the inconsistency in Hoover's policies. The Hawley–Smoot Tariff, which limited international trade, made things even worse. Meanwhile, by supporting insolvent companies and keeping people in work, Hoover simply extended the agonies of the Depression. He should have let the economy right itself.

KEY TERM

New Deal President Roosevelt's programme to end the Depression and restore prosperity.

David M. Kennedy

Kennedy agreed in part with Hoover that economic problems in Europe made the Depression worse in the USA. He sees as a catalyst the progressive abandonment of the Gold Standard. Keeping to the Gold Standard guaranteed the value of money across frontiers. Nations issued currencies in amounts fixed by the ratio of money to the amount in their gold reserves. In theory, gold coming in from other countries would expand the monetary base in the country which received it. This would mean the amount of money in circulation could be increased. This would in turn inflate prices and lower interest rates as more money for borrowing became available.

A fall in gold stocks had the opposite effect: it shrank the domestic money supply, deflated prices and raised interest rates. Any country whose supply of gold was falling was expected to deflate their economy, to lower prices to stimulate exports and raise interest rates. This would reverse the outflow of capital. By tying foreign economies together, the Gold Standard in theory ensured economic fluctuations in one country would be spread to others.

However, because of the Depression, by 1931 huge amounts of gold were lost. To protect themselves countries raised tariffs, imposed controls on the export of capital and abandoned the Gold Standard. Britain was the first country to do this, in September 1931. Hoover felt that Britain was acting like a failed bank that cheated its creditors. This may be true, but Britain was also at the heart of the global financial structure. Therefore, when Britain abandoned the Gold Standard, other countries followed suit. This produced a crisis in the global economy and led to other countries protecting themselves through tariffs, like the Hawley–Smoot Tariff in the USA. The value of global business fell from $36 billion in 1929 to $12 billion by 1932.

This affected the USA in three main ways:

- US banks held worthless assets from foreigners as they had defaulted on repayment.
- Foreign investors began to withdraw capital from US banks.
- Insecurity led to domestic runs on US banks.

During the months of September to October 1931, following Britain's abandonment of the Gold Standard, 2294 US banks failed (double the number that did so in 1930). The Fed responded by further deflating the economy at a time when it should have inflated it, for example, by increasing the stock of money. To stop the outflow of gold, the Fed raised the rediscount rates. If Hoover was at fault it was in his refusal to change his ideas. Many countries at least partially recovered after abandoning the Gold Standard. Hoover persisted with it.

Lee E. Ohanian

Ohanian, a Professor at the University of California, surveyed current thinking in 2009. He showed that economic historians have been focusing more attention on labour markets. Usually during depression, high unemployment and low living standards drive wages down, lowering the costs of output so the depression eventually rights itself.

However, during the Great Depression this did not happen. Wages for those in work actually rose. The reason most commonly offered is that government intervention, particularly during the New Deal years (see Chapter 4), restricted competition between businesses. Ohanian gives the examples of the National Industrial Recovery Act (see pages 89–91) that allowed cartels to operate, restricting price reductions and production, and the National Labor Relations Act (see page 107) that allowed workers' unions to negotiate for higher wages. Through its intervention therefore, the federal government actually prolonged the Depression by not allowing free-market forces to operate.

Federal government policies

> ▶ *Key question: How successfully did President Hoover's administration tackle the Great Depression?*

Although President Hoover eventually intervened more than any former president in the economy, the measures he was prepared to take were wholly insufficient to meet the demands of the economic crisis. Above all he could not, and importantly, neither would his own supporters, accept the need for direct government involvement. This section will look at the measures he took – summarized in the table on the next page.

Year	Economic factors and statistics	Government action
1929	Unemployment 3.2% GNP $203.6 billion Growth rate 6.7% October: price of shares fell by $14 billion	Agricultural Marketing Act
1930	Unemployment 8.9% GNP $183.5 billion Growth rate 9.6% Serious drought south-east of Rockies	Voluntarism Hawley–Smoot Tariff $49 million in loans to drought victims
1931	Unemployment 16.3% GNP $169.5 billion Growth rate 7.6%	Moratorium for 18 months on collection of war debts National Credit Corporation set up with funds of $500 million
1932	Unemployment 24.1% GNP $144.2 billion Growth rate 14.7%	Federal Home Loan Bank Act Reconstruction Finance Corporation set up with funds of $2 billion Emergency Relief and Construction Act Dispersal by force of 'Bonus Army'

Government action in response to economic factors 1929–32

The role of President Hoover

President Hoover worked tirelessly to combat the Depression. He worried constantly and gave generously to charity. He cut his own and state officials' salaries by 20 per cent to help provide revenues for his recovery measures. Hoover worked all day, every day and long into the night with scarcely a break for meals.

Hoover well understood the seriousness of the Depression, which overshadowed all but the first seven months of his presidency. In public, however, he had to be optimistic in spite of all the problems; this has led many to argue that he quite lost touch with reality. When, for example, he told the press that unemployment was falling, this created considerable resentment among many of the jobless, and led others to argue that the unemployed were simply too lazy to get a job.

As a result of his constant public optimism, Hoover gradually lost all credibility. 'Hoovervilles' – the shanties where homeless lived – were named after him, as were 'Hoover blankets' – the newspapers in which they wrapped themselves to keep warm.

Hoover's problem was that he would not abandon his two central beliefs of self-reliance and American individualism.

> **How effectively did President Hoover work to combat the Depression?**

Having said this, Hoover involved the government more in the economy than any other previous president. However, he could not bring himself to accept what many increasingly argued was necessary: direct government relief. He continued to believe that the economy had to right itself. 'Economic depression', he said, 'cannot be cured by legislative action or executive pronouncement. Economic wounds must be healed by the action of the cells of the economic body – the producers and consumers themselves.'

Hoover certainly understood the need for the government to take action to help this to happen. He had no patience, for example, with his Treasury Secretary, Andrew Mellon, who was advising businessmen who were still solvent to fire their workers and sell everything until the crisis was over. Hoover called these ideas 'child-like' and removed Mellon from his post by sending him to London as ambassador.

However, as we shall see, Hoover's policies were simply not far reaching enough to address the scale and seriousness of the Depression. He was prepared to do something, but nowhere near enough.

? What is the value of the photograph in Source E in showing how American people lived during the Depression?

SOURCE E

Hooverville in New York City. Note the squalor in which people lived.

Agriculture

→ **How did President Hoover try to help the agricultural sector?**

Hoover called a special session of Congress in April 1929, before the Wall Street Crash, to deal with the pressing problems of agriculture. He would no more intervene to help farmers than his predecessors, but he was prepared to help farmers to help themselves.

The Agricultural Marketing Act of 1929 established a nine-person Federal Farm Board with funds of $500 million to create farmers' marketing co-operatives called 'stabilization corporations'. These were to be given the task of buying, storing and eventually disposing of farm surpluses in an orderly way. However, they had no power to order reductions in production. Huge surpluses in 1931 and 1932 both at home and abroad saw prices fall and the corporations paying above-market values for produce. The Grain Stabilization Corporation, for example, bought wheat in Chicago at 80 cents a bushel while the world price had fallen to 60 cents. By the time it ceased its purchases in summer 1931, it had paid an average of 82 cents per bushel for 300 million bushels while the world price had fallen to 40 cents a bushel.

The Corporation might have been helping farmers, but it was also accused of throwing taxpayers' money away. It was buying farm produce at well over the market price and therefore was seen to encourage farmers to keep producing more, when, in fact, they should have been encouraged to produce less. By 1932 the world price of wheat was between 30 cents and 39 cents a bushel, less than harvesting costs in the USA. When Congress did propose a bill to subsidize farmers to reduce production, Hoover threatened to veto it because it undermined the principle of voluntary action. In the event, the bill failed without any need for a veto. It was too radical a measure for the time.

The agricultural policy failed mainly, then, for two reasons:

- It was paying American farmers artificially high prices and this could not continue in the long term.
- It treated agriculture as a domestic issue and, therefore, failed to take account of foreign considerations. Without high tariffs, there was little point in trying to keep the American price artificially high. The answer to the problem of cheap foreign imports, then, seemed to be even higher tariffs.

Tariffs

→ **What was the impact of the Hawley–Smoot Tariff?**

The Hawley–Smoot Tariff, which came into force in June 1930, was the highest in American history, with average duties of 40 per cent on both agricultural and industrial items. It led to most European nations abandoning free trade and to even fewer American goods being exported. This was of no advantage to farmers with their huge surpluses. Knowing this, farming interests in Congress fought hard against the measure, and it passed the Senate by only two votes. Hoover could have vetoed the bill but chose not to.

What was the purpose of repudiating war debts?

Repudiation of war debts

Hoover blamed the Depression on Europe but he was probably not entirely correct in doing so. Others have argued that it was the American depression that spread to Europe and not vice versa. Certainly after the Wall Street Crash, American credit dried up. The Hawley–Smoot Tariff made things worse. In the years 1929 and 1930 the value of international trade fell in total by $500 million and in the following year it fell by $1.2 billion. This led to European countries **repudiating their war debts**.

Germany was particularly affected by the withdrawal of American credit. When the German government became virtually bankrupt it announced the suspension of reparations payments and said that it might also have to refuse to pay back loans. Hoover feared a European war over this. He knew that the French, in particular, might resort to military action to get their reparations. Moreover, refusal to repay debts would badly affect American banks, which were already struggling to keep solvent.

On 21 June 1931, Hoover announced the USA would postpone the collection of its debts for 18 months if other countries would do the same. This, he hoped, would release monies for investment. It is generally known as the **moratorium**. In the event, it was too little too late to stop the collapse of European economies.

Interestingly, when the proposed moratorium came up for renewal in December 1932, it was during the period of Hoover's **lame duck presidency**. Hoover advised Roosevelt to continue the moratorium. However, Roosevelt, sensing hostility in Congress, agreed to the passage of the Johnson Act. This made it illegal to sell in the USA the securities of any country that had refused to repay its debts. As the stock market was still stagnant, this had little effect except to make European countries even more resentful of the USA. Finland was the only country that continued to pay its debts.

How effective was voluntarism in halting the Depression?

Promotion of voluntarism

At first, Hoover hoped to persuade businessmen and state governments to continue as if there was no Depression, to solve it through their own voluntary efforts. He called meetings of businessmen in which he implored them not to reduce their workforce or cut wages, but rather to maintain their output and urge people to buy. He encouraged state leaders to begin new programmes of public works as well as continuing with the old.

As the Depression worsened, business had little choice but to cut back. Workers were laid off, most investment was postponed and wages of those still in work were reduced. As we have seen, states also had to reduce their spending. The problems were simply too great for **voluntarism** to work, particularly when it went against customary business practice. Bankers, for example, set up the National Credit Corporation in October 1931 with the

KEY TERM

Repudiation of war debts Where countries ceased repaying their war debts.

Moratorium Term given to Hoover's offer to postpone debt repayment for 18 months.

Lame duck presidency The period between one president coming to the end of his term and his successor taking over.

Voluntarism The notion that business and state government should solve the Great Depression through their own voluntary efforts.

task of helping failing banks to survive. It began with a capital fund of $500 million donated by the major financial institutions.

With banks continuing to fail at unprecedented rates, the Corporation had spent only $10 million by the end of 1931. Bankers were simply too ingrained in their ways to begin investing in failing concerns. The Corporation faded away, showing again that individual financial concerns would almost always put their own interests before those of their country.

Unemployment relief

← **How effective was Federal government relief?**

Hoover secured additional amounts from Congress to the tune of $500 million in 1932 to help the various agencies to provide relief. However, this was wholly inadequate to meet the scale of the problem. He set up the President's Emergency Committee for Employment to help the agencies to organize their efforts. But, again, he would not countenance direct federal relief, arguing that this destroyed self-help and created a class of people dependent on the government for handouts. Even during the severe drought of 1930–1, which saw near-starvation conditions in much of the south, he baulked at direct relief. In the end, Congress allocated a pitifully small sum, $47 million, and even that was to be offered as loans that must be later repaid.

By 1932, with no easing of the Depression, Hoover introduced two more radical measures, which again were insufficient in themselves but marked a significant shift in the level of government involvement.

Federal Home Loan Bank Act

This measure, passed in July 1932, was intended to save mortgages by making credit easier. A series of Federal Home Loan banks was set up to help loan associations to provide mortgages. However, as the maximum loan was only 50 per cent of the value of the property it was largely ineffective. It was simply another example of help that failed because it was insufficient to deal with the seriousness of the situation, in this case homes being repossessed.

Reconstruction Finance Corporation

This was undoubtedly Hoover's most radical measure to combat the Depression and was a forerunner of the New Deal initiatives of Franklin D. Roosevelt. The Reconstruction Finance Corporation (RFC) was established in January 1932 with authority to lend up to $2 billion to rescue banks, insurance companies, railroads and construction companies in distress. The new Treasury Secretary, Ogden Mills, said the RFC was 'an insurance measure more than anything else'. It was designed to restore confidence, particularly in financial institutions.

Of its loans, 90 per cent went to small and medium banks, and 70 per cent to banks in towns with a population of less than 5000. However, critics of the RFC pointed to the size of individual loans, not the actual number. They argued that 50 per cent of loans went to the seven per cent of borrowers who happened to be the biggest banks. Moreover, of the first $61 million committed by the RFC, $41 million was loaned to no more than three institutions. One alone, the Central Republican National Bank and Trust Company, received $90 million in total. This came soon after the return to the bank of its president, who had been seconded to run the RFC. The $90 million, incidentally, was almost as much as the bank held in total deposits at the time. Similarly, the biggest loans also went to the biggest railroads and public utilities.

The government argued its case by saying that the largest firms were the biggest employers, so it made sense to help them in the war against unemployment. However, many critics saw the RFC as giving direct relief to large concerns while none was offered to individuals in distress.

In fact, the clamour for direct relief became so great that in summer 1932 Hoover finally agreed. He gave his support to the Emergency Relief and Construction Act, which authorized the RFC to lend up to $1.5 billion to states to finance public works. However, to be eligible the states had to declare bankruptcy and the works undertaken had to produce revenues that would eventually pay off the loans. When Hoover agreed to this, many of his erstwhile supporters felt he had gone too far. In 1932 James M. Beck, a former Solicitor General, compared Hoover's government to that of Soviet Russia! Many members of the Republican Party believed strongly in policies of non-intervention. However, in the end, the RFC offered far too little far too late. By this time, in the words of Calvin Coolidge's former secretary, Edward Clark, 'Today, there seems to be no class nor section where Hoover is strong or where a decision is respected because [he] made it.'

Hoover's credibility, which was already severely damaged, was finally destroyed by his role in an event that made him seem cruel as well as unfeeling. This was the treatment of the 'Bonus Army'.

What was the 'Bonus Army' and how was it dealt with?

 **KEY TERM**

Veterans' Administration
An organization to help ex-servicemen.

War veterans and the 'Bonus Army'

Ironically, it was Hoover who had set up the **Veterans' Administration** for those who had seen military service. Annual federal expenditure on veterans' disabilities was $675.8 million. However, Hoover will always be remembered for what happened to the 'Bonus Army'.

Congress had agreed a veteran's 'bonus' in 1925. Based on the number of years of service, it was to be paid in full to each veteran in 1945. But, quite understandably, as the Depression, hit many veterans said they needed it immediately. A march to Washington was organized to publicize their cause. By 15 June 1932, 20,000 people were camped in the capital, mainly around the Anacostia Flats region. On that day the House of Representatives voted by 226 votes to 175 to allow immediate payment of the bonus.

However, two days later, largely because of the cost, the Senate vetoed this. Feeling for the veterans' plight, but insistent that nothing could be done for them, Hoover offered $100,000 to pay for their transportation home.

Many refused to budge. Some were squatting in derelict buildings in Pennsylvania Avenue with the tacit support of the district police superintendent who sympathized with them. Hoover increasingly feared violence and even revolution. The White House was protected with barricades and its gates were chained.

The Secretary of War, determined to move the squatters, called in troops under General Douglas MacArthur. Tanks and infantry not only shifted the squatters, but chased them back to the main camp on Anacostia Flats where tear gas was used to disperse them. The camp was destroyed, many marchers were injured, and two babies died from the effects of the gas. The Assistant Secretary of War publicly called these men, who had previously been regarded as heroes, 'A polyglot mob of tramps and hoodlums with a generous sprinkling of Communist agitators.'

Although MacArthur had gone beyond his authority in attacking the camp on Anacostia Flats, the deed was done and Hoover came out in his support. Later, in the election campaign he even blurted out, 'Thank God you have a government that knows how to deal with a mob.' However, Americans had been horrified at the scenes and whether they were his fault or not, Hoover was blamed. The violent dispersal of the 'Bonus Army' by the military was a major political blunder.

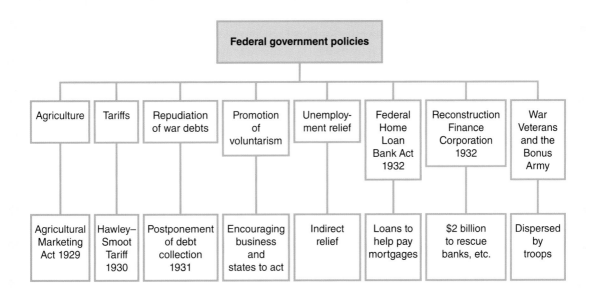

SUMMARY DIAGRAM

Federal government policies

5 The 1932 presidential election

> ▶ **Key question:** Why was the 1932 presidential election so significant?

The USA had been in Depression for most of Hoover's presidency, and despite his efforts there appeared no easing in sight. Hoover was exhausted and, as we have seen, was blamed by many for his failed policies. Some questioned whether the US system of capitalism could survive and offered extremist alternatives. The Democrats meanwhile selected a candidate of great charisma who engendered confidence and faith even though he offered little of actual substance in his electoral programmes.

Parties of the extreme right and left

> **How significant were the extremist alternatives on the right and left wings of politics?**

The extent of the Depression undoubtedly led some to wonder whether the American system was doomed. Extremism usually thrives on hopelessness and despair, and there was certainly enough of both during the Depression. However, there is very little evidence that the USA was anywhere near revolution and, unlike in European countries, extremist parties never received more than a small amount of support.

The extreme right

There were the beginnings of an American **fascist** movement, called the Silver Shirts. Despite the increasing interest shown in it by disaffected members of the Ku Klux Klan, its membership was estimated to be less than 700. Certainly its effects at this time were insignificant.

The extreme left

The extreme left offered policies of public ownership and equalization of wealth. The American right in particular saw them as traitors in the pay of the USSR.

Communists

American **Communists** expected the Depression to lead to revolution. They set up unemployment councils with the slogan, 'Fight – Don't Starve' and organized marches against unemployment. The Communists were a small, highly disciplined party in the revolutionary tradition of underground activity. They took their orders from Moscow. The Soviet government insisted they refuse to work with the Socialists or any non-communist organization.

Indeed, its lack of understanding of the USA is shown in some of its orders. African-Americans, for example, were viewed as a persecuted nationality and the party was persuaded to campaign for the creation of a separate African-American state in those parts of the south-east where they were in the majority. Even when Communists did work with African-Americans to improve their living standards, as in the Sharecroppers' Union set up in 1931, their efforts achieved little. Local authorities often supported the violence and intimidation from the Ku Klux Klan, for example, that destroyed the Sharecroppers' Union members' will to fight. During the 1932 presidential election the Communists spent much of their time sniping at the Socialists. This helped to account for their poor showing in the election.

Socialists

The decade of the 1920s was a difficult one for the Socialists. Their opposition to American entry into the First World War and split with the Communists in 1919 had lost them the support of many intellectuals. They were committed to working with the **American Federation of Labor** (AFL), which was conservative and often racist in nature. In the 1932 election the Socialist candidate, Norman Thomas, polled fewer than one million votes. Many of his own supporters felt it was more important to defeat Hoover than to vote for socialism. Many gave their support to the Democratic candidate, Franklin D. Roosevelt, simply for that reason. To others Roosevelt really did symbolize new hope, offering the real change they were clamouring for.

> **KEY TERM**
>
> **American Federation of Labor** An organization representing American workers' unions.

The election campaigns

> Why did Roosevelt win the 1932 presidential election?

Roosevelt was by far the strongest Democratic nominee for candidate. Hoover was too busy fighting the Depression to campaign effectively. The members of his re-election team were themselves short on ideas. One slogan they thought up but wisely decided not to use was 'Boy! Wasn't that some Depression'.

Hoover generally had poor relations with the press; Roosevelt courted them. Hoover lacked charisma; Roosevelt exuded it. However, many historians have argued that there was little to choose between the candidates in terms of economic policies. Certainly, Roosevelt did not promise government action to solve economic problems. In fact, he even made a speech on 19 October attacking Hoover's 'extravagant government spending' and pledging a 25 per cent cut in the federal budget.

The most important factor was that Hoover expected to lose, while his opponent was determined to win. Many of Roosevelt's promises were vague and even contradictory. In San Francisco he made a speech advocating economic regulation only as a last resort, while, at Oglethorpe University, Georgia, he spoke of 'bold experimentation' to beat the Depression and of a redistribution of national income. However, Roosevelt did say things that captured the public imagination. In a national radio address in April 1932, before his nomination, he called for government to help 'the forgotten man'. In his acceptance speech, after receiving the nomination he repeated this idea (see Source F).

Explain how effectively
Roosevelt uses language and
tone to engender support in
Source F. Support your
answer with examples from
the source.

SOURCE F

An extract from a speech by Franklin D. Roosevelt accepting the Democratic Party nomination in 1932.

On the farms, in the large, metropolitan areas, in the smaller cities and in the villages, millions of our citizens cherish the hope that their old standards of living and of thought have not gone forever. These millions cannot and shall not hope in vain.

I pledge you, I pledge myself, to a new deal for the American people. Let us all here assembled constitute ourselves prophets of a new order of competence and of courage. This is more than a political campaign; it is a call to arms. Give me your help, not to win votes alone but to aim in this crusade to restore America to its own people.

In this speech Roosevelt created a name for his programme, the 'New Deal', whose operation will be discussed in detail in the next chapter. Traditionally the victorious nominee waited at home for the party elders to visit him and to offer the nomination. However, Roosevelt took the unprecedented step of flying to Chicago, where the convention was being held, to accept it. This had the effect of showing to the rest of the USA that here was a man who meant business, who recognized there was a grave crisis and could not wait to get on with the job of solving it.

Americans were voting above all for change. This, above all, is what Roosevelt seemed to offer.

1932 Presidential election	
Herbert Hoover	Franklin Delano Roosevelt
Self-help Voluntarism Community responsibility	'New Deal for the American People' Restoration of confidence in the USA
15.7 million votes	22.8 million votes

SUMMARY DIAGRAM

The 1932 presidential election

Chapter summary

President Hoover and the Great Depression

Many Americans had high hopes of Hoover as president, but his term of office coincided with the onset of the Depression. While he was prepared to do more than any previous president, the intensity of the economic downturn was too great for his policies to address effectively. Above all he would not consider direct government intervention.

- The Depression eventually affected every aspect of the US economy and the financial and banking sectors remained in turmoil.

- Millions became unemployed. Many became homeless too, crossing the continent in search of work.
- Hoover's policies were inadequate to meet the scale of the problem. Although he repudiated foreign war debts, the high tariffs probably made matters worse.

Despite the scale of the Depression there was little enthusiasm for extremist politics. People still believed in the main in the strength of the American system of government. Franklin Delano Roosevelt won the 1932 presidential election. People had great hopes that he could solve the economic problems, not because he had any concrete policies but because he wasn't Herbert Hoover.

 # Examination advice

How to answer 'examine' questions

Questions that ask <u>examine</u> are prompting you to consider a variety of explanations. Each of these will need to be explained in full. It is also possible to question the question. This means that you can disagree with the basic premise of the question. In this case, you must present full counter-arguments and be prepared to expound on these.

Example

> <u>Examine</u> the reasons why President Hoover's attempts to deal with the Great Depression were unsuccessful.

1 In the case of this specific question, you should be prepared to write about exactly what President Hoover did from October 1929 until he left office in early 1933. For each of his policies you should explain why it was unsuccessful. Successful responses will also explain what the specific problem was that Hoover hoped to overcome.

   An alternative if more difficult approach to answering this question would be to challenge the question. You could take the point of view that depressions were cyclical in nature and that the economy would have eventually recovered. You could also add that the US government and Hoover should not have interfered in the economy since rarely in the nation's history had it done so.

2 First, take at least five minutes to write a short outline. In your outline, list the initial problem, Hoover's actions, and the result. You are not expected to know each and every action but be prepared to discuss at least four in depth. An example of an outline for an answer to this question might be as follows.

Problem	Action	Result
Farm surpluses, falling prices	Agricultural Marketing Act, 1929	Stabilization corporations bought up surplus farm produce above market value. Farmers produced more instead of less. Could not continue in the long term. Very costly
Imported industrial and agricultural products which were cheaper than US ones	Hawley–Smoot Tariff 1930. Hoover could have vetoed this but did not	High protective tariffs led most Europeans to abandon free trade and to purchase fewer US goods
Falling wages and reduced workforce	Hoover encouraged voluntarism	As Depression worsened, businesses felt they had to fire workers and cut wages to stay in operation. Voluntary efforts failed to take hold
Millions of unemployed	Emergency Committee for Employment to co-ordinate agencies' efforts but no direct federal relief	Inadequate for scale and scope of problems
Failing banks, insurance companies, industries	Reconstruction Finance Corporation 1932	Much aid went to small number of companies instead of to suffering individuals
Foreclosures on home mortgages	Federal Home Loan Bank Act, 1932	Because maximum loan was only 50% of property value, it was largely ineffective

3 In your introduction, you should discuss the major problems, what Hoover did, and why such efforts were largely unsuccessful. Be sure to state your thesis. This could well be that Hoover's efforts failed because they did were usually too timid in the face of the gravity of the situation. An example of a good introduction is given below.

> When Herbert Hoover became president in March 1929, the future of the nation seemed bright. However, within seven months, the USA entered an economic downturn that would destroy Hoover's presidency. Most, if not all of his attempts to counter the deteriorating economic situation were not successful. As millions lost their jobs, homes, farms and faith in America, the government responded with measures that fell far short of what was needed. Hoover believed Americans should be responsible for their own welfare and that they could overcome difficulties by working harder. Unfortunately, the scale of the nation's economic ills was such that this was not possible. Among the major issues in the Depression were home foreclosures, unemployment, failing businesses and banks, and falling exports. In responding to each of these, Hoover's policies did not help to alleviate the continuing and deepening problems.

4 The body of your essay should explain in detail the problems, solutions and results of several major issues from 1929 to 1933. Be prepared to devote at least one paragraph to each issue. One unifying point that could be stressed was the paltry efforts made by the Hoover administration in almost all cases. You should also consider why that might have been the case. Hoover instinctively did not think the US government should deprive its citizens of the desire to work by offering handouts. In his opinion, the economy would right itself through volunteerism, hard work and self-reliance. Unfortunately, these were not sufficient to address the falling economy. Similarly, when specific policies were adopted, the results were not positive.

5 In the conclusion, you should tie together the ideas you have explored and how they relate directly to the notion that Hoover's efforts were unsuccessful because the measures taken were insufficient in the face of such major problems. An example of a good concluding paragraph is given overleaf.

President Hoover's efforts to tackle the increasingly grave problems facing the USA during the first years of the Great Depression were inadequate. His core beliefs that hard work and sacrifice would overcome the difficulties played a part in his less than aggressive measures. When he did make specific decisions, the results were insufficient in dealing with the difficulties facing the country. In virtually every case, the measures proposed and enacted were far too small to solve the scale of the problems. It would be up to his successor, Franklin D. Roosevelt, to involve the government much more deeply in confronting the greatest economic problems ever faced by the USA.

6 Now try writing a complete answer to the question following the advice above.

 Examination practice

Below are two exam-style questions for you to practise on this topic.

1 Examine why relief agencies were unable to cope with the Great Depression during Hoover's administration?

2 Discuss the social impact of the Great Depression from 1929 to 1933.
(For guidance on how to answer 'discuss' questions, see page 228.)

CHAPTER 4

The USA 1933–45: New Deals and economic recovery

This chapter investigates domestic issues during the period of Roosevelt's presidency from 1933 to 1945. It looks at the First New Deal from 1933 to 1935, Roosevelt's presidential style, the effectiveness of the legislation introduced during the first 100 days, and alternatives from the political left and right in the build-up to the 1936 presidential election. It analyses the nature and meaning of the First New Deal before going on to look at how the New Deal programmes developed in the years 1935–41, asking how successful they were in addressing the continuing problems caused by the Depression. The impact of the period on arts and literature will be discussed. Finally, it examines the impact of the Second World War on the US economy.

The chapter examines the following key questions that you need to consider:

✪ How far were the beginnings of Roosevelt's presidency a significant break with the past?

✪ How significant were the alternatives to the New Deal?

✪ Was the First New Deal a planned programme or simply a series of unrelated measures to deal with specific problems?

✪ How successfully did the Second New Deal address the problems faced by the USA?

✪ How effectively did Roosevelt deal with the problems of his second term?

✪ Were the measures taken during the Third New Deal more radical than those that had gone before?

✪ How and when did the New Deal come to a close?

✪ How much impact did the New Deal have on American politics and the economy?

✪ How effectively did the New Deal improve conditions for women and African-Americans?

✪ What conclusions can be drawn about the impact of the New Deal?

✪ How did literature and the arts respond to changes in American society?

✪ What was the political and economic impact of the Second World War on the USA?

1 The first 100 days and the First New Deal

▶ **Key question:** *How far were the beginnings of Roosevelt's presidency a significant break with the past?*

Two weeks before his inauguration on 4 March 1933, Franklin Delano Roosevelt addressed a meeting in Miami, Florida. Joseph Zangara fired five bullets at him from close range. All missed their target. Zangara opposed capitalism and sought to kill the man pledged to save it. Fittingly, Roosevelt did go on to save the capitalist system in the USA through his New Deal programme.

Historians speak of two and even three different New Deals in the 1930s. These will be examined in this chapter.

Roosevelt's inauguration

How different were the policies of Hoover and Roosevelt?

Roosevelt's **inauguration** was in March 1933. This was four months after the election in November 1932. Hoover was still in office and clearly Roosevelt must have been frustrated waiting to take over.

During this period, the Depression worsened considerably, with the outgoing president, Hoover, unable to introduce effective measures to combat it. Hoover sought to involve Roosevelt in a smooth transition and to agree on common policies. However, Roosevelt was non-committal to these offers. He wanted neither to be associated with Hoover, whose credibility was shattered, nor to tie himself to shared policies with political opponents.

KEY TERM

Inauguration The ceremony that begins the president's term of office.

?
How fair is the cartoon in Source A to Hoover's record as president? Explain your answer carefully using evidence from the source.

SOURCE A

Cartoon of Roosevelt throwing out Hoover's rubbish on taking office in March 1933.

Later, Hoover was to accuse Roosevelt of stealing his policies and taking credit for them. Indeed, it was alleged by some critics that Roosevelt wanted the Depression to get worse so he could take credit for launching a rescue operation after his inauguration. Hoover could then be accused of having done nothing to halt the Depression.

In fact there was little difference at first between the policies of Roosevelt and Hoover. It was the two men who were different. Roosevelt came across as dynamic, charismatic and someone in whom people were ready to have faith. Hoover, as we have seen, was tired, jaded and dull by comparison.

There was tremendous expectation and excitement about Roosevelt's presidency; people were willing it to be something special. Certainly no incoming president since the Civil War had faced so many problems. Roosevelt's inaugural speech seemed to offer everything that people wanted to hear. 'The only thing we have to fear', Roosevelt said, 'is fear itself'. He called for 'action and action now'.

SOURCE B

Extract from Roosevelt's inaugural address, March 1933.

Our greatest primary task is to put people back to work. This is no unsolvable problem if we face it wisely and courageously.

It can be accomplished in part by direct recruiting by the government itself, treating the task as we would treat the emergency of war, but at the same time, through this employment, accomplishing greatly needed projects to stimulate our use of natural resources.

> How does Roosevelt emphasize the urgency of the task faced by his government in Source B?

Roosevelt's presidential style

> **What was different about Roosevelt's presidential style?**

Many historians, for example William E. Leuchtenburg, have claimed that the modern presidency begins with Roosevelt. There is little doubt that the New Deal expanded the roles of the president and state in the running of the USA. However, Roosevelt also brought a new style to the presidency. He appeared full of infectious optimism and confidence. A few weeks after Roosevelt's inauguration, one business journal commented, 'The people aren't sure where they're going but anywhere seems better than where they've been.' Roosevelt's style differed from that of his predecessors in two ways:

- his use of the media
- his appointment of personnel.

Use of the media

Roosevelt was perhaps the first president to understand the power of the media. He developed the twice-weekly press conferences into cosy conversations. He got to know members of the press corps by name, he explained policies carefully and he invited questions. This contrasted with his predecessors, who had only accepted questions written out and presented in advance. Hoover's relationship with the press had been so frosty that he had been accused of using the secret service to investigate any leakage of information to the press.

The result of this new friendliness and 'openness' towards the press corps was that Roosevelt got them on his side. He could release information as and when he thought it necessary, forestall criticism and effectively control much of the newspaper reporting about him.

Fireside chats

Roosevelt was said to have 'the first great American radio voice'. He spoke directly to the electorate on issues in 'fireside chats'. These became so popular that those without a radio would visit those who had to ensure they did not miss the president. The mass media was still in its infancy. Until Calvin Coolidge began to enjoy being photographed, few Americans had ever seen a picture of their president, let alone heard his voice. Now the reassuring voice of Roosevelt in living rooms throughout the nation restored confidence and helped people to believe that everything was going to be all right. After he told people over the radio to tell him their troubles, it took a staff of 50 to handle his mail, which arrived by the truckload. By contrast, one person had been employed to deal with Herbert Hoover's correspondence.

Appointment of personnel

Previously, presidents had tended to appoint political allies or at best other members of their party to help them to govern. Roosevelt tended to look for the best people for the job irrespective of political affiliations. Most of the 'Brains' Trusters' (see page 58) followed him to the White House. In addition, he appointed Henry A. Wallace, a farming expert, as Secretary for Agriculture.

Roosevelt encouraged rivalry and disputes among his appointees. He would listen to their disputes and then make up his own mind between them. Sometimes he used personal appointees to investigate issues, bypassing proper channels. Often when appointing people to office he made their job specifications deliberately vague so their responsibilities would appear to overlap with others'. He knew this would make people more dependent on him as they asked him to intervene in disputes or sought his favour or support.

This strategy of personnel management worked. Roosevelt inspired intense loyalty. He could enthuse with a smile or small favour. As Harold Ickes, his Secretary of the Interior said, no matter how jaded you were, you came out of a meeting with Roosevelt like 'a fighting cock'. His appointees would need their energy. The first 100 days of Roosevelt's administration set the scene for the transformation of the USA.

The first 100 days

Roosevelt asked Congress to grant him powers as great as those it would have given him had the USA been invaded by a foreign enemy. He called Congress into a special session, which was to last for 100 days. These first 100 days of Roosevelt's presidency were possibly the most frenzied and energetic of any presidency, with a considerable amount of emergency legislation and the setting up of many 'alphabet agencies'. Many historians have categorized the measures into those intended to bring about 'relief, recovery or reform', but as we shall see it is dangerous to assume Roosevelt had a blueprint to transform American life greatly.

However, it is no exaggeration to say that, intentionally or not, at the end of the 100 days the USA had been transformed.

Banking and finance

The most pressing concern was undoubtedly the collapse of the American banking system. By 1932 banks were closing at the rate of 40 per day. In October of that year, the Governor of Nevada, fearing the imminent collapse of an important banking chain, declared a bank holiday and closed every bank in the state. By the time of Roosevelt's inauguration, banks were closed in many states.

One important effect of these bank closures was a flow of gold from the Federal Reserve and New York banks to local banks that were still functioning. This was to support those banks so they had enough capital to continue to function. Between January and the inauguration in March, the nation's gold reserves fell from $1.3 billion to $400 million because of this shift. Nevertheless, American banks had only $6 billion available to meet $41 billion worth of deposits. In the two days before the inauguration $500 million was withdrawn. The situation was so fraught that Washington hotels would not accept out-of-town cheques from inauguration guests.

Emergency Banking Relief Act

On 6 March Roosevelt closed all the banks in the country for four days to give Treasury officials time to draft emergency legislation. The ensuing Emergency Banking Relief Act was passed by Congress after only 40 minutes of debate. All the measures it contained had already been considered by Hoover. However, they had been rejected because he feared the panic that may have resulted from the closing of the banks. Roosevelt had no such fear. Although his action may have been unconstitutional, people were expecting him to act decisively and, while the banks were closed, they improvised using barter, foreign currencies and stamps as units of exchange.

The aim of the Emergency Banking Relief Act was simply to restore confidence in the American banking system. It gave the Treasury power to investigate all banks threatened with collapse. The Reconstruction Finance Corporation (RFC, see page 67) was authorized to buy their stock to support

How effective were the measures taken during the first 100 days?

🔑 KEY TERM

Alphabet agencies New government bodies set up to tackle problems. They were so called because they became known by their initials, for example AAA, CCC.

them and to take on many of their debts. In doing so the RFC became in effect the largest bank in the world.

In the meantime, Roosevelt appeared on radio with the first of his 'fireside chats'. He explained to listeners, in language all could understand, the nature of the crisis and how they could help. The message on this occasion was simple: place your money in the bank rather than under your mattress. It worked. Solvent banks were allowed to reopen and others were reorganized by government officials to put them on a sounder footing. By the beginning of April, $1 billion in currency had been returned to bank deposits and the crisis was over. Raymond Moley, one of the 'Brains' Trusters', and Roosevelt's speechwriter, felt that 'American capitalism was saved in eight days'.

The Glass–Steagall Act

Roosevelt later drew up legislation to put the banking system on a sounder long-term footing. The Glass–Steagall Act of 1933 had the following effects:

- Commercial banks that relied on small-scale depositors were banned from involvement in the type of investment banking that had fuelled some of the 1920s' speculation.
- Bank officials were not to be allowed to take personal loans from their own banks.
- Authority over **open-market operations** such as buying and selling **government securities** was centralized by being transferred from the Federal Reserve Banks to the Federal Reserve Board in Washington.
- Individual bank deposits were to be insured against bank failure up to the figure of $2500 with the insurance fund to be administered by a new agency, the Federal Deposit Insurance Corporation (FDIC).

Reactions

The banking legislation, despite its success, was not without its critics. Some criticized Roosevelt for adopting Hoover's policies and for not being radical enough. Raymond Moley admitted that Hoover might have passed similar legislation if he had had the power. Moreover, the measures were carried out by officials appointed by Hoover such as Ogden Mills, whom Roosevelt had kept on.

While the Federal Reserve Board had been given more control, many critics nevertheless wanted to see more government supervision of banking, possibly through nationalization. Some felt that Roosevelt had even rewarded bankers for their past incompetence. Many banks had been given government subsidies to help them to stay in business. By requiring that state banks join the Federal Reserve system to qualify for insurance, large banks were given more control over smaller ones. Although this was to protect them from failure, it all seemed to favour the rich and powerful. However, what these critics failed to appreciate was that this was precisely Roosevelt's intention. He saw his task as the saving of, rather than the destruction of, American capitalism.

 **KEY TERM**

Open-market operations
Buying and selling of government securities on the open market to control the monetary supply.

Government securities
Bonds and bills issued by the government to raise revenue.

Finance

Roosevelt saw his role in finance as two-fold:

- to stop the flow of gold out of the country
- to increase the amount of money in circulation in the USA, thus raising prices.

In a series of measures taken in March and April 1933, he effectively took the USA off the Gold Standard by forbidding the export of gold except under licence from the Treasury and prohibiting the trading-in of currency for gold. Those holding gold were required to turn it in to the Federal Bank for $20.67 an ounce.

The main objective of these measures was to bring down the value of the dollar abroad. Once the dollar was no longer tied to the value of gold, it could find its own level in international markets. This meant in theory that foreigners could afford to buy more American goods. The measure did seem to work, because the international value of the dollar fell to $0.85 in gold, meaning that foreigners could buy 15 per cent more American goods than before for their money.

Effects of Roosevelt's financial measures

This success did leave Roosevelt in a dilemma abroad. European countries in particular had great hopes that the London Economic Conference, which met on 6 July 1933, would help to solve their financial problems. Delegates from these countries wanted a general stabilization of currencies. Roosevelt believed the falling value of the dollar was revitalizing the American economy and so refused to make any agreement. This led directly to the collapse of the Conference. It showed how Roosevelt was concentrating on American recovery and how the New Deal was essentially a domestic programme. The stabilization of foreign economies was simply not on his agenda.

Roosevelt wanted the dollar to fall even further by being left to find its own level. On 22 October 1933, he announced that the RFC would buy gold above the market price, which was then $31.36 an ounce. As the price of gold rose, the value of the dollar fell because it needed more dollars to buy it. On 30 January 1934, the Gold Reserve Act pegged the price of gold at $35 an ounce, and the dollar had effectively been devalued by nearly 60 per cent since March 1933 when gold had been worth $20.67 an ounce.

At home, the effect of all this was to increase the amount of money in circulation. This, it was hoped, would raise prices. The theory behind this was, as the volume of money rose, its relative value would fall simply because there was more of it around. On the other hand, if the value of money fell it bought less, thus causing prices to rise. It was hoped that the rise in prices would in turn help to revitalize American industry and agriculture. However, while prices did rise somewhat, juggling the price of gold and currency mechanisms did not effect any major economic recovery because the nature of the Depression was too complex for any single measures to work.

The Silver Purchase Act, June 1934

Roosevelt also sought to raise prices by introducing more silver into the coinage. He was persuaded in this by some of his supporters from silver-mining states such as Colorado. They had seen the value of silver fall to an all-time low and were looking for government help to improve this situation. Late in 1933 the federal government began to buy up all the silver produced domestically, at an artificially high price. The Silver Purchase Act of June 1934 stated that the Treasury would buy silver until its monetary value equalled 33 per cent that of gold; or alternatively the market price of silver reached what should be its monetary value. However, in effect this measure had little impact beyond subsidizing the domestic silver industry. It offered a further lesson that prices could not be raised without real economic recovery.

Regulation of the Stock Exchange

To ensure that the excesses of the 1920s, which had caused the Wall Street Crash, were not repeated two measures were passed:

- The Truth-in-Securities Act, 1933, required brokers to offer clients realistic information about the securities they were selling.
- The Securities Act, 1934, set up a new agency, the Securities Exchange Commission (SEC). Its task was to oversee stock market activities and prevent fraudulent activities such as insider dealing, where brokers agreed to artificially raise prices before selling, as in the Bull Pool (see page 41). Roosevelt appointed Joseph Kennedy to head the Commission. Cynics held that Kennedy, who had been a major speculator in the 1920s, could exploit the situation. The Act was highly successful despite the opposition of Wall Street insiders, some of whom had threatened to move the exchange to Canada if it was passed. When the system caught and imprisoned Richard Whitney for embezzlement in 1938, the SEC demonstrated that it could now search out its own rotten apples. Wall Street had gained a new credibility.

Economies in government

Roosevelt was a conservative in financial matters and, like his predecessors, he believed strongly in a balanced budget. Care was taken to distinguish between the budget for normal government business and that for emergency relief to deal with the Depression. He expected the budget for normal business to balance. He also sought to make all his recovery programmes self-financing and often they began with loans rather than grants. It was hoped that as money began to be made from the programmes, these loans would be repaid.

The Economy Act, 1933, meanwhile, slashed government salaries and cut ex-soldiers' pensions. Roosevelt, like Hoover, refused to give the veterans their bonus. However, when a second 'Bonus Army' arrived in Washington, Roosevelt greeted them with refreshments and entertainment. His wife was sent to charm them without giving in to any of their demands. As a result of the charm offensive, this time, they departed peacefully.

Agriculture

Agricultural recovery was given a higher priority than industrial recovery. This was for a variety of reasons:

- Thirty per cent of the labour force worked in agriculture. If agricultural workers could afford to buy more, industry would be stimulated.
- If agriculture became more profitable, there would be a reduction in farms being repossessed by the banks.
- As we have seen (page 28), the farming lobby in Washington had always been influential in the past but now felt under threat. Democratic politicians representing agricultural interests in the south and west had been among Roosevelt's earliest political supporters and he certainly felt he owed them something.
- Roosevelt took a personal interest in agriculture. He regarded the farmer as the backbone of the USA. This is an aspect of Roosevelt's thinking that is often forgotten. He remained passionately concerned with conservation and ecology, as illustrated by his personal interest in the work of the **Civilian Conservation Corps** (see page 92).

The increasingly militant **Farmers' Holiday Association** in the midwest threatened farm strikes if effective legislation was not forthcoming. The same organization had disrupted the repossession of farms. It both threatened and carried out acts of violence against officials trying to implement these.

In the long run, the aim of agricultural policies was to make farming more efficient by ending overproduction. This would be done by taking the most uneconomic land out of production and resettling displaced agricultural workers. However, in the short term, farming crises had to be addressed. This was done through a series of measures.

Extension of farm credit

The Farm Credit Act of March 1933 brought all the various agencies dealing with agricultural credit into one body, the Farm Credit Administration. This helped the co-ordination of agricultural issues. In April, the Emergency Farm Mortgage Act loaned funds to farmers in danger of losing their properties. The Frazier–Lemke Farm Mortgage Act of June went a stage further. It lent money to farmers whose lands had already been repossessed so they could recover them; interest was set at only one per cent.

Agricultural Adjustment Act, May 1933

Overproduction had been the greatest problem of American agriculture. Government measures such as Hoover's Federal Farm Board (see page 65)

 **KEY TERM**

Civilian Conservation Corps An alphabet agency that employed young people to work on agricultural and conservation projects.

Farmers' Holiday Association A pressure group set up to improve pay and conditions for farmers.

had not addressed this problem. While industrial production had declined by 42 per cent in the years 1929–33, agriculture had fallen by only six per cent. It was extremely difficult to tell farmers to cut back their production. If the cutbacks were to be voluntary, an individual farmer would be very unlikely to make the first move to do so in case none of his neighbours followed suit; if compulsory, there would need to be new and far-reaching enforcement agencies set up. Nevertheless, the main principle behind the Agricultural Adjustment Act was that the government would subsidize farmers to reduce their acreage and production voluntarily.

The overall aim was of the Agricultural Adjustment Act was to increase farmers' incomes. A new agency was set up, the Agricultural Adjustment Administration (AAA), which agreed to pay farmers to reduce their production of 'staple' items, initially corn, cotton, milk, pigs, rice, tobacco and wheat. The programme was to be self-financing through a tax placed on companies that processed food. It was assumed that these companies would in turn pass on the increased cost to the consumer.

Reduction of cotton production was perhaps the most pressing need. At the beginning of 1933, unsold cotton in the USA already exceeded the total average annual world consumption of American cotton. Moreover, farmers had planted 400,000 acres more than in 1932. They were, quite simply, paid to destroy much of this. A total of 10.5 million acres were ploughed under, and the price of cotton accordingly rose from 6.5 cents per pound in 1932 to 10 cents in 1933.

However, it was one thing to destroy cotton but it was far more contentious to destroy food when so many Americans were hungry. Six million piglets were bought and slaughtered. Although many of the carcasses were subsequently processed and fed to the unemployed, the public outcry was enormous.

SOURCE C

? Read Source C. Why do you think there was such an outcry about slaughtering the pigs?

An extract from C.B. Baldwin, Assistant to the Secretary of Agriculture Henry Wallace in *Hard Times: An Oral History of the Great Depression* by Studs Terkel published in 1970.

They decided to slaughter piggy sows. You know what a piggy sow is? A pregnant pig. They decided to pay the farmers to kill them and the little pigs. Lot of 'em went into fertilizer. This is one of the horrible contradictions we're still seeing.

They lowered the supply goin' to market and the prices immediately went up. Then a great cry went up from the press, particularly the Chicago Tribune *about Henry Wallace slaughtering these little pigs. You'd think they were precious babies. The situation was such, you had to take emergency measures. Wallace never liked it.*

In fact, the AAA destroyed only cotton and piglets. Drought helped to make the 1933 wheat crop the poorest since 1896, and agreements were reached to limit acreage in other crops in subsequent years.

Total farm income rose from $4.5 billion in 1932 to $6.9 billion in 1935. The percentage of farmers signing up for AAA agreements was high at first – 95 per cent of tobacco growers, for example – and the Act was very popular with farmers.

Faced by drought, western ranchers sought to bring beef cattle under the protection of the AAA in 1934. By January 1935 the government had purchased 8.3 million head of cattle, in return for which ranchers agreed to reduce breeding cows by 20 per cent in 1937. Overall, it would appear that the AAA worked effectively to deal with the crisis of overproduction, although there were problems and these will be considered later (see page 114).

Tennessee Valley Authority, May 1933

The Tennessee Valley Authority (TVA) was one of the most grandiose schemes of the New Deal. It was created to harness the power of the River Tennessee, which ran through seven of the poorest states in the USA. It was hoped that by so doing the region of 80,000 square miles with a population of two million would become more prosperous. The TVA had several major tasks:

- to construct 20 huge dams to control the floods which periodically affected the region
- to develop ecological schemes such as tree planting to stop soil erosion
- to encourage farmers to use more efficient means of cultivation, such as **contour ploughing**
- to provide jobs by setting up fertilizer manufacture factories
- to develop welfare and educational programmes
- most significantly perhaps, to produce hydroelectric power for an area whose existing supplies of electricity were limited to two out of every 100 farms.

 **KEY TERM**

Contour ploughing
Ploughing across hillsides so that the crested grooves retained the soil. Prior to this farmers had often ploughed up and down. In heavy rain the soil could get washed away.

The designers of the TVA deliberately stated in the Act that the production of electricity was only a by-product. This was because they knew private companies would oppose the right of a government agency to manufacture and sell it. Moreover, the electricity generated was cheaper than elsewhere. The TVA effectively became a central planning authority for the region. It was largely responsible for the modernization and improved living standards that saw its residents increase their average income by 200 per cent in the period from 1929 to 1949.

Explain how the two sides of the hill are different in Source D. What do you think was the purpose of this photograph?

SOURCE D

The owner of the farm on the left agreed to become a test farmer using contour ploughing. Photo courtesy of the Tennessee Valley Authority.

Industrial recovery

Industrial recovery was a priority for the New Deal. However, it had only limited success due to the scale of the industrial collapse. Although the economy grew 10 per cent per year during Roosevelt's first term from 1933 to 1936, output had fallen so low since 1929 that this still left unemployment at 14 per cent.

Roosevelt's primary aims were to get people back to work and to increase consumer demand. To do this, he needed both to act quickly before the situation got even worse and to gain the co-operation of businessmen. He knew he could achieve little without the latter; there was simply no alternative structure to change things without the active support of businessmen. They would hardly consent to radical policies such as nationalization or **anti-trust legislation** (see page 15).

The problem was that there was no consensus about how to go about ensuring industrial recovery.

Some businessmen still supported policies of *laissez-faire*; others wanted massive government intervention. Some felt competition should be ended; others believed it to be the keynote to recovery. Again, it is important to note that Roosevelt was in the business of saving the American system of capitalism, not replacing it. This came as a disappointment to many who had hoped for more radical objectives.

🔑 **KEY TERM**

Anti-trust legislation
Laws to break down trusts.

Roosevelt was forced to act quickly and under pressure, as Congress was about to pass a measure to restrict the working week to 30 hours with the hope of sharing out the existing jobs. He opposed this scheme because he feared that rather than raise overall purchasing power it would simply share out more thinly what already existed. Instead, he replaced it with the National Industry Recovery Act (NIRA) of June 1933.

The Act came in two parts:

- National Recovery Administration (NRA)
- Public Works Administration (PWA).

National Recovery Administration

The NRA was set up to oversee industrial recovery. Headed by General Hugh Johnson, it seemed to offer something to all groups involved in industry. Powerful businessmen, for example, benefited from the suspension of anti-trust legislation for two years. The argument behind this was that if industrial expansion was to be promoted, it was crazy to maintain laws that, in fact, restricted it. Firms were encouraged to agree to codes of practice to regulate unfair competition such as price-cutting, and to agree on such matters as working conditions and minimum wages in their industry.

Elsewhere in the NRA legislation, 'yellow dog' clauses (see page 30) were outlawed and Section 7(a) declared employees had a right to join trade unions and participate in **collective bargaining**. This meant that employers would have to recognize trade unions to negotiate on behalf of their members. Roosevelt had not welcomed this clause, which had been forced on him by Congress. He was more interested in reducing unemployment than legalizing unions. His fears that this could lead to industrial unrest seemed proven by the wave of violent strikes that were alleviated only with further legislation.

A hectic promotional campaign took place to promote the NRA and the codes. The national response to the campaign was tremendous. Eventually, 557 codes were drawn up covering most industries, and firms which agreed to them were entitled to display what would become one of the most enduring symbols of the New Deal: a blue eagle, with the logo underneath, 'We do our part'. It was hoped that consumers would support those firms that bore the blue eagle and boycott those which did not. To hasten proceedings, Hugh Johnson had drawn up a blanket code known as the President's Re-employment Agreement. This was particularly intended for small firms to subscribe to in order to take advantage of the blue eagle and the increased custom it would presumably attract.

Problems with the codes

Problems with most of the operations of the NRA became quickly apparent. Many of the codes, for example, turned out to be unworkable. This was in part because they were adopted so quickly, often without proper thought or planning, but also because they were often contentious. Many large

 **KEY TERM**

Collective bargaining
Discussions between employers and employees (usually represented by trade unions) about working conditions and pay.

manufacturers, notably Henry Ford, never subscribed to them and yet, as we shall see, small firms complained that they favoured big business. Many small firms found it difficult to comply with all the regulations, particularly the minimum wage clauses. It was hoped, for example, that the firms signing the codes would introduce a minimum wage of $11 for a 40-hour week. Few small firms could afford this.

In March 1934 Congress set up the National Recovery Review Board to investigate whether small firms were disadvantaged by the codes; it reported that indeed they were. The codes seemed to favour large companies that could take advantage of them to restrict competition and increase their profits. They could, for example, work together to draw up codes in which they agreed to raise prices while keeping wages low. Some agreed to limit output to raise prices and could therefore afford to cut back on their workforce or pay lower wages.

Unions said that Section 7(a) was too weak for their needs and that many employers, including those who did subscribe to the codes, were still riding roughshod over them. Ford, who did not subscribe to any codes, kept a gang of union bashers on the payroll (see page 13). Johnson created labour advisory boards to mediate in disputes but because these were advisory, they had little influence.

The argument that the NRA favoured big business was particularly persuasive. The codes were largely drawn up by representatives from big business, often with the assistance of inexperienced White House officials. One of the first tasks of a newly appointed young government official, for example, was to meet sharp company lawyers to draw up the petroleum codes, even though he knew nothing about the industry.

Ultimately, despite the fanfare, the codes did not help economic recovery. This led Johnson to attempt a 'Buy Now' campaign in October 1933 to encourage people to spend and therefore stimulate production. He also advocated an overall 10 per cent wage increase and 10-hour cut in the working week. Neither was successful.

In reality, the NRA codes looked impressive but they could not bring about an economic recovery. Many critics argued that, in practice, they did little except give large firms the opportunity to indulge in unfair practices – the very opposite of what had been intended. Johnson, a successful businessman himself, believed very firmly in self-regulation by business. There were to be no new government powers over companies. Indeed, as mentioned earlier, the government had agreed to suspend anti-trust legislation for two years.

Johnson had made many powerful enemies with his high-handed ways. The press had a field day not only over his excessive drinking but also over the high salary he gave to his secretary, Frances Robinson, whom he admitted was 'more than a stenographer'. He began to be an embarrassment to the administration and had to go. Roosevelt dismissed him in September 1934. After his departure some of the codes were relaxed but the Supreme Court dealt the death blow in May 1935 when it declared the NRA unconstitutional (page 113).

Public Works Administration

The second part of NIRA set up an emergency PWA to be headed by the Secretary of the Interior, Harold Ickes. It was funded with $3.3 billion and its purpose was '**pump priming**'. It was hoped that expenditure on public works such as roads, dams, hospitals and schools would stimulate the economy. Road building would lead to increased demand for concrete, for example, which would lead the concrete companies to employ more workers, who would therefore have more money to spend, and so on.

A cautious administrator, Ickes made slow progress. In fact, he was criticized for spending only $110 million of his funding in the first six months. His strength was that he demanded value for money and would only fund worthwhile projects. He did not want to have the agency jeopardized by criticisms that it was wasting taxpayers' money, or 'boondoggling', in popular speech. This viewpoint was fully supported by the president. Moreover, public works projects involve lengthy preparations with design, planning and submission of contracts. Eventually the PWA put hundreds of thousands of people to work, building, among other things, nearly 13,000 schools and 50,000 miles of roads.

It pumped billions of dollars into the economy and was responsible for massive public works schemes, particularly in the west, where it enabled dams to be built to help irrigate former semi-desert land, electricity to be produced and four vast National Parks to be created.

Relief

There were millions of needy people in the USA. One major difference between Roosevelt and Hoover was the willingness of the former to involve the government in direct relief measures.

Federal Emergency Relief Act, May 1933

This act established the Federal Emergency Relief Administration (FERA). It was given $500 million to be divided equally among the states to help provide for the unemployed. Half the money was to be granted to states for outright relief and, with the remainder, the government would pay each state $1 for every $3 it spent on relief.

Roosevelt chose Harry Hopkins, whom he had first appointed to run social welfare schemes when he was Governor of New York state, to run this programme. He had administered the relief programmes that the president had introduced when Governor of New York. The Act said that each state should set up a FERA office and organize relief programmes. It should raise the money through borrowing, tax rises or any other means. When some

KEY TERM

Pump priming Expression used to suggest that government spending would lead to economic growth.

states such as Kentucky and Ohio refused to comply, Hopkins simply threatened to deny them any federal monies.

Many states were wedded to the idea of a balanced budget and found expenditure on relief extremely distasteful. It was still felt by many that to be poor was your own fault. Those requiring relief were often treated abominably. One FERA worker reported that in Phoenix, Arizona, over 100 claimants were jammed into a small room in temperatures of over 100 degrees (38°C), while an overflow queue was waiting in a nearby garage. In many places there could be interminable waits and delays. Hostile policemen often guarded the long queues of claimants, while uncaring officials completed endless numbers of forms. Even after this there were usually long delays before any kind of relief was forthcoming. The bottom line was that they knew Hopkins could not refuse them funds as the only people who would suffer were those the funds were meant to help, the needy and unemployed themselves. One governor even boasted that he had cut relief spending but still received FERA funds.

In the face of such opposition, FERA's effectiveness was limited. Its workers were refused office space in some states and often their caseloads were numbered in thousands. Its funds were limited too. In 1935 it was paying about $25 per month to an average family on relief, while the average monthly minimum wage for **subsistence** was estimated at $100.

However, although its effects were disappointing, it did set the important precedent of federal government giving direct funds for relief.

Civilian Conservation Corps 1933

Unemployed young men between the ages of 17 and 24 (later 28) were recruited by the Department of Labor to work in the Civilian Conservation Corps (CCC) in national forests and parks and public lands. The CCC was organized along military lines, but its tasks were set out by the Departments of the Interior and Agriculture.

At an estimated cost of $5500 million in the first year, 250,000 recruits worked on reforestation, soil conservation and forestry management projects. Initially they served for nine months to give as many as possible the opportunity to join; they were paid $30 per month, of which $25 had to be sent home to their families. Among the first recruits were 2500 of the second 'Bonus Army' (see page 85); Roosevelt waived the age restrictions on their behalf.

The CCC was originally set up for two years but Congress extended this for a further seven years in 1935, when its strength was increased to 500,000. In the period of its life, the CCC installed 65,100 miles of telephone lines in inaccessible areas, spent 4.1 million man-hours fighting forest fires and planted 1.3 billion trees. The CCC gave countless young men a new self-respect and, particularly those from the cities, valuable experience of both comradeship and life in the 'great outdoors'. In addition, 100,000 of its recruits were taught to improve their literacy skills. However, this experience was primarily available to young *white* men and, of course, their time in the CCC was no guarantee that they would not return to the ranks of those on relief when it was over.

Civil Works Administration

The Civil Works Administration (CWA) was created in November 1933, with a $400 million grant from the PWA, primarily to provide emergency relief to the unemployed during the hard winter of 1933–4. Although it put four million people to work on public works projects, it was closed down in March when the winter was over. However, FERA agreed to fund more public works projects itself.

Native Americans

The Indian Reorganization Act recognized and encouraged Native American culture in a shift from the former policy of assimilation (see page 27). Tribes were reorganized into self-governing bodies that could vote to adopt constitutions and have their own police and legal systems. They could control land sales on the reservations, while new tribal corporations were established to manage tribal resources.

These measures in no way relieved Native American poverty. Indeed, 75 out of 245 tribes vetoed them when asked to vote on the measures. However, officials did their best to ensure Native Americans could take advantage of New Deal agencies such as the CCC and PWA. Having said this, one must remember that Native American poverty was so great that these measures for all their good intentions could at best have only a very limited effect. As New Deal programmes wound down in the 1940s, Native Americans began to set up pressure groups but often remained among the poorest people in the USA.

Housing

Housing remained a problem because many homeowners were having problems repaying their mortgages, while there was a shortage of public sector accommodation.

Home Owners Refinancing Corporation, June 1933

This agency helped homeowners in difficulties by offering new mortgages at low rates of interest over longer periods.

Federal Housing Administration

The Federal Housing Administration (FHA) was established in June 1934 to offer federal insurance to protect the ability to repay low-interest, long-term mortgages taken out by those buying new homes. Clearly, this was an attempt to stimulate the building industry. However, the loans were solely for newly purchased single-family homes; they could not be used to renovate existing properties or for buildings set out as apartments where several people may live.

The FHA therefore did nothing to help the increasingly poverty-stricken inner cities. In fact, one of the agency's unanticipated effects was to encourage the movement to the suburbs. And with 65 per cent of new houses costing over $4000 it was estimated that less than 25 per cent of urban families could afford to take out any kind of mortgage on them. The agency mainly benefited white, middle-class families. Increasingly, inner-city areas tended to be run down and left to poorer ethnic minorities who were forced to rent squalid properties.

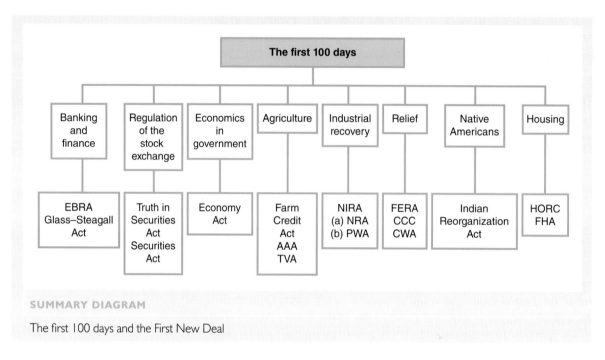

SUMMARY DIAGRAM

The first 100 days and the First New Deal

②Alternatives to the New Deal

▶ Key question: How significant were the alternatives to the New Deal?

The New Deal attracted much opposition, from the political right because it was too radical and from the political left because it was not radical enough. In this section the alternatives put forward by some of these opponents will be examined.

Why did members of the wealthy classes oppose the New Deal?

→ The right

Many of the wealthy, who had supported Roosevelt in the darkest days of the Depression as the saviour of capitalism, now turned against him when it seemed that capitalism had, in fact, been saved. This was in part because of the increases in taxes, which they opposed, and also what they perceived as too much continued government involvement in the economy. The Republican Party, still associated with its failures during the early 1930s, was rebuilding and preparing for the 1936 election, but they were finding it difficult to field a strong candidate.

Liberty Leaguers

The Liberty League was organized in April 1934 by many conservative Democrats as well as Republicans to promote private property and private enterprise unregulated by law. Among its leaders were Al Smith, who had been the Democratic candidate in the 1928 presidential election, and John Jacob Raskob, a former Democratic Party chairman. Increasingly, its members saw Roosevelt as a traitor to his class; some refused even to speak of him by name but used cruel jibes like, 'that cripple in the White House'. Some likened the New Deal to communism in the USSR. There is even a suggestion that the far right planned a *coup d'état* against Roosevelt in 1934 and that this was foiled by the very general who had been asked to lead it. The Liberty Leaguers attacked Roosevelt throughout the New Deal years and formed the basis of right-wing opposition to him. By July 1936, it had 125,000 members; after Roosevelt's victory in the elections of that year, however, it became less significant.

The left

At the time, Roosevelt was more concerned about threats from the left. This was particularly because left-wing groups might join together to form a third party to challenge him in the next presidential election. The threats varied from those advocating radical schemes such as Revolving Old Age Pensions to popular leaders such as Huey Long and Father Charles Coughlin.

What were the left-wing alternatives to the New Deal and how great a threat were they?

End Poverty in California

The novelist Upton Sinclair came up with a scheme whereby the unemployed would be put to work in state-run co-operatives. They would be paid in currency, which they could spend only in other co-operatives. For a time, Sinclair's ideas gained credibility and he won the Democratic nomination as state governor for California in the 1934 election. However, well-organized opposition, particularly from the movie industry in Hollywood, ensured that he was soundly defeated by the Republican candidate. Nevertheless, his many supporters remained and proved useful recruits for more serious alternative movements as discussed below.

'Share Our Wealth'

As an energetic Governor of Louisiana, Huey Long had ordered massive public works programmes – over 3000 miles of paved highways were built between 1928 and 1933, besides new public buildings and an airport at New Orleans – and ambitious adult literacy schemes. However, he did govern as a dictator and opponents were treated quite brutally by his bullyboys.

In February 1934, Long moved on to the national scene with his 'Share Our Wealth' programme. He advocated that all private fortunes over $3 million should be confiscated and every family should be given enough money to buy a house, a car and a radio. There should also be old-age pensions, minimum wages so that every family would be guaranteed $2000–$3000 per year and free college education for all suitable candidates. Long's ideas proved very popular and 'Share Our Wealth' clubs grew to 27,431 in number, with 4.6 million members spread across the states. Long began to talk of joining forces with other radicals to form a third party to oppose Roosevelt in the 1936 presidential election.

In 1935, Postmaster General James A. Farley took a secret poll to assess Long's popularity and was shocked to discover that up to four million people might vote for him in 1936. This meant that Long might hold the balance of power in the election. The Louisiana senator was, in fact, gunned down in September 1935. Rumours circulated by his supporters that Roosevelt's hand was somehow behind the assassination. While these accusations were unfounded, the president must nevertheless have breathed a sigh of relief at the news of Long's death.

Old Age Revolving Pensions Inc.

Francis Townsend was a retired doctor who advocated old-age pensions with a difference. Everyone over 60 years of age who was not in paid employment should be given $200 per month on the understanding that every cent of it was spent and none saved. The idea was that this would boost consumption and thereby production and so pull the USA out of the Depression. Moreover, encouraging people to retire at 60 would provide more jobs for the young. Soon Townsend Clubs had 500,000 members and Congress was being lobbied to put the plan into operation. It was, of course, totally impractical; payments to recipients would have amounted to 50 per cent of national income and an army of bureaucrats would have been necessary to ensure pensioners were spending all their $200. Nevertheless, the level of support showed that the movement had to be taken seriously.

Father Charles Coughlin

Charles Coughlin was a priest whose radio programme, *The Golden Hour of the Little Flower*, was enormously influential during the first half of the 1930s. It regularly commanded an audience of 30–40 million, and listeners contributed more than $5 million per year to his parish in Detroit. At first, Coughlin had supported Roosevelt, telling his audience, 'The New Deal is Christ's Deal'. However, he later felt that Roosevelt had not done enough to change the banking system: Coughlin believed that banks should be nationalized. He contradicted himself by arguing that the New Deal was both a communist conspiracy and a means by which Wall Street financiers could keep ordinary people enslaved.

In 1934, Coughlin founded the National Union for Social Justice with the aim of monetary reform and redistribution of wealth. Roosevelt was afraid of Coughlin's influence, particularly when a possible alliance with Huey Long was mooted. However, Long was assassinated and Coughlin became increasingly anti-Semitic; he blamed Jews for both the New Deal and control of Wall Street. Inevitably, perhaps, he began to look with admiration to the **European fascist dictators** and this, together with government-inspired attacks, led to Coughlin's influence declining as the decade wore on. This was due to many Americans' dislike of Hitler and Mussolini, and increasing fears of being involved in war against them.

Thunder on the left

This is the name given to various political developments that are credited with moving Roosevelt and the New Deal further to the left in 1935 and 1936. Governor Floyd B. Olson of Minnesota, for example, led the Farmer–Labor Party which proposed far-reaching economic reforms. It advocated the state take control of idle factories to put the unemployed to work, nationalization of public utilities and a postponement of farm mortgage foreclosures. However, the movement died with Olson, who developed terminal cancer in 1936. Robert Lafollette Jr and his brother Philip founded a new Progressive Party, which had the support of eastern intellectuals and called for collective bargaining, unemployment insurance and old-age pensions.

Impact of the opposition

Although, with hindsight, we can see that these movements did not constitute a serious threat to Roosevelt, this was not how they were perceived at the time. At best, from Roosevelt's point of view, their popularity showed the level of support there might be for more radical presidential measures to combat the Depression. At worst, there was the possibility that millions of Americans were so frustrated with the established order that they were prepared to vote for radical or even revolutionary change. Although few of Roosevelt's advisers seriously believed this, the prospect of a third party at the 1936 presidential election was worrying. In a three-way presidential election it might hold the balance of power. Roosevelt may need to put forward many of the measures it favoured in order to get its support to hold onto office.

Roosevelt, meanwhile, had learned of the mood of the country. In the 1934 mid-term congressional elections, the Democrats had made gains in both houses, with 69 out of 96 seats in the Senate, the biggest Democratic majority to date. Roosevelt was preparing a second New Deal that was influenced not only by the demands of radical politicians but also by the increasing opposition of big business to his measures.

 **KEY TERM**

European fascist dictators Extreme right-wing, nationalist leaders such as Hitler in Germany and Mussolini in Italy, who seemed to offer a viable alternative to democracy, and whose countries at the time seemed to be tackling the problems of the 1930s more successfully than the USA.

How much impact did the opposition have on Roosevelt?

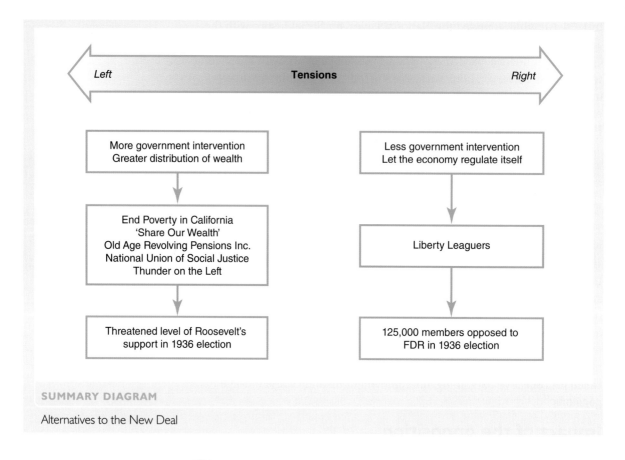

SUMMARY DIAGRAM

Alternatives to the New Deal

③ Key debate

▶ *Key question: Was the First New Deal a planned programme or simply a series of unrelated measures to deal with specific problems?*

 Historians often seek patterns in past events. To what extent is this possible in assessing the construction of the New Deal? (Reason, History.)

The First New Deal transformed the USA. No government had previously been so energetic in peacetime; no government had taken so much upon itself. However, the main question to consider is whether the First New Deal was a coherent attempt to change the political, social and economic structure of the USA or whether it was simply an *ad hoc* series of measures taken to deal with crises as they arose.

It must be said from the outset that Roosevelt did employ some people who had a radical vision. They saw, for example, a permanent need for the government to take responsibility for the running of the economy and for people's welfare. No doubt the New Deal was their blueprint for action. However, these people were not of one mind; they did not make up one radical group that was in agreement. They tended to offer different, often conflicting advice.

A blueprint for change

Many historians such as Michael Parrish and William E. Leuchtenburg have argued that it seems best to regard the First New Deal as a series of measures in response to crises. There seems to have been no master plan or blueprint for radical change behind them, certainly on the part of the president. However, not all share this view.

There is an argument that because the New Deal set so many precedents, it did, in fact, act as a blueprint for major change, whatever the president may have wished. Never before, for example, had any US government intervened to such an extent in the economy and society. Never before had people begun to look to the government for help to such an extent. Never before had there been such regulation. Never before had there been so many minds at work in Washington to effect change. Together these factors did, in fact, even if unintentionally, lead to significant changes in the role that many citizens expected of the government.

As it was, Roosevelt was building up both a considerable body of opposition to the measures he had taken and, conversely, powerful pressure for more radical change. Increasingly, as problems with his measures emerged, he found himself beleaguered.

Some of those involved in the First New Deal were under no doubt that it represented a momentous departure. Many critics agreed with Representative Joseph W. Martin from Massachusetts who believed the New Deal would lead to communism, saying, 'We are on our way to Moscow'. However, others at the time thought it lacked coherence. Historians since have debated its character and meaning. While many emphasize how it met the need for a greater role for government in addressing the crises caused by the Depression, others more recently have argued that the New Deal actually made the economic situation worse.

Contemporaries

Gardiner C. Means, a New Deal staffer, argued that the real revolution was not in the measures taken as such but in the determination to look at the problems and find solutions. The USA had been locked into nineteenth-century institutions that no longer met the needs of the American people. The New Deal examined the realities and found solutions – for example before the New Deal it was assumed that people were unemployed because they were lazy; the New Deal realized this was not the case and set about creating jobs for them.

Raymond Moley felt that the New Deal enhanced the power of central government because the economy was in a state of anarchy and extensive measures were necessary.

Later historians

A left-wing historian, Christopher Lasch, writing in the late 1960s, tended to agree. He did not see a revolutionary situation in the USA but there was a demand for strong leadership, which Roosevelt offered. Even businessmen clamoured for strong leadership in the midst of the Depression.

In 1959, Arthur J. Schlesinger Jr published *The Coming of the New Deal*, one of the most penetrating analyses of the measures. He argued that there was no blueprint except to save the capitalist system, and the environment through the conservation schemes. He felt indeed it was a conservative programme with roots in the past, in the presidencies of Jefferson (1801–9) and Jackson (1829–37), and movements such as **Populism** and **Progressivism**. The measures themselves were responses to crises, 'scrambled' together.

Writing in 2001, William E. Leuchtenburg tended to agree that the purpose of the First New Deal was to preserve the social order rather than to effect revolution, although he emphasizes the significance of the farming legislation as a crucial solution to the problems of the Depression.

Critics

Conservative historian Paul Johnson denies that there was any coherent economic policy behind the New Deal, and argues that it really did little more than develop Hoover's meddling and thereby impeded recovery. In *FDR's Folly*, published in 2004, Jim Powell echoed the argument that the New Deal prolonged the Depression by ill-advised economic policies; he particularly attacked the banking legislation, arguing that the biggest problem for most banks was not having enough reserves to back their activities; the answer would have been to allow more profitable banks to open more branches, which the legislation prohibited them from doing. As evidence in support, Powell cites the case of Canada, which, as we shall see in Chapter 5, allowed branch-banking and suffered hardly any bank failures during the Depression.

Writing in 2009, Burton Fulsom argued that the New Deal did little to solve the Depression – in fact, some New Deal policies such as the price fixing in the NRA simply made it worse. He was particularly scathing about the AAA in paying farmers to cut production. Fulsom believed Roosevelt should have cut taxes instead of raising them; he compared the high taxes of Roosevelt's era unfavourably with the low taxes of the 1920s which he felt stimulated investment and economic prosperity.

It can be seen then that while some commentators see the early New Deal as an attempt to save the capitalist system, others see it as an unnecessary expansion of federal government power. All agree, however, that the First New Deal, whether conservative and based on precedent or radical, did mark a major shift in the role of federal government.

🔑 KEY TERM

Populism Nineteenth-century political movement favouring greater government intervention and policies such as nationalization of the railroads.

Progressivism Late nineteenth- and early twentieth-century political movement to expand the role of government in dealing with social and economic problems and tackle corruption and abuses.

The Second New Deal 1935–6

▶ **Key question:** *How successfully did the Second New Deal address the problems faced by the USA?*

SOURCE E

A letter to the President received in 1936.

Dear Mr President,

This is just to tell you everything is all right now. The man you sent found our house all right and we went down the bank with him and the mortgage can go a while longer. You remember I wrote you about losing the furniture too. Well, your man got it back for us. I never heard of a President like you, Mr Roosevelt. Mrs — and I are old folks and don't amount to much, but we are joined with those millions of others in praying for you every night.

God bless you, Mr Roosevelt.

What is the value of Source E as evidence of how popular Roosevelt was as president?

This is one of the thousands of letters Roosevelt received every day. He insisted that his staff answer every one of them. Many ordinary people regarded Roosevelt as their saviour. He once said that everyone was against him except the electorate. He never lost the support of the mass of the population. People believed he cared about and understood their problems.

The nature of the Second New Deal

What was the significance of the Second New Deal?

Many historians have argued that the New Deal became more radical in the years after 1935, that Roosevelt was genuinely trying to change the face of the USA and that he was favouring the poorer classes at the expense of the rich. They point in particular to the measures that made up the Second New Deal as evidence of this.

In the 1936 presidential election Roosevelt won a great victory. He was at the height of his success. And yet, after this the New Deal was beset with problems and according to some historians petered out in 1938 and 1939. They argue that it was ultimately a failure because it did not radically change the face of the USA. However, this can only be considered a failure of the New Deal if it was actually one of its objectives.

When the 75th Congress met early in 1935, Roosevelt presented it with a major legislative package. There was considerable excitement among the White House staff. Harry Hopkins said, 'Boys, this is our hour. We've got to get everything we want in the way of relief, **social security** and minimum wages.' Eighty-eight days later most of Roosevelt's objectives had been achieved. Some measures that he had not particularly supported had also been passed, for example, in the field of labour relations.

 **KEY TERM**

Social security Relief and benefits for those in need of government support, for example the old and sick.

Some historians, notably Arthur Schlesinger Jr, have seen the Second New Deal very much as a change in direction. They see the early New Deal as an attempt to reduce business competition in favour of greater co-operation through planning and government guidance. Clearly the NRA and AAA were examples of this in action (see pages 85–91). However, they believe the Second New Deal saw a reintroduction of competition but with regulations about fair play. Examples of this were:

- fair representation for all sides in industry through the National Labor Relations Act (see page 107)
- the Public Utility Holding Company Act that broke up holding companies (see page 108)
- a national system of benefits for those groups who could not participate in the system, through measures such as the Social Security Act (see pages 108–9).

Nevertheless, as we will see, in attacking big business the New Deal's bark was always worse than its bite.

Before considering the legislation of the Second New Deal, we need to examine in some detail the motivation behind it and the conditions that made it possible.

Why did the government feel a second New Deal was necessary?

Reasons for the Second New Deal

Historians have suggested a variety of reasons behind the Second New Deal:

- Roosevelt needed to respond to the radical forces described on pages 94–7. He was politically astute enough to understand the need to take the initiative from people such as Huey Long, Francis Townsend and Charles Coughlin, to avoid possibly millions of voters supporting politicians with extreme views.
- The mid-term congressional elections in 1934 had returned a more radical House of Representatives, which was expecting wide-ranging legislative action and was prepared to support it. The Farmer–Labor Party (see page 97) could rely on possibly as many as 50 supporters in both houses. They were preparing their own programme that would have effected quite radical changes. For example, they spoke of maximum hours of work and minimum wages, greater investment in public works, higher taxes for the wealthy and social security. Meanwhile, radical senators such as Lafollette and Wagner were also preparing their own proposals.
- The climate in the new Congress was for action and Roosevelt wanted to prevent this. He did not wish to surrender the initiative to Congress in preparing New Deal legislation.
- Roosevelt was increasingly frustrated by the Supreme Court, which was beginning to overturn New Deal legislation. He believed it was opposing

him. This in itself made him more radical in outlook. He also needed to
introduce new measures to replace those such as the NRA, which the
Supreme Court had declared unconstitutional (see page 113).

- Roosevelt was also increasingly frustrated with the wealthy and with the
forces of big business, who were opposing him more and more. He was
particularly angry when the **US Chamber of Commerce** attacked his
policies in May 1935. He believed he had been elected to save American
business and he felt let down by its lack of continued support. Moreover,
small businesses had benefited little from measures so far adopted. We
have seen, for example, how many of the NRA codes discriminated
against them (see pages 89–90). New Deal officials in Washington were
becoming aware that small firms had a crucial role to play in economic
recovery. Many of the measures taken in the Second New Deal, for
example the Public Utility Holding Company Act, were designed with
them in mind.

- Some historians have argued that politics in the USA was becoming more
divided and extreme. Roosevelt was seeking the support of the political
left.

Each of these reasons contains elements of truth. Many of Roosevelt's
supporters were forecasting widespread support, particularly for Huey Long
if he chose to run for president (see pages 95–6). The new Congress was
preparing a programme of far-reaching reforms.

We have already seen that members of big business – which Roosevelt still
largely saw as the lynchpin of recovery – were organizing opposition to him
(see pages 94–5). However, one should not overestimate Roosevelt's
apparent shift of focus. On 22 May 1935 he again vetoed the veterans' bonus
payments and also said the government had to be careful that it did not
spend public funds wastefully. Many of the ideas encompassed in the
Second New Deal were not new to him. Indeed, as Governor of New York,
he had considered several of them, such as old-age pensions and the
regulation of public utilities. The appointment of new advisors as many of
the original 'Brains' Trusters' moved on, did not necessarily herald a change
in direction. As discussed on page 80, Roosevelt liked differences of opinion
among his advisers and encouraged their rivalry. However, when it came to
making decisions, he was his own man.

Finally, there was no more coherence to the Second New Deal than there
had been to the First. Much of it emerged both in response to new and
continuing crises and because the First New Deal had not brought about the
economic recovery hoped for.

KEY TERM

**US Chamber of
Commerce** Non-
governmental organization
responsible for speaking for
business in the USA.

?

Look at Source F. What happens to the numbers of

a) Democrat and
b) Republican Congressmen between 1932 and 1938? How would you explain these changes on the basis of what you have read so far?

Return to this question when you have completed this chapter. Are your answers to the question still the same?

SOURCE F

Make-up of Congress during the New Deal years.

Senate

Year	Democrat	Republican	Progressive	Independent	Farm–Labor
1932	59	36	0	0	1
1934	69	25	1	0	1
1936	76	17	1	1	1
1938	69	23	1	1	2

House of Representatives

Year	Democrat	Republican	Progressive	Independent	Farm–Labor
1932	313	117	0	0	5
1934	322	103	7	0	3
1936	334	88	8	0	5
1938	262	169	2	1	1

How effective were the measures of the Second New Deal?

Legislation

Emergency Relief Appropriation Act, April 1935

This measure saw the authorization of the largest appropriation for relief, at that time in the nation's history, to set up new agencies to provide employment through federal works. The $45.5 billion allocated was the equivalent of over $20 billion at 1930 values and well over $400 billion today. It set up the Works Progress Administration (WPA).

Works Progress Administration

Harry Hopkins was given control of the new WPA. The WPA recruited people for public works projects. It became a major employer. At any one time it had about two million employees and, by 1941, 20 per cent of the nation's workforce had found employment with it. Wages were approximately $52 per month, which were greater than any relief but less than the going rate in industry. The WPA was not allowed to compete for contracts with private firms or to build private houses. However, it did build 1000 airport landing fields, 8000 schools and hospitals, and 12,000 playgrounds.

Most people agreed with Hopkins when he said, 'Give a man a dole and you save his body and destroy his spirit. Give him a job and pay him an assured wage and you save both the body and the spirit.' The WPA gave an employment opportunity to those who would otherwise have been unemployed. It took people on for one year only and did not compete with private enterprise. It employed no one who could have been employed elsewhere. Many of its projects such as surveying historic sites would not have been carried out by the private sector. In the south, some farmers complained that field-hands and domestic servants were hard to find because of the WPA. The agencies came under attack from all quarters. Conservatives predictably argued that WPA projects were of dubious value and that little real work was involved.

Although it was not supposed to engage in large-scale projects, it did so. Among other things it was responsible for cutting the Lincoln Tunnel, which connects Manhattan Island to New Jersey, and building Fort Knox, home of the USA's gold reserves, in Kentucky.

Writers and photographers were employed to record American life and culture, and the theatre was also encouraged.

National Youth Administration

The National Youth Administration (NYA) was set up to encourage education and to provide part-time jobs for students so they could complete their studies. The African-American educator Mary McLeod Bethune was placed at the head of the NYA's Division of Negro Affairs to make sure young African-Americans got a fair chance. For example, she had her own fund specifically for African-American students, and she encouraged state officials to make sure African-Americans were signing up for programmes. Eleanor Roosevelt also encouraged women and members of the ethnic minorities to participate in government schemes.

Rural Electrification Administration, May 1935

The Rural Electrification Administration (REA) was formed to build generating plants and power lines in rural areas. In 1936, only 12.6 per cent of farms had electricity, often because it was not profitable for private companies to provide it to out-of-the-way areas. Where rural co-operatives were formed to develop electricity, banks were reluctant to lend them money because the organizations could rarely afford the rates of interest. However, the REA offered loans at low rates of interest and farmers were encouraged to form co-operatives to acquire supplies of electricity. By 1941, 35 per cent of farms had electricity; 773 systems, with 348,000 miles of transmission lines, had been built in six years.

Resettlement Administration, May 1935

It was decided to merge all rural rehabilitation projects into one new agency, the Resettlement Administration (RA). This was run by an agricultural economist, Rexford Tugwell, who had ambitious plans to move 500,000 families from overworked land and resettle them in more promising surroundings elsewhere. This necessitated the agency buying good land, encouraging farmers to move to it and teaching them how to farm it effectively, using modern machinery and efficient techniques.

KEY TERM

Greenbelt communities
New towns in rural areas based on careful planning with residential, commercial and industrial sectors separated.

Tugwell also envisaged the building of whole new **greenbelt communities**. In the event, partly due to underfunding, only three were ever completed: Greenbelt, Maryland; Greenville, Ohio; and Greendale, Wisconsin. Rural problems such as poverty and the natural catastrophe of the Dustbowl (see page 115) were too great to be solved merely by the construction of three new towns.

Overall, the agency only ever resettled 4441 families and as such could not be judged a success. The reasons for its apparent failure were partly to do with the costs involved and partly the reluctance of people to move. While the 1930s were a restless age and, as we shall see (page 116), there were significant migrations, the strength of the ties people felt for their own home region proved very powerful. Net migration from farms was lower in the 1930s than in the 1920s. One of the main reasons for people moving was not so much the promise of new communities as the lack of jobs in existing ones. With work in short supply everywhere, people tended to stay put despite the efforts of the RA. In addition, the government set up various schemes to help farmers remain on their land (see page 121). This left the RA policies at variance with those followed elsewhere in the administration.

SOURCE G

An Oklahoma worker, formerly a farm-owner, works in the fields at 30 cents an hour in 1939. He is probably one of those resettled as a result of the Dustbowl.

Describe the nature of the work the farm worker is undertaking in Source G.

Revenue (Wealth Tax) Act, June 1935

This act was implemented to pay for New Deal reforms and was perceived by those affected by it to be an attack on the fundamental right of Americans to become rich. The newspaper tycoon William Randolph Hearst called it the 'soak the successful' tax. However, Roosevelt's main aim was not to see any major redistribution of wealth but rather to reduce the need for **government deficit spending**. Quite simply, the government sought to raise more revenue through taxation and it seemed logical to do this by targeting those who could most afford it. Before this, it should be remembered, taxes on the rich had been minimal – those earning more than $16,000 per year paid on average less than $1000 tax.

The Act, drafted by Treasury officials, caused long and heated debate. Many of their original proposals such as a **federal inheritance tax** were defeated. Legislation finally created a graduated tax on corporate income and an excessive profits tax on corporations. The maximum tax on incomes of over $50,000 was increased from 59 per cent to 75 per cent.

In fact, the new taxes raised comparatively little: about $250 million. For example, the laws regulating taxes paid by corporations contained loopholes, which clever lawyers could easily exploit. Only one per cent of the population earned more than $10,000 and so the increased income taxes did not raise large amounts of revenue. However, if Roosevelt had taxed the middle classes more, as he was urged to do by more radical colleagues, he would have cut their spending power and thus delayed economic recovery. While the Act did little in itself, it did act as a precedent for higher taxes during the Second World War from 1941 to 1945 (see page 138).

Wagner–Connery National Labor Relations Act, July 1935

Roosevelt was reluctant to become involved in labour relations legislation for many reasons. In part he was simply uninterested in the subject. There was also a mistrust of labour unions in the USA. This was particularly the case among conservative politicians such as the southern Democrats whose support he needed. He had no more wish to become the champion of unions than to upset big business further – and big business generally loathed unions.

The Act, therefore, was not initiated by Roosevelt. Indeed, he approved it only when it had passed through the Senate and looked likely to become law. Nevertheless, the National Labor Relations Act is generally seen as an important part of the Second New Deal and was a milestone in American labour relations. It was born out of the disappointment with the Labor Advisory Boards set up under the NRA (see page 90). It was one thing to allow unionization but quite another to get employers to accept it and the Board was generally felt to be powerless.

The Act guaranteed workers the rights to collective bargaining through unions of their own choice. They could choose their union through a secret

 **KEY TERM**

Government deficit spending When the government spends more than it receives in income.

Federal inheritance tax Government tax on the estate of the deceased.

ballot and a new three-man National Labor Relations Board was set up to ensure fair play. Employers were forbidden to resort to unfair practices, such as discrimination against unionists.

It was the first Act that effectively gave unions rights in law and in the long term committed federal government to an important labour relations role. However, Roosevelt still did not see it that way and preferred to continue to take a back seat in labour relations.

Public Utility Holding Company Act, August 1935

There had been many problems resulting from the existence of giant holding-company structures (see page 16), as they were often powerful enough to bribe legislators either to stop legislation that threatened them or to promote policies beneficial to them.

The Public Utility Holding Company Act ordered the breaking up of all companies more than twice removed from the operating company (some of Samuel Insull's companies, it will be remembered, were more than 24 times removed). It did this by making all holding companies register with the Securities Exchange Commission (SEC), which could decide their fate. Any company more than twice removed from the utility that could not justify its existence on the grounds of co-ordination of utilities or economic efficiency was to be eliminated by 1 January 1940.

The SEC was also given control of all the companies' financial transactions and stock issues.

Social Security Act, August 1935

It has already been suggested that the provision made by states for social security was wholly inadequate. For example, only Wisconsin provided any form of unemployment benefit and this was to be paid by former employers as a disincentive to laying-off their workers. Roosevelt had long been interested in a federal system of social security. However, what he came up with was both conservative and limited.

Nevertheless, despite this, the Social Security Act was the first federal measure of direct help as a worker's right and would be built upon in the future. The Act provided for old-age pensions to be funded by employer and employee contributions, and unemployment insurance to be paid for by **payroll taxes** levied on both employers and employees. While the pension scheme was a federal programme, it was anticipated that states would control unemployment insurance.

There was much resentment that the wealthy were not made to contribute more to the scheme. In considering this criticism we need to remember that, despite what many might have wished, Roosevelt was not really interested at this time in a major redistribution of wealth.

 **KEY TERM**

Payroll taxes Taxes paid by employers for each of their employees.

Limitations of the Act

The Social Security Act was generally inadequate to meet the needs of the poor. Pensions were paid at a minimum of $10 and a maximum $85 per month according to the contribution that recipients had paid into the scheme. They were not to be paid until 1940 so everyone first receiving them had paid something in. Unemployment benefit was a maximum of $18 per week for 16 weeks only.

Assistance programmes for blind people, disabled people and families with dependent children were also set up by the Act. However, although states received the same amount per child from federal government, the amounts paid varied widely. In 1939 Massachusetts paid poor children $61 per month while Mississippi paid $8 per month.

The people needing most help, such as agricultural workers, domestic servants and those working for small-scale employers, were actually excluded from the Act. This was because it was felt employers could not afford to pay the contributions and it would in any event cost the Treasury too much to collect them. It was hoped that these workers would be included in the schemes later, once the Act had had time to embed itself.

Health insurance was not included largely due to the opposition of the **American Medical Association**, which would not agree to any measure that limited its right to decide what fees to charge patients.

Assessment

Although the Social Security Act had serious flaws, it should not be forgotten that it was a major break with American governmental tradition. Never before had there been a direct system of national benefits. However, it is important to stress that this was not direct relief. Roosevelt refused to allow general taxes to subsidize the system. It had to be self-financing. Recipients had to pay into the system. The pensions were paid not at a flat rate but according to how much the worker had previously contributed. Unemployment benefits were low and paid for a very limited period.

Many conservatives argued that even this was too much. It would destroy individual initiative. It would make people dependent on the state. It took powers away from individual states and concentrated them in Washington. Many states compensated for unemployment benefits by cutting back on other schemes of relief. They increased **residence qualifications** and they made **means-tested benefits** more rigorous.

However, despite the limitations and drawbacks, the Act signified a massive break with the traditional role of federal government. It was also sending out a loud message that it cared about people. It was said that Roosevelt took more satisfaction in this measure than anything else he had achieved on the domestic front.

 **KEY TERM**

American Medical Association US doctors' professional association, governing medical practices.

Residence qualifications People had to be resident in a certain area for a specified period of time to qualify for benefits there.

Means-tested benefits Where the levels of welfare benefits are based on the recipient's income.

Banking Act, August 1935

This Act was intended to give the federal government control of banking in the USA. Each Federal Reserve Bank could elect its own head but that person had to be approved by the Federal Reserve Board. The decisions on reserve requirements and rediscount rates were to be given to the Federal Reserve Board. All large banks seeking new federal deposit insurance were required to register with the Board and accept its authority.

In these ways the control of banking was removed from private banking to central government and the centre of financial management shifted from New York to Washington.

What was the impact of the Second New Deal?

Assessing the Second New Deal

The Second New Deal saw an important expansion of the role of federal, state and local government. There was much that was new.

- The banking system was centralized.
- Some of the worst excesses of capitalism, such as the colossal power of the holding companies, were addressed. The attack on unfair competition helped small businesses.
- Labour unions were given a legal voice.
- The Social Security Act created the first national system of benefits, although individual states operated the parts they had control over very differently.
- There was also the further development of existing policies, as with the creation of the WPA to aid both relief and recovery.
- The REA helped the process of modernizing the rural areas of the USA.

However, not all of the legislation was particularly effective. The REA enjoyed only limited success. The Revenue Act of 1935 angered people out of all proportion to its actual effect. Some historians have argued that the Second New Deal differed from the first in that the first was primarily about relief and recovery from the Depression, while the second was about the creation of permanent reforms.

Whatever the merits of individual pieces of legislation, whatever the significance of the Second New Deal in terms of its philosophy, the key element was that the administration was seen to be acting, to be doing something and to be addressing issues and concerns. The Second New Deal continued, of course, to involve itself particularly in everyday issues that were important to those individuals whose concerns probably would previously have been ignored. It was for this reason that the administration could enter the 1936 presidential election with confidence.

However, many thought Roosevelt was doing too much, that his policies should be scaled down. Conservatives variously thought he was unfairly attacking business, encouraging welfare dependency and expanding government to an unacceptable degree. However, the New Deal was clearly popular with the millions of ordinary voters who still blamed the wealthy and privileged for what they perceived as their callous attitudes during the Depression.

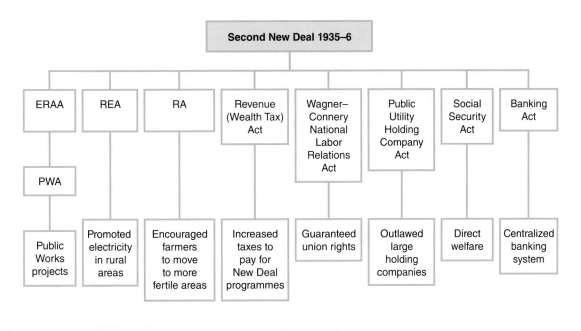

The Second New Deal 1935–6

5 Problems in Roosevelt's second term

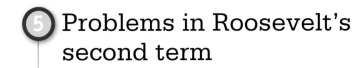

▶ *Key question: How effectively did Roosevelt deal with the problems of his second term?*

All parties agreed that the 1936 presidential election would be significant. If the electorate voted for Roosevelt for a second term, they would be supporting the changes in the role of government he had made.

The 1936 presidential election

In the election Roosevelt was triumphant. With the smaller alternative parties barely raising a million votes among them, Roosevelt won 60.8 per cent of the popular vote to his opponent's 36.5 per cent and carried all but two states, Vermont and Maine, which were memorably shown in a

Why did President Roosevelt win the 1936 election?

subsequent cartoon to be in the doghouse. The Democrats also appeared to control both houses of Congress (see Source F, page 104). As ever, Roosevelt had offered little in the way of concrete promises in his election speeches but people expected much of him.

What is the political message of the cartoon in Source H?

SOURCE H

Cartoon showing Maine and Vermont in the doghouse, 1936.

Roosevelt had fought the election largely on his personality and the trust ordinary people had in him. He was certainly aided by the lack of organization of his opponents and the fact that the Republicans could not possibly gain support by attacking measures that had benefited so many. Perhaps his victory made him overconfident and even arrogant. However, during his second term problems multiplied until his presidency seemed at times on its last legs.

How and why did the Supreme Court threaten New Deal legislation?

The Supreme Court

Given Roosevelt's flexible ideas on the workings of the Constitution, it was perhaps inevitable that he would come into conflict with its guardian, the Supreme Court. Although he had not directly attacked the Court during the election campaign, he was very concerned about its operations and felt it was in need of reform. Although the Court had supported New Deal laws in the days of crisis, it had increasingly declared legislation unconstitutional as Roosevelt's first term of office came to an end. In the 140 years before 1935, the Supreme Court had found only about 60 federal laws unconstitutional; in 18 months during 1935 and 1936, it found 11 to be so.

Indeed, on one day, 'Black Monday', 27 May 1935, the Supreme Court attacked the New Deal in several ways. For example, it found the Farm Mortgage Act (see page 85) unconstitutional. It argued that the removal of a trade commissioner, which Roosevelt sought, was the responsibility not of the president but of Congress. Most importantly, it found the NIRA to be unconstitutional through the 'sick chicken' case.

The 'sick chicken' case

This was possibly the Court's most serious decision and it motivated Roosevelt into action. The case involved the Schechter Brothers, a firm of butchers in New York who were selling chickens unfit for human consumption. Prosecuted by the NIRA for breaking its codes of practice, the Schechter Brothers appealed against the verdict to the Supreme Court. It decided that their prosecution should be a matter for the New York courts not the federal government, and the poultry code was declared illegal.

In effect, the decision meant that federal government had no right to interfere in internal state issues. While recognizing that the federal government had powers to intervene in **inter-state commerce**, the court found that it had none to do so in the internal commerce of states.

 **KEY TERM**

Inter-state commerce
Trade between different states.

Moreover, if the federal government could not prosecute individual firms for breaking the NIRA codes, it followed that all the codes themselves must be unconstitutional. This was because they were developed by federal government but affected individual firms in individual states. The argument went that the executive branch had acted unconstitutionally in giving itself the powers to implement the codes in the first place. This was because it had no authority to intervene in matters that were the preserves of individual states. Given that the codes were at the heart of NIRA, it could not survive without them. More significantly, the ruling seemed to imply that the government had no powers to oversee nation-wide economic affairs except in so far as they affected inter-state commerce.

Judiciary Reform Bill

Roosevelt believed the justices on the Supreme Court were out of touch. None were his appointees. He increasingly saw the issue of the Supreme Court as one of unelected officials stifling the work of a democratically elected government. Members of the Supreme Court meanwhile saw it as them using their legal authority to halt the spread of dictatorship. The scene was set for battle.

On 3 February 1937, Roosevelt presented the Judiciary Reform Bill to Congress. This proposed that the president could appoint a new justice whenever an existing judge, reaching the age of 70, failed to retire within six months. He could also appoint up to six new justices, increasing the possible total from 9 to 15. Roosevelt argued that the Supreme Court could not keep up with the volume of work and more justices would help. However, everyone knew that it was really a proposal to pack the court with his own nominees who would favour New Deal legislation.

Failure of the Judicial Reform Bill

In the event, the whole thing backfired. It was not a matter of the most elderly justices being the most conservative; in fact the oldest, Justice Brandeis, was, at 79, the most liberal. Nor was the Court inefficient. Chief Justice Hughes could show that the Court was necessarily selective in the cases it considered and that, given the need for considerable discussion on each one, a greater number of justices would make its work far more difficult.

Roosevelt had stirred up a hornet's nest. Many congressmen feared he might start to retire them at 70 next. He had also greatly underestimated popular support and respect for the Court. In proposing this measure, Roosevelt was seen as a dictator. In July the Senate rejected the Judiciary Reform Bill by 70 votes to 20. However, it was not a total defeat for Roosevelt.

- Justice Van Devanter, who was ill, announced his retirement.
- The Supreme Court recognized that Roosevelt had just won an election with a huge majority. Most of the electorate clearly supported his measures. Therefore the Court had already begun to uphold legislation such as the National Labour Relations and the Social Security Acts – possibly, as one wag commented, because 'a switch in time saves nine'.
- As more justices retired, Roosevelt could appoint his supporters, such as Felix Frankfurter, to replace them.

However, Roosevelt did not again attempt to reform the Court.

What problems did Roosevelt face in regard to agriculture and rural poverty?

Problems with agriculture

Roosevelt faced further challenges with agriculture and rural poverty. There were significant problems with the working of the AAA, but then came the natural disaster of the Dustbowl, which led to one of the biggest migrations in US history, with attendant issues with which the government had to deal.

Problems with the AAA

Although the AAA (see pages 85–7) was generally regarded as successful, various problems had emerged as time went on.

At the local level, the AAA was usually run by county committees, and so tended to be dominated by the most powerful landowners. If, for example, they were paid to take land out of production, they thought little about turning out their sharecroppers or tenants despite the attempts of AAA officials to mediate.

In addition, there was an increasing feeling that the AAA only really benefited the wealthy. While farm income doubled overall during the 1930s, it had only reached 80 per cent of the amount farmers were receiving before 1914. By and large, the agricultural sector remained depressed.

The Dustbowl

To add to the problem, there was a natural catastrophe taking place over much of rural America. As in Canada (see page 152), years of over-ploughing in the agricultural regions had made much of the soil fine and dusty. This had been of little importance in years of heavy rain, but in dry years that were coupled with high winds, the topsoil literally blew away. There was a series of droughts in the early 1930s, which one weather scientist described as 'the worst in the climatological history of the country'.

Beginning in the eastern states, the drought headed west. By the winter of 1933–4 the snowfall in the northern Rockies was only 33 per cent that of normal times and in the southern peaks there was hardly any. High winds led to massive erosion; the topsoil blew away in great clouds. The Natural Resources Board estimated in 1934 that 35 million acres of previously arable land had been destroyed and the soil of a further 125 million acres was exhausted. One storm between 9 and 11 May 1934 saw an estimated 350 million tons of soil transplanted from the west of the country and deposited in the east. Chicago received 1.8 kg of soil for every one of its citizens.

SOURCE I

A dust storm in Oklahoma.

What would conditions be like inside the house in Source I?

The effects

The effects were horrendous. Day became night as whole landscapes were covered with swirling dust. Homes were buried and formerly arable land was exposed as bare rock. Thousands lost their farms and were forced to migrate. It has been estimated that the state of Oklahoma alone lost 440,000 people during the 1930s, while Kansas lost 227,000. Many left to try their luck in neighbouring states. Usually their quest was unsuccessful. The plains states had little large-scale industry. Unemployment stood at 39 per cent in Arkansas in 1933, and about 30 per cent in Missouri, Oklahoma and Texas.

Migration of farm workers

Around 220,000 people migrated to California in search of work. The 'Golden State' did not welcome them. The authorities patrolled their borders, sending migrants back. They also expelled many Mexican immigrants. Despite these efforts, the state still had a drifting population of 200,000 migrant agricultural labourers, 70,000 in the fertile San Joaquin Valley alone.

Government measures

To combat erosion, the government had set up the Soil Erosion Service in August 1933. This was later renamed the Soil Conservation Service and became part of the Department of Agriculture. It divided farms into soil conservation districts, and encouraged farmers to consider new ideas such as contour ploughing to hold the soil (see page 87). Test farmers were used and evidence of their efforts was publicized to promote the effectiveness of their methods. The CCC planted trees and shelter-beds. However, all in all it was too little too late; and indeed if the land was reclaimed, farmers often began to over-plough again and the Dustbowl returned in some areas, for example to Lubbock, Texas in 1973–4.

When the rains finally did come, they would not stop. On 23 January 1937 the *New York Times* reported that floods across 12 states had made 150,000 people homeless. Nearly 4000 were killed in the windstorms and floods.

Long-term effects

Although these events were disastrous for farmers in the short term, in the long term they were beneficial for American agriculture. Many of the surplus workforce left and many of the remaining farms became bigger and more efficient. The Agricultural Bureau estimated that in 1933 about one in every 10 farms changed hands and that about half of those sales were forced. This figure did not notably fall at any time during the 1930s. The human cost was incalculable, despite the fact that measures were taken to alleviate some of the misery during the latter years of the New Deal.

Labour relations

What problems arose in industrial relations?

The mid-1930s was a time of difficult labour relations. Labour unions wanted to exercise the rights afforded them by Section 7(a) of NIRA and the Wagner Act (see page 107). However, many employers did not recognize these. At a time when many large-scale employers such as Henry Ford employed strong-arm men, strikes could often result in violence. There was also considerable anger at the use of '**blackleg**' labour during disputes, particularly if the 'blacklegs' were of a different ethnic group from the strikers.

One infamous example of violence towards strikers was the 'Memorial Day Massacre', which took place in Chicago on 30 May 1937. The dispute began when Republic Steel refused to recognize trade unions. As protesters marched on the mill, Chicago police fired into the unarmed crowd, killing 10 and wounding 30, some of whom were permanently disabled. No policemen were ever prosecuted for this.

 **KEY TERM**

Blacklegs People who break strikes by going into work.

Creation of the Committee of Industrial Organizations

There was, moreover, an important new development in American labour unionism. The American Federation of Labor (AFL) traditionally favoured craft unions and did not encourage the semi-skilled and unskilled to unionize. John Lewis, President of the United Mine Workers, in particular, wanted to see large industry-wide unions set up rather than small individual craft-based ones. If this happened it would be possible for any dispute to paralyse an entire industry. When the AFL continued to show little interest in this idea at its 1935 conference, Lewis and others who thought similarly broke away to form the Congress of Industrial Organizations.

This was later renamed the Committee of Industrial Organizations (CIO).

Achievements of the CIO

Using the threat of massive strikes, the CIO had achieved union recognition in the automobile, steel, rubber, electricity, textile and farm implement industries by the end of 1937. Firms could not afford long drawn-out strikes at a time of economic recovery. Union membership rose from four million in 1936 to seven million in 1937. The number of strikes rose from 637 in 1930 to 2172 in 1936 and 4740 in 1937. Managers were worried by this and the accompanying threat to their profits. The unions meanwhile were concerned about the level of violence used against them, which was often condoned and even perpetrated by the authorities.

SOURCE J

Policemen tussle with pickets as disorder breaks out at the gates of the Pontiac Fisher body plant in July 1939.

What could be inferred from the photograph in Source J about industrial relations in the USA in the 1930s?

Both sides looked to Roosevelt for help, but he upset both by doing nothing. He felt that the two sides had to solve the problems for themselves. He had never been especially sympathetic to labour unions; hardly any of the New Deal legislation supporting them had been initiated by him. Indeed, as we have seen, he had only given his support to the Wagner Act when it had already passed through the Senate (see page 107). However, as the unions gained in strength, Roosevelt could not continue to ignore them, and by 1940 they made the largest contribution to the Democratic Party's campaign funds; in return, their leaders expected consultations at the highest levels.

The 'Roosevelt Recession' 1937–8

What were the effects of the downturn in the economy?

KEY TERM

'Roosevelt Recession'
Downswing in the economy associated with Roosevelt's cutbacks in government spending in 1937.

Federal expenditure was cut in June 1937 to meet Roosevelt's long-held belief in a balanced budget. He hoped business had by this time recovered sufficiently to fill the gaps caused by government cutbacks. It had not. The cutbacks led to what became known as the **'Roosevelt Recession'**. The graph below shows how unemployment rose, particularly among farm workers, in 1937–8. With the numbers of unemployed rising from 7,000,000 to 10,390,000 in 12 months, social security payments swallowed $2 billion of the nation's wealth.

SOURCE K

Unemployment 1935–9.

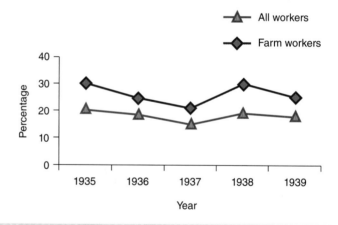

? What can be inferred from the figures in Source K?

The same problems of human misery that had been witnessed in the early years of the decade returned in full force.

- In the manufacturing industries, employment fell by 23 per cent and the production of such items as motor cars fell by as much as 50 per cent.
- Overall, national income fell by 13 per cent. Recovery suddenly seemed as far away as ever.
- According to the Federal Reserve Board's index of industrial production, 66 per cent of the gains made during the New Deal years were lost.

- The fall in the index above from 117 in August 1937 to 76 by May 1938 was faster than at any time during the earlier depression of 1929–33.

The 'Roosevelt Recession' and big business

Big business was made a scapegoat for the collapse. A Temporary National Economic Committee (TNEC) was speedily set up to investigate price fixing among large corporations. Many government officials thought these practices were responsible for the recession.

In the event, the mass of evidence that the Committee had collected led to little in the way of government action because by the time it reported, the recession was over. In any case, there was little political will to take on the giant corporations. While there was much popular sympathy for small companies and their difficulties, people increasingly realized the benefits of large ones with their relatively cheap, mass-produced goods that small companies could not provide.

In this sense, the New Deal always supported big business, even though it often verbally attacked it. This perceived hostility led to a lack of morale among businessmen and accounts for their frequent opposition to the New Deal. We must remember that, despite his attacks, Roosevelt expected big business to lead the USA out of the recession. However, it was ill disposed to do so because of the attacks. Representatives of big business in their turn blamed too much government and high taxes for their problems. Many sought a return to the policies of the 1920s.

Roosevelt's attempts to end the recession

Roosevelt seemed undecided in the face of the mounting economic problems. His Treasury Secretary, Henry Morgenthal, was advising him to balance the budget, while the chief of the Federal Reserve Board, Marriner Eccles, insisted that he return to deficit spending. In April 1938, Roosevelt finally chose the latter and asked Congress to vote him a $3.8 billion relief budget with the lion's share going to the PWA and WPA.

However, recovery was slow and in 1939 unemployment still stood at nine million. Roosevelt did appear to be moving towards policies of massive government intervention in the economy and deficit spending. However, his conversion was slow and reluctant. Yet, by the later 1930s he did seem to give more credence and support to those advisers such as Harry Hopkins and Frances Perkins who had advocated more government involvement, and conservative Democrats were increasingly frozen out. As the decade drew to a close, the European war began to dominate Roosevelt's policies. War contracts and the opening of markets unable to be met by those at war brought about recovery and concealed the failings of the New Deal.

Problems of second term	How addressed	Level of success
Supreme Court opposed New Deal legislation	Judicial Reform Bill	Bill rejected in Congress – but Supreme Court began to pass New Deal legislation

Agriculture
1 Working of AAA unfair to tenant farmers and share-croppers
 	
2 Dustbowl
	1 (a) AAA officials try to persuade local committees to act more fairly
	    (b) Second AAA
	2 (a) Farm Tenant Act
	    (b) Farm Security Administration
		1 (a) Largely failed
		    (b) Mainly helped large farmers
		
		2 (a) Partial success
		    (b) Partial success

Labour relations	(a) Did little to intervene in industrial disputes (b) Fair Labor Standards Act	(a) Upset both sides (b) Affected industries involved in inter-state commerce but many sectors excluded
'Roosevelt Recession'	$3.8 billion in relief	Inadequate to meet needs or to inflate the economy

SUMMARY DIAGRAM

Problems in Roosevelt's second term

 The Third New Deal 1937–9

▶ **Key question:** *Were the measures taken during the Third New Deal more radical than those that had gone before?*

Some commentators have spoken of a 'Third New Deal' between 1937 and 1939. This, they argue, was characterized by Roosevelt adopting the idea of permanent government spending to solve economic problems. They cite as a particular example his response to the 1937 recession. However, this argument may not be sustainable. It could imply a consistency where there was none. It could be counter-argued that the measures of the later New Deal were more piecemeal than ever. As it turned out, much of Roosevelt's programme failed to pass through an increasingly hostile Congress. The national mood was for a reduction in government spending, not expansion. This naturally limited the scope of what was passed.

We have seen above how the 'Roosevelt Recession' took his administration by surprise and he seemed uncharacteristically uncertain as to how to address it. However, problems in getting legislation through Congress were already appearing before this. There is broad agreement that Roosevelt's second administration was something of a disappointment. The increasing hostility of Congress, compounded by the president's increasing concentration on foreign affairs, has led some to argue that it ran out of steam.

Certainly, Roosevelt was frustrated in many of his legislative requests. He wanted, for example, the encouragement of more privately built housing and the creation of seven more planning authorities along the lines of the TVA (see page 87). Nothing came of either. As we will see, he went through with his plan to reorganize the executive in the face of congressional disapproval. This is not to suggest that pressing concerns were not addressed or that advances were not made. However, on the whole the legislation of Roosevelt's second administration seems nowhere near as comprehensive as that of his first.

Agriculture Acts

The government continued to take action to try to alleviate the problems faced in the agricultural sector.

How was agriculture dealt with in the Third New Deal?

Bankhead–Jones Farm Tenant Act, July 1937

This was passed partly in response to a report showing that as banks foreclosed on farms, farm ownership was declining. The Act created a Farm Security Administration (FSA), which replaced the RA. Its primary aim was to help tenants to acquire low-interest loans to buy and restock their farms. The Act was, of course, contrary to the RA, which was intended to resettle farmers elsewhere. The FSA was intended to redress some of the ill effects of the first AAA (see pages 85–7) and helped tens of thousands to stay on their land. It also established about 30 camps to provide temporary accommodation for displaced families.

The FSA also provided medical and dental centres, and funded loans to enable owners of small farms to purchase heavy machinery. By 1947, 40,000 farmers had bought their own farms through its efforts and 900,000 families had borrowed $800 million to rehabilitate their farms. Because of the return to prosperity as a result of the Second World War, the vast majority of the loans were repaid.

Second Agricultural Adjustment Act, February 1938

This was based on storing surplus produce in good years for distribution in poor ones. It established that quotas in five staple crops – rice, tobacco, wheat, corn and cotton – could be imposed by a 66 per cent majority of farmers in a vote. Those who then kept to the quotas received subsidies. By concentrating on quotas the Act was meant to be fairer to small farmers than the first AAA, which had given most subsidies to those with the most land. In case of overproduction, a Commodity Credit Corporation could make loans to enable the farmer to store his surplus produce. If, in other words, the market price fell, the farmer could store his crop. When the price rose the farmer could repay the loan and sell the surplus. Moreover, the Food Stamp Plan allowed for farm surpluses to be distributed to people on relief: they would receive 50 cents worth of such commodities for every $1 spent on other groceries.

The AAA's complexity left the county committees with too much to do and so they had little time to explain its provisions to individual farmers. It was widely distrusted therefore and believed to be unfair. This was particularly true for the small farmers it was designed to help. They had no time to study its details and had to rely on the county committees largely made up of the large-scale farmers they distrusted. It also came into operation too late for some farmers. They had already overproduced before they knew of the quotas for 1938. The resentment of the farmers was expressed in the 1938 Congressional elections, when Republicans and opponents of the New Deal made sizeable gains. The two politicians who introduced the measure into Congress were both defeated. Nevertheless, the principle behind the Act – that of subsidies for farmers adhering to quotas – essentially remained in force until recent years.

What was the purpose of housing legislation?

Wagner–Steagall National Housing Act, September 1937

This Act was designed to meet the needs for slum clearance and the building of public housing. It was largely the brainchild of Senator Wagner of New York state. Roosevelt had little enthusiasm for the scheme because he did not understand the scale of the problem of housing in the cities and preferred to support home ownership schemes. The measure established the US Housing Authority (USHA) to act through the public housing bureaux in large cities to provide loans of up to 100 per cent at low rates of interest to build new homes.

Congress allocated $500 million, only half of what had been requested. The biggest problems lay in the great north-eastern cities. However, in a slight to them, it was stipulated that no more than 10 per cent of USHA could be spent in any one state. By 1941, 160,000 homes had been built for slum dwellers at an average rent of $12–15 per month.

This was wholly inadequate to meet the problem. It was a clear example of Congressmen from the west and south failing to agree on the needs of the northern cities. They increasingly saw these as getting the lion's share of the benefits of New Deal legislation. They were determined to reverse this trend. In addition, conservatives feared public housing was a threat to capitalism, driving away the private landlord.

The result of the limitations of the Act was that millions of people remained in poor housing. It was only when urbanization developed throughout the USA in the post-war period that Congress began to provide adequate means for public housing developments.

Fair Labor Standards Act, June 1938

> **How did the government help pay and working conditions?**

This Act fixed minimum wages and maximum hours of work in all industries engaged in inter-state commerce. The minimum wage was set at 25 cents per hour, intended to rise eventually to 40 cents, and maximum hours should be 44 per week, with the hope that they would fall to 40 within three years. The wages of 300,000 people were immediately increased and the hours of 1.3 million were reduced. The inter-state shipment of goods made by children working under the age of 16 was forbidden. Children under 18 years were forbidden to work in hazardous employment.

To supervise the legislation, a wages and hours division was set up in the Department of Labor. This had the power to impose hefty fines. However, to get the Act accepted, particularly by southern politicians, Roosevelt had to make exemptions, notably domestic servants and farm labourers. As with the Social Security legislation, it was hoped that these would be included in the future. Moreover, as the omissions were mainly jobs associated with African-Americans, it could be argued that this group was losing out yet again. It was another example of New Deal legislation bypassing them, an issue that will be more fully addressed on pages 128–9.

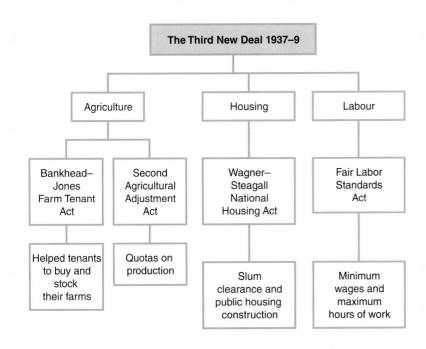

SUMMARY DIAGRAM

The Third New Deal 1937–9

Political developments 1938 and 1939

> ▶ *Key question: How and when did the New Deal come to a close?*

In the mid-term elections of 1938 the Republicans doubled their seats in the House of Representatives and also made gains in the Senate (see Source F, page 104). The tide appeared to be turning against Roosevelt politically. Although he was to break with tradition and stand for a historic third (and later a fourth) term of office, this was not known at the time.

Increasingly, as his second term drew to a close, he was seen as a lame duck president whose New Deal policies had failed to deliver economic recovery to the extent hoped for. There were no new New Deal measures passed after January 1939. Increasingly thereafter foreign affairs began to dominate.

However, one can discern a shift in Roosevelt's thinking. He began to realize that a balanced budget might not be possible in the modern world and that involvement in the economy and in the provision of relief might become permanent features of American government. This was quite different from his earlier ideas. In fact, some commentators have argued that when the USA was ready for radical change in 1933, Roosevelt adopted a conservative stance but when he tried to impose radical change during the later 1930s, the country was too conservative to accept it. In 1939, for example, opinion polls found that only 20 per cent of Americans were prepared to accept the idea of an unbalanced budget. Roosevelt faced two significant defeats during this period which resulted in the creation of the Executive Office of the President. His defeats included:

- the Revenue Act
- his attempted purge of Democrat opponents.

Revenue Act 1938

Roosevelt's **Revenue Act** of 1938 was considerably weakened when Congress removed the proposed tax on company profits. Allowing firms to keep more of their revenue, would, it was hoped, help to stimulate industrial recovery. Nevertheless, the message seemed to be that Roosevelt could not rely on the support of the legislature, that it was 'business as usual', and the mood was for lessening government involvement.

In other words, Roosevelt had, in his increasing radicalism, gone beyond the mood of the politicians in Congress. The message from the legislature suggested that many of the powers he had accumulated in the past were now going to be taken away from him.

What lessons could be learned from the watering down of the 1938 Revenue Act?

 **KEY TERM**

Revenue Act States how the government aims to raise money that year.

Roosevelt's attempted purge of the Democrats

How successfully did Roosevelt purge the Democrat Party of opponents?

When Roosevelt tried to purge his own party by getting rid of conservatives this also failed. In summer 1938 the mid-term primary elections for Democratic candidates to Congress took place. The president travelled the country supporting liberal candidates and opposing conservative ones. However, the conservative candidates he opposed still made a show of publicly supporting him. Moreover, these elections tended to be very much about local issues. Roosevelt's interventions had little effect but they did make the president seem ham-fisted. The attempt also made for difficult working relationships with the new Congress when it met.

Executive Office of the President

Roosevelt recognized that the increased role of government would be permanent. He planned to accommodate this through the creation of the **Executive Office of the President**. This would lead to an expanded White House staff, a system of promotion by merit in the civil service and development of more government departments. He was surprised by the general hostility to the idea. There was a fear that he was seeking to acquire too much power, that he wished to become a dictator and that his appointees would use their new unelected positions to stay in power.

Others felt that the president was encroaching on the powers of Congress, which was supposed to initiate legislation. Some, of course, opposed it simply because it was promoted by Roosevelt. In any event, the House of Representatives rejected the measure in April 1938 by a vote of 204 to 196. Roosevelt, in fact, created the Executive Office by **Executive Order** in September 1939 as was his right. But it is important to note that this was in defiance of Congress.

KEY TERM

Executive Office of the President The president's staff.

Executive Order An order by which the president could force through any decision he made despite Congressional opposition.

Gallup Poll A survey of people's views made by the Gallup organization.

Effects of these defeats

What was the impact of these political defeats?

Although each of these attempts to impose his will ended in defeat, collectively they made more people suspicious of Roosevelt's intentions. In August 1938 a **Gallup Poll** showed that 50 per cent of Americans feared the development of dictatorship in the USA, compared with 37 per cent in a similar poll the previous October. With anxious eyes looking towards Europe and the growth of dictatorships, the tide seemed to have turned against Roosevelt and the expansion of American government. Moreover, Roosevelt was blamed for the recession, which is why it was named after him.

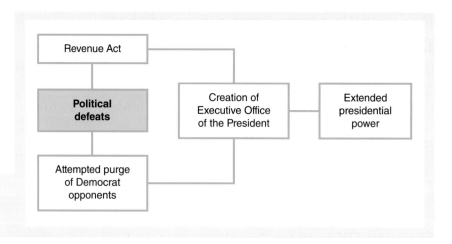

SUMMARY DIAGRAM
Political developments 1938 and 1939

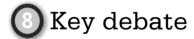 **Key debate**

> ▶ *Key question: How much impact did the New Deal have on American politics and the economy?*

There has been heated debate among historians as to what the New Deal achieved. In this section we will analyse some the key elements of these debates.

In the years following the New Deal, historians and commentators were generally supportive of it. People involved in the process knew they were making history. Studs Terkel, a broadcaster and oral historian, interviewed various participants in the 1960s including Gardener C. Means and Raymond Moley (see page 99). Means felt that it marked a turning point in American government, with the end of nineteenth-century ideas of a limited government role; Moley agreed that it led to a growth in government power but felt the opportunities for radical change were lost during the second New Deal. Some argued that the enhanced role of the government in responsibility for people's welfare marked the growing maturity of the nation, bringing about what American historian Carl Degler called 'a third American Revolution'. He meant by this the huge growth in government and break with *laissez-faire*. William E. Leuchtenburg, a historian of the New Deal, wrote that 'it is hard to think of another period in the whole history of the republic that was so fruitful or a crisis that was met with such imagination'.

Schlesinger and Leuchtenburg

Arthur M. Schlesinger Jr and William E. Leuchtenburg, writing in the late 1950s and early 1960s, both felt that the New Deal showed a compassionate response to crisis. Leuchtenburg argued that the New Deal created a more just society by recognizing previously unrecognized groups such as organized labour. However, it only partially addressed these issues; groups such as slum dwellers, share-croppers and African-Americans still felt excluded in a society that was still racially segregated.

The New Left

In the 1960s historians of the **New Left** such as Howard Zinn, Paul Conkin and Barton J. Bernstein became more critical of the New Deal. They tended to see the New Deal as a wasted opportunity for radical change. It was felt that the piecemeal solutions of the New Deal enabled capitalism to prevail. In the words of Paul Conkin, 'the story of the New Deal is a sad story, the ever recurring story of what might have been'. Bernstein wrote that it 'failed to solve the problem of the depression, it failed to raise the impoverished and it failed to redistribute income'. Conkin argued that the New Deal should have improved social justice and produced a more contented, fulfilled population.

It was felt by historians of the New Left, for example, that the New Deal never consulted people as to their needs, which would have involved them in the political process, although this was not strictly true, for example where ordinary people were involved in running the Tennessee Valley Authority (see page 87).

More recent views

In addressing the points raised by the New Left, the New Deal was not intended to effect radical change. Historians of this school have therefore tended to criticize it for something it was not rather than to examine it on its own merits. In the 1970s, historians and economists, notably Milton Friedman, whose monetarist theories were discussed on page 58, often attacked the New Deal for the opposite reasons: that it had set the USA on the wrong course. Government spending, they argued, fuelled inflation; governments taking responsibility for people's livelihoods fostered **welfare dependency** and stifled entrepreneurial creativity. These historians favoured the working of the free market. They saw the election of President Reagan in 1980 as a turning-point, reversing the movement begun by the New Deal for governments to take responsibility for people's lives.

Leuchtenburg has more recently argued that since the writings of the New Left, it has generally been assumed that the New Deal failed. Historians tended to debate whether it failed because of the deficiencies of Roosevelt or the powerful conservative forces that opposed radical change. Leuchtenburg, on the other hand, feels that the New Deal achieved a lot, not least the dramatic growth in federal government. Ordinary citizens looked increasingly to it to solve many of their problems where previously they had looked to it to solve none of them. The legacy of this increased role was, moreover, permanent. British historian D.K. Adams showed that President Kennedy's speech outlining his **New Frontier** programme in 1961 was a paraphrase of a 1935 one by Roosevelt.

 **KEY TERM**

New Left School of historians critical of the New Deal for not adopting more radical changes.

Welfare dependency Where people come to rely on state benefits.

New Frontier President Kennedy's reform programme 1961–3.

David Kennedy goes on to acknowledge that there was much the New Deal did not do, for example, bring economic recovery, redistribute national income or end capitalism. However, it achieved much, notably the reform of the economy so that the benefits of a capitalist system could be more evenly distributed. Methods of achieving this included:

- the recognition of organized labour
- greater regulation of abuses in the economic system
- greater financial security through, for example, the introduction of old-age pensions.

It is important to consider not what the New Deal failed to do but what it did achieve in a political system designed originally to prevent the growth of federal government. In so doing, the New Deal mended the failings of capitalism through the existing system and therefore possibly averted a far more radical programme.

9 The impact of the Great Depression on society: African-Americans and women

▶ **Key question:** *How effectively did the New Deal improve conditions for women and African-Americans?*

We have already seen that the New Deal did more for Native Americans than past administrations (see page 93), but critics have argued that it did little for African-Americans and women.

African-Americans

How far did life improve for African-Americans?

Roosevelt needed the vote of southern Democrats, who were often racist. A realist, he said, 'I did not choose the tools with which I must work.' Certainly, early in the New Deal, southern politicians were often his most loyal supporters. Not surprisingly, therefore, the New Deal saw no civil rights legislation. As we have seen (see page 114), many measures – the AAA for instance – worked against African-Americans.

African-Americans suffered particularly badly in the Depression, often being the last to be taken on and the first to be fired. Many poorly paid, menial jobs previously reserved for them were now taken by whites. NRA codes allowed for African-Americans to be paid less than whites for doing the same jobs. Some African-Americans called the NRA the 'Negro-run-around' because it was so unfair to them. The CCC was run by a southern racist who did little to encourage African-Americans to join: those who did faced strict segregation. Anti-lynching bills were introduced into Congress in 1934 and

SOURCE L

African-American share-croppers being evicted from their home in 1939. This was a photograph taken by Arthur Rothstein, who created a photographic survey of the nation paid for by the Farm Security Administration.

How well might the photograph in Source L indicate what the New Deal did for African-Americans? **?**

1937, but Roosevelt did nothing to support either and both were eventually defeated.

Nevertheless, many African-Americans saw him as much a saviour as poor whites did. His portrait hung in many African-American homes.

The president did employ more African-Americans in government, notably, as we saw on page 105, Mary McLeod Bethune at the NYA. The civil service trebled the number of African-Americans in its employment between 1932 and 1941 to 150,000. There was also some **positive discrimination**, notably again in the NYA where African-American officials were usually appointed in areas where African-Americans predominated.

Although there were few official measures specifically to benefit African-Americans, there were important gestures of support. There were more African-Americans with the ear, if not of the president, then of important figures close to him, and millions of African-Americans benefited from relief measures that, even if still favouring whites, gave them more help than they had ever previously received.

 **KEY TERM**

Positive discrimination
Where members of one group are favoured over those of others.

Women

Women held more important posts in government during the New Deal era than at any time before or after until the 1990s. Mrs Roosevelt was one of the most politically active first ladies; as Secretary of Labor, Frances Perkins was

← **How far did New Deal measures improve opportunities for women?**

only one of many women holding government office; and Ruth Bryan Owen became the first female ambassador (to Denmark). Many prominent women had come together through expertise in social work, which was, of course, an asset for designing many New Deal measures. Unfortunately, when government priorities changed with the onset of war, much of their influence was lost.

The New Deal, in fact, did little for women. Unlike African-Americans, they did not tend to vote as a group. As a result politicians did not set out particularly to win their support. Much New Deal legislation worked against them. In 1933, for example, the Economy Act forbade members of the same family from working for federal government and so many wives lost their jobs. A total of 75 per cent of those losing their jobs through this measure were women. We have seen on page 52 that many measures to curb the Depression took jobs away particularly from married women.

The New Deal did nothing to reverse this process. NRA codes allowed for unequal wages and some agencies such as the CCC barred women entirely. Women suffered particularly in the professions where, even by 1940, about 90 per cent of jobs were still filled by men. There was a strong emphasis that in the job market, men should be the principal wage earners with women's wages only supplementing this. Where women did find employment – which many had to do to balance the family budget – it tended often to be in low-status, poorly paid jobs. On average during the 1930s, at $525 per annum, women earned half the average wage of men.

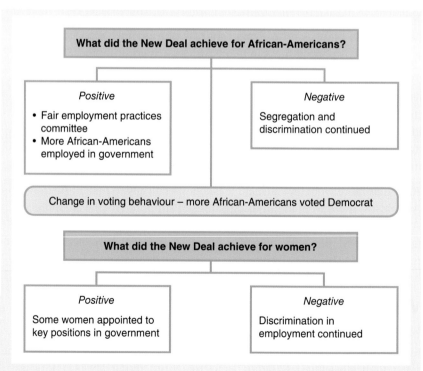

SUMMARY DIAGRAM

The impact of the Great Depression on society: African-Americans and Women

10 The New Deal: an evaluation

▶ **Key question:** *What conclusions can be drawn about the impact of the New Deal?*

The first decades of the twentieth century had seen an unprecedented growth in government. Of the three Republican presidents of the 1920s, only Coolidge sought to reverse this trend. Therefore, the New Deal continued a process already underway.

Industrial relations had moved into the modern era with more of a partnership between government, employers and unions. The government also recognized the importance of big business. While small self-reliant businessmen may have been heroes in the American dream, as we have seen, American capitalism developed in reality through the power of big business. Although it may not always have been realized at the time, it was largely the interests of big business that the economic measures of the New Deal benefited. The gains of this were clear during the war, when businesses were relatively easily able to adapt to large-scale armaments production.

The people and the states increasingly looked to the government for help with their problems. The USA was becoming urbanized to a noticeable degree, and legislation such as the 1937 National Housing Act recognized this. Many of Roosevelt's supporters in the south later turned against him because they felt legislation was increasingly favouring northern cities to the detriment of rural areas.

However, even in the countryside things had changed. Agencies such as the TVA and REA had helped rural areas to move into a modern era with their provision of facilities such as electrical power. Farmers were now expecting loans and subsidies from the government through the AAA. The tentacles of government, it seemed, were everywhere. The USA had moved from a land of self-reliant individualism with very little government interference to one where the government increasingly took responsibility for people's lives and welfare. The Depression had shown that the economy was not self-righting and that the American dream was largely impossible to realize unaided, however much initiative and ability to work hard one might possess. In the end, the Depression had eroded much of the American dream, particularly the notion of self-reliance. It became necessary in the 1930s to address a harsh reality and the significance of the New Deal was that it did precisely this.

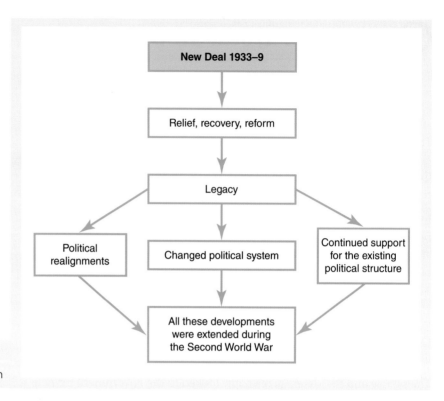

The New Deal: an evaluation

11 Literature and the arts during the Great Depression

▶ Key question: How did literature and the arts respond to changes in American society?

Literature

Overall, the response to the Depression was pessimistic, with realistic novels from major authors such as John Steinbeck, John Dos Passos and William Faulkner focusing on tragedy and the hopelessness of humans in the face of such adversity. Conservatives accused many of these writers of supporting Communist ideas.

Communists

It might be expected that the Communist Party would support literature to emphasize the miseries caused by the failures of capitalism and the need for revolution. However, the party, through its main voice, the magazine *New Masses* insisted that writers toe the party line and stifled creativity. One leading Communist critic, Michael Gold, wrote, 'Every poem, every novel and drama must have a social theme or it is merely confectionary.' Others went further insisting that pieces conformed to Communist theory. As a result many pieces were sterile and dull. The Communists rejected work by Steinbeck and Richard Wright. In Wright's 1940 novel *Native Son* he refused to idealize a Communist lawyer or explain his hero's tragedy solely in terms of the socio-economic forces ranged against him.

John Dos Passos

John Dos Passos (1896–1970), a journalist and novelist, produced his three-part masterpiece, *USA*, during the 1930s. Using experimental prose forms including stream of consciousness writing and written equivalents of 'newsreels', the novel featured a vast gallery of characters, both real and fictional but the overall mood, as it plots the gradual abandonment of the American dream, was one of despair.

Thomas Wolfe

Wolfe (1900–38) tried to embrace the range and diversity within the USA in a series of mainly autobiographical novels published between 1929 and his death 10 years later. In these works, beginning with *Look Homeward Angel* and ending with the posthumously published *You Can't Go Home Again*, Wolfe captured the frenetic energy of urban life coupled with the confusion and vulnerability of Americans.

William Faulkner

Faulkner (1897–1962), a Nobel Prize winner, wrote about his home state of Mississippi, with the added features of southern pride and racism. Many of his books were set in the fictional county of Yoknapatawpha and focused on the trials of the aristocratic Sartoris family and the newly wealthy Snopes. Faulkner was fascinated by the heavy weight of southern history and most of his characters were trapped by it.

John Steinbeck

John Steinbeck (1902–68), another Nobel Prize winner, may be the writer who most accurately caught the mood and despair of people caught up in the Depression, most notably in his novel *The Grapes of Wrath*, published in 1938 and filmed by John Ford in 1940.

The novel follows the fortunes of the Joad family, forced off their land in the midwest by the Dustbowl and seeking work in California. The novel is a devastating indictment of the waste and cruelty occasioned by the Depression, where families become non-persons forced into a nomadic existence, constantly moved on by the authorities and yet maintaining their dignity despite the hopelessness of their plight.

Steinbeck had the advantage of not only being able to draw realistic characters caught up in dramatic tragedy, but also being a talented naturalistic writer who could draw unforgettable word pictures.

Federal Writers' Project

The Federal Writers' Project was set up under Henry Alsbury, a theatrical producer and journalist, largely to provide employment for authors, and developed into a scheme employing 6600 of them. In Indiana for example, 150 were employed at any one time, working between 20 and 30 hours per week.

The work of the Federal Writer's Project was possibly far more significant than originally intended. It complied works of local and oral history that may not otherwise have been created, including, for example, 2300 first-person slave narratives, which were subsequently published, accompanied by 500 photographs as 'Unchained Memories'. The project's authors also produced a detailed guidebook for each state which included history, culture, photographs and detailed descriptions of every settlement.

Let Us Now Praise Famous Men

This work was intended to have a similar impact to *The Grapes of Wrath*. A writer, James Agee, and photographer, Walker Evans, were commissioned by *Fortune* magazine in 1936 to record the lives of poor tenant farmers. They showed the immense dignity of the farmers despite their poverty. Perhaps the magazine was expecting a piece about downtrodden victims; in any event it refused to publish the work, which did not appear until 1941 when the worst of the Depression was over.

How far did cinema offer an escape from the problems of the Depression?

The cinema

Hollywood was the centre of the world's largest cinema industry. Millions of people all over the world saw its productions every week. On one level, the cinema fulfilled the main avenue of temporary escape for millions of people caught up in the Depression. They could follow the glamorous life of the stars, and indulge in fantasy through Busby Berkley musicals, gangster movies in which the Warner Studios excelled and epics such as *Gone with the Wind* (1939).

Americans flocked to sentimental movies such as *Mr Deeds Goes to Town* (1936) with their idealized view of small-town USA where, despite adversity, everything turns out right in the end. There were **screwball comedies** such as *It Happened One Night* (1934) and *Bringing Up Baby* (1938) with no hint of any Depression.

John Wayne was only one actor whose tough independence in countless Westerns suggested people could overcome all their problems through determination and honesty. However, Hollywood portrayed the reality of the Depression too. The same director who made *Gold Diggers of 1933* (1933) had earlier made *I am a Fugitive from a Chain Gang* (1932) about how easy it was for the unemployed to fall into crime. On the whole, however, cinema-goers preferred to escape from their everyday lives into the darkened hall where they could fantasize for a few hours that they lived in a more pleasant world.

KEY TERM

Screwball comedies
Absurd but very funny comedies with richly comic characters and crazy situations.

Possibly the most powerful movie about the Depression was *The Grapes of Wrath* (1940), which actually used much of Steinbeck's dialogue and brought the miseries of the Joads to powerful visual light. Other movies criticized realities, however: Charlie Chaplin, the famous comedian, writer and director, attacked the monotony and inhumanity of factory life in *Modern Times* (1936); the Ku Klux Klan was arraigned in *Black Legion* (1937), while *Make Way for Tomorrow* (1936) explored the difficulties of being old and poor.

Radio

Radio was hugely popular in the 1930s, bringing distant worlds and escape from reality into people's homes as opposed to their having to go out to the cinema. It is possible that people in debt generally tried to hang on to their radios after all their other luxury items had been sold. The success of the radio can be gleaned from revenues from sponsors: NBC received $21,452,732 in 1933 and CBS $10,063,566.

While there were concert recitals and serious programmes, **soap operas** held sway in the afternoons when it was believed the main audience would be women at home. In the early evening families would gather to listen to Westerns such as *Gunsmoke*, comedies like *Amos an' Andy* and quizzes such as *The Sixty-four Dollar Question*. Even without the Depression, radios kept many people in isolated areas in touch with an imagined outside world.

Popular music

Perhaps the one piece that symbolized the depression years was a song: Yip Harburg's 'Brother Can You Spare a Dime?'

SOURCE M

Lyrics to 'Brother Can You Spare a Dime?', Yip Harburg, 1932. ['Brother, Can You Spare a Dime?' by E.Y. 'Yip' Harburg and Jay Gorney. Published by Glocca Morra Music (ASCAP) and Gorney Music (ASCAP). Administered by Next Decade Entertainment, Inc. All Rights Reserved. Used by Permission.]

They used to tell me I was building a dream, and so I followed the mob,

When there was earth to plow, or guns to bear, I was always there right on the job.

They used to tell me I was building a dream, with peace and glory ahead,

Why should I be standing in line, just waiting for bread?

Once I built a railroad, I made it run, made it race against time.

Once I built a railroad; now it's done. Brother, can you spare a dime?

Once I built a tower, up to the sun, brick, and rivet, and lime;

Once I built a tower, now it's done. Brother, can you spare a dime?

How popular was radio?

KEY TERM

Soap operas Romantic serials, so called because many of the sponsors were soap companies.

How far did popular music reflect the realities of life during the Depression?

How does the lyricist capture the despair of the singer? Explain your answer by close reference to Source M.

This song was all the more poignant for coming out during the veterans' march on Washington (see pages 68–9). Others were more upbeat, for example 'Life is Just a Bowl of Cherries' by Lew Brown and Ray Henderson (1931) and 'We're in the Money' by Al Dubin and Harry Warren, which featured in the film, *Gold Diggers of 1933*.

What was the impact of photographing life during the Depression?

Photography

SOURCE N

'Migrant Mother'– an image of Florence Owens Thompson, a destitute worker in a pea-picking camp, not looking into the camera but lost in her own thoughts. Photographed by Dorothea Lange in 1936.

In Source N, what might Mrs Thompson be thinking?

The period saw the production of intensely moving photographs of victims of the Depression, often under the auspices of the Farm Security Administration and given without charge to newspapers to publish. Under the head of the historical section, Roy Stryker, talented photographers compiled over 80,000 images of life during the Depression. Notable among them were Dorothea Lange, Walker Evans, Ben Fields and Arthur Rothstein. Lange probably created one of the most iconic photographs in 'Migrant Mother' (Source N).

The same phenomenon took place in Canada, where photographers captured the misery of displaced and poverty-stricken farmers in Saskatchewan.

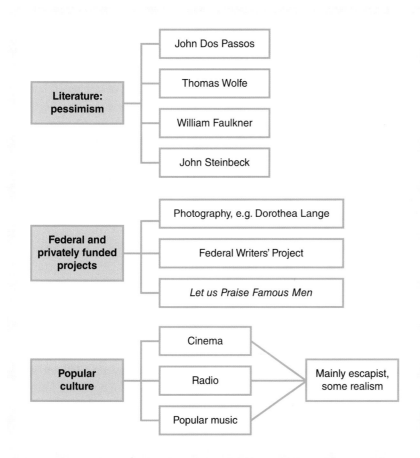

SUMMARY DIAGRAM

Literature and the arts during the Great Depression

The impact of the Second World War on the USA

> ▶ **Key question:** *What was the political and economic impact of the Second World War on the USA?*

There is no doubt that involvement in the Second World War rather than the New Deal brought prosperity back to the USA. Roosevelt, however, did not live to see these fruits. Having won a fourth term of office in the 1944 presidential election, he died in April 1945.

Political effects

How did the government take more control of people's lives?

The government took over more control of people's lives. In 1940 the Smith Act had been passed which made it illegal to threaten to overthrow the government of the USA. Originally aimed at supporters of fascism, it later became associated with the post-war attack on Communists. The Selective Service Act of the same year had introduced conscription. As the war developed the Office of War Mobilization was created to control the supply of goods and prices; the National War Labor Board set wages. As we shall see, these measures had a huge effect on the wartime economy and the freedoms of the labour force.

Economic effects

What impact did war production have on the economy?

American involvement in war production made the New Deal irrelevant. Between 1941 and 1945 the USA produced 86,000 tanks, 296,000 aircraft and 15 million rifles. Farm income grew by 250 per cent. Unemployment effectively ceased by 1942; in 1944 it stood at 1.2 per cent, having fallen from 14.6 per cent in 1940. In 1944 alone, 6.5 million women entered the labour force; by the end of the war almost 60 per cent of women were employed. The number of African-Americans working for the federal government rose from 50,000 in 1939 to 200,000 by 1944. In the years between 1940 and 1944 five million African-Americans moved to the cities, where a million found jobs in defence plants. Gross national product (GNP) meanwhile rose from $91.3 billion in 1939 to $166.6 billion by 1945.

However, under the Office of War Mobilization, food prices and rents were strictly controlled. Some items such as meat, sugar and petrol were rationed, and the production of cars for ordinary motorists stopped entirely. While many consumer items such as clothes were made from far less material and became simpler in style and others disappeared from the shops, most Americans were comparatively well paid during the war and did not suffer the deprivations of those in other belligerent countries. Although prices rose by 28 per cent during the war years, average wages increased by 40 per cent;

people may not have had much to spend these wages on, but they could and did save. It was the spending power of these consumers which helped to fuel the post-war boom period.

As a result of the costs of the war, the national debt, which stood at $41 billion in 1941, had risen to $260 billion by 1945. The federal government spent twice as much between 1941 and 1945 as it had before in 150 years.

Roosevelt hoped to pay for much of the war production by increased taxes. The highest earners paid 94 per cent tax. This gave a sense of greater equality. The poor grew more wealthy during the war years and the rich received a smaller proportion of national income, as Source O shows.

SOURCE O

Percentage of national income taken by the richest one per cent of the population.

Year	Percentage of national income taken by richest 1% of the population
1939	13.4
1944	11.5
1945	6.7

What can be inferred from the figures in Source O?

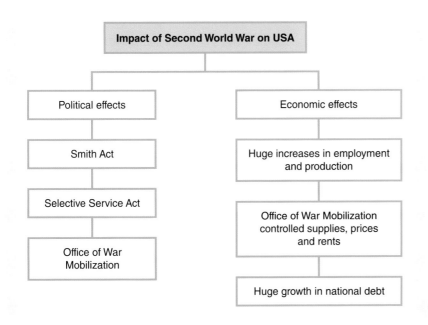

SUMMARY DIAGRAM

The impact of the Second World War on the USA

Chapter summary

The USA 1933–45: New Deals and economic recovery

Roosevelt arrived at the presidency on a tide of goodwill, but was faced with huge problems. Although there was no developed blueprint for reform, the first 100 days saw a tide of legislation to address these problems:

- Banking and finance were reformed.
- Alphabet agencies were set up to deal with specific problems, for example in agriculture, industry, housing.
- States were offered direct relief to distribute among the needy.

Roosevelt faced powerful opposition, however, from both the right and the left. The latter included Huey Long, the influential politician from Louisiana who could have fought Roosevelt in the 1936 presidential election.

While Roosevelt was a fiscal conservative who did not seek radical change in the USA, the First New Deal nevertheless set important precedents in the growth of the executive power in the USA.

Roosevelt introduced the Second and Third New Deals as the problems caused by the Depression persisted. He gradually came around to the view that federal intervention in the economy would be a permanent rather than temporary feature and so accepted deficit spending as an inevitable consequence of this. Some of his measures appeared radical because he sought to maintain the initiative and not have to accept more radical measures proposed by Congress. However, the limitations of the New Deal measures were shown by the Roosevelt Recession.

- The Second New Deal continued measures for recovery but also introduced emergency relief, and for the first time, social security measures.
- Roosevelt won a decisive victory in the 1936 election.
- His second term was beset by problems including opposition from the Supreme Court and the natural catastrophe of the Dustbowl.
- Roosevelt attempted to formalize the growth of government by the creation of the Executive Office of the President.

The Depression stimulated achievements in arts and literature, not least the photography which showed the human cost of the economic collapse.

While the New Deal was accused of running out of steam and the real economic recovery was more to do with the onset of the Second World War, its achievements should not be minimized. As a result of the New Deal, the USA was changed forever.

However, the Second World War saw real prosperity return to the USA which continued after 1945.

 # Examination advice

How to answer 'compare and contrast' questions

For <u>compare and contrast</u> questions, you are asked to identify both similarities and differences. Better essays tend to approach the question thematically. It is best not to write half of the essay as a collection of similarities and half as differences. Finally, straight narrative should be avoided.

Example

> <u>Compare and contrast</u> the effectiveness of the First and Second New Deals.

1 You are asked to discuss to what degree both the First and Second New Deals were effective. Here, effective can mean successful. You will need to distinguish clearly the two New Deals and state what you mean by effectiveness. Be sure to consider for whom the New Deals were effective. And did they solve problems? Finally, was one set of government programmes more effective than the other?

2 Take five minutes before writing your essay to identify the key elements of each New Deal. Also be sure to include whether or not the specific programmes within each New Deal were successful. One difficulty you may face is that there were so many elements to the New Deals and that the amount of information is overwhelming. Try to focus on the programmes which best support your thesis. Below are some examples of what might be included as key areas.

First New Deal
- The Emergency Banking Relief Act, 1933 (see page 81)
- The Glass–Steagall Act, 1933 (see page 82)
- Agricultural Adjustment Act (AAA), 1933 (see pages 85–6)
- Tennessee Valley Authority (TVA), 1933 (see page 87)
- National Industry Recovery Act (NIRA), 1933; two parts: National Recovery Administration (NRA) (see pages 89–91) and Public Works Administration (PWA) (see page 91).

Second New Deal
- Emergency Relief Appropriation Act, 1935 (see page 104)
- Works Progress Administration (WPA), 1935 (see pages 104–5)
- Rural Electrification Administration, 1935 (see page 105)
- Social Security Act, 1935 (see pages 108–9).

3 In your introduction, you should begin by defining the two New Deals. Next, you will need to state your thesis. This might well be that elements of one New Deal were more effective than those of another. You could also briefly discuss why this might have been the case. An example of a good introductory paragraph is given below.

President Franklin D. Roosevelt initiated a series of reforms and government programmes meant to tackle the severe economic problems the USA faced during the Great Depression. These can broadly be divided into two phases, the First New Deal in 1933 and the Second New Deal in 1935–6. In the case of the former, some semblance of financial stability was created and immediate problems were confronted. To a certain extent, Roosevelt was able to save US capitalism. However, because of continued economic difficulties and political challenges, Roosevelt embarked on a second phase of reforms, known as the Second New Deal. Both sets of programmes were attacked by those who felt the government had no business in interfering with the economy. Nonetheless, for the many millions of unemployed and the poor, it was no small comfort to know that the government was doing something to alleviate their situations. While achievements were made with the First New Deal, the lack of a coherent overall plan limited its effectiveness. The Supreme Court also declared unconstitutional several of the more important acts such as the National Recovery Administration. In the Second New Deal, Roosevelt changed direction and it seemed as though the worst excesses of capitalism would be addressed, which many at the time thought had not been done under the First New Deal.

4 The bulk of your essay will be discussing the various key points outlined in your introduction. Your argument should focus on both similarities and differences. You could, for example, look at government policies to address severe problems with agriculture. What aid was offered to farmers in the First New Deal and in the Second? How were they different? Which of the two had the larger impact? Other paragraphs might include how each Deal addressed mass unemployment and how the government approached big business.

5 In your concluding paragraph, you should refer to your thesis and the major points you raised in order to support this. Do not introduce any new material here. An example of a good concluding paragraph is provided below.

The administration of Franklin D. Roosevelt tried a wide variety of methods to tackle the effects of the Great Depression. During the First New Deal, confidence in the banking system was restored and over-production of some agricultural products was curtailed. However, unemployment remained a persistent problem and many citizens felt that the rich were not made to pay their fair share. In the Second New Deal, Roosevelt tried to address these problems. Again, there were certain significant achievements such as the Social Security Act but many citizens were not covered. Finally, both programmes represented a drastic and heretofore unheard of involvement of the US government in the lives of Americans. For many, this was a welcome intervention and provided some hope where there had been none.

6 Now try writing a complete answer to the question following the advice above.

Examination practice

Below are three exam-style questions for you to practise on this topic.

1 Evaluate how effective Roosevelt's political opponents were in blunting the impact of the New Deal.
(For guidance on how to answer 'evaluate' questions, see page 178.)

2 'Roosevelt's New Deals did not solve the economic problems of the country.' To what extent do you agree with this statement?
(For guidance on how to answer 'to what extent' questions, see page 44.)

3 Discuss how literature and the arts responded to the changes in American society during the Depression.
(For guidance on how to answer 'discuss' questions, see page 228.)

CHAPTER 5

The Great Depression in Canada

This chapter examines how the Great Depression affected the political and economic development of Canada. It starts by looking at the apparent prosperity of Canada in the 1920s before going on to consider the causes and effects of the Depression. It then examines how Canadian governments responded to the problems caused by the Depression, emphasizing the contributions of Mackenzie King and R.B. Bennett.

You need to consider the following questions throughout this chapter:

✪ How healthy was Canada's political system and economy in the 1920s?

✪ What were the causes and effects of the Great Depression in Canada?

✪ How effectively did federal governments respond to the Depression?

✪ Why did Bennett change his view on the extent of government intervention?

✪ What alternative approaches were promoted to address Canada's problems?

✪ What were the main features of Mackenzie King's domestic policies to 1939?

✪ How far did Canada become a planned economy during the Second World War?

✪ How far did the Great Depression lead to the growth of the role of federal government?

① Canada in the 1920s

▶ *Key question: How healthy was Canada's political system and economy in the 1920s?*

As in the USA, many in Canada were growing in confidence as the 1920s progressed. Having performed very well in the First World War and enhancing its national standing as a result, there was a renewed feeling of independence from Britain. The economy was also booming; this signified, it was assumed, a mature and stable infrastructure. The decade was characterized by a consumer boom and good living. Many Canadians thought the good times would never end. However, there were worrying trends and indicators for those who scratched beneath the surface.

 KEY TERM

Dominion status Semi-independent within the British Empire.

> **What was the significance of the political developments that took place in the 1920s?**

→ **Political developments**

Canada was governed according to the British North America Act which had granted it **dominion status** in 1867. The intention had been to create a strong central government based in Ottawa with national responsibilities such as oversight of the economy, and weaker provincial authorities tasked with more localized issues. In effect, however, the **provinces** rigorously defended their own powers such as responsibilities for the health and welfare of their citizens and, as we shall see, the federal authorities were limited in what actions they could take when faced with national issues. Also, ultimate authority as to the division of powers lay with the **Privy Council** in Britain. If, therefore, Canadians wished to change their constitution they had to appeal to the British government.

Canadian governance was complicated by the fact that it was divided into English- and French-speaking areas. The inhabitants of the latter were largely descendants of settlers to the original French colonies in Canada, located mainly in the south-eastern province of Quebec (Québec). Often tensions would arise between the different groups in Quebec and sometimes there would be nationalist movements seeking at least partial independence (see page 148).

In the late nineteenth century a two-party system had emerged, the Conservatives and Liberals. However, the 1921 federal elections saw a third force emerge, the Progressive Party. This was formed by a coalition of farmers' interests and dissident Liberals who opposed the tariff policies of the mainstream parties. This was important because they won 64 seats in the ensuing election out of 235 and controlled the balance of power.

Post-war problems

There was a short-term recession after the war from 1919 to 1921 which was important in the way it signposted future issues in the Great Depression such as overproduction, inflation and unrest.

- There was a fall in demand for wheat following the war as peacetime conditions returned. Moreover, the former **belligerent countries** returned to domestic production, which led to more wheat being produced and resulting in a collapse in prices. Coupled with the onset of drought, this brought a hardship to the prairies from which they never really recovered. In 1921, for example, the price of wheat was $2 per bushel; by the following year this had halved.
- Wartime inflation due to shortages of goods was not really controlled until 1923.
- There was a series of industrial disputes about pay and working conditions which often resulted in violence. The most serious precursor of future unrest was in the city of Winnepeg, paralysed by strikes in May 1919. Many of those in dispute sought the creation of One Big Union (OBU) to speak for all workers. When strikers paraded on 21 June, the mayor read the **Riot Act** and the demonstration was dispersed with force. In future the authorities would be prepared to use police and militias to quell demonstrations. Strikes were particularly prevalent in the coalfields of the west, for example 22,000 people were on strike there in August 1922.

KEY TERM

Provinces Different political regions of Canada, such as Quebec and Ontario.

Privy Council Council made up of members of the British government and charged with interpreting matters of government such as which body holds which responsibilities.

Belligerent countries Countries involved in war.

Riot Act Call for demonstrators to disperse before the authorities use force.

What problems did Canada face after the First World War?

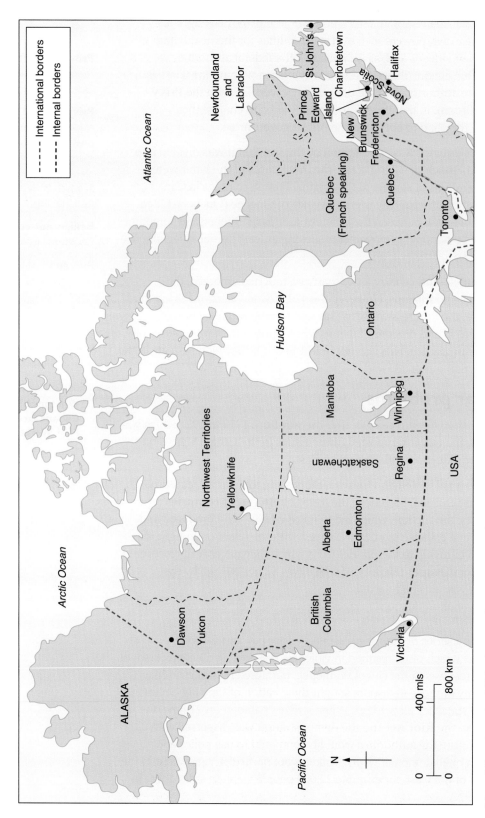

Map of Canada in the 1920s showing the provinces and capital cities

- The maritime provinces of New Brunswick, Nova Scotia and Prince Edward Island felt they were being marginalized as their percentage of Canadian population fell *vis-à-vis* other areas, and formed the Maritime Rights Movement. They particularly felt aggrieved that freight prices were too high for them to compete with other provinces. When it seemed that the three maritime provinces (see map, page 146) would shift their allegiance to the Conservatives, Liberal Prime Minister Mackenzie King offered a Royal Commission to investigate their grievances. As a result freight charges were reduced, but the discontent continued.

Economic prosperity

In the 1920s, many Canadians were enjoying what appeared to be unparalleled prosperity in one of the fastest growing economies in the world.

What were the indicators of Canadian prosperity in the 1920s?

The same sorts of factors featured in Canada as in the USA. After a short post-war slump, the economy recovered and the growing prosperity seemed endless.

New industrial development
Canadian prosperity had been fuelled in the later nineteenth century in part by wheat production on the vast prairies. The boom period had lasted for 30 years during which Canada's share of the international wheat market had shot up by 50 per cent. This, in turn, had led to railroad construction with intercontinental lines straddling the vast nation. The west having been settled, the early twentieth century saw the development of the vast mineral deposits and timber of the far north in the so-called Precambrian Shield. There was a huge growth in mining, pulp and paper production and in hydro generating plants to produce cheap energy.

Urbanization
As in the USA, more people were moving into cities. The percentage of the population who lived in urban areas increased from 50 to 54 per cent during the course of the decade. This led to a boom in house-building and consumer spending. Plentiful employment opportunities were available in factories producing consumer goods such as electrical appliances and clothing. Average per capita income was $500, which afforded a good standard of living. Radios proliferated. Foster Hewitt began a national institution in 1923 when Saturday night ice hockey coverage started. Advertising, movies – overwhelmingly from the USA – and leisure pursuits all thrived.

Motor vehicles and roads
Cheap motor vehicles were available largely through US branch plants such as those at Oshawa and Windsor in Ontario. In 1904, there were fewer than 1000 motor vehicles across the whole of Canada; by 1918, there were 500,000. Canada became the second largest motor manufacturer in the world, exporting one-third of the cars it manufactured – despite having no

indigenous manufacturers by the 1920s. For example, one of the largest, McLaughlin Motor Company, had sold out to General Motors in 1918. Road mileage grew from 385,000 in 1922 to 565,000 in 20 years. Tax revenue from motor sales and gasoline and fuel became an important source of revenue for provincial governments.

The stock market

As in the USA, many people bought shares, often on the margin (see page 32). However, the risks seemed slight. Shares bought in Okalta Oil Company in January 1929 for $30 sold for $300 in March while 100 shares in Home Oil costing $350 in January sold for $1575 in March. One firm of stockbrokers, Solloway, Mills & Co. Ltd, offers one example of growth. Between 1926 and 1929 they expanded from one small office in Toronto to 40 across Canada, with 1500 employees. As in the USA, new millionaires became folk heroes; British Columbia alone boasted 83 in the 1920s.

What political and economic problems lay beneath the surface?

Political and economic problems

Despite the prosperity, there were underlying political and economic problems in Canada.

Provincial governments

Most growth areas such as mineral extraction fell under provincial rather than federal government jurisdiction, and the provinces saw a huge growth in their responsibilities, for example in awarding contracts to develop hydroelectric power. However, they lacked the infrastructure or other funding to deal with these enhanced responsibilities.

Social tensions

Some Canadians welcomed the 'Americanization' of Canadian culture. Others loathed it. There was also growing resentment of English hegemony in the French-speaking areas. In Quebec, for example, the Anglo community controlled virtually all economic activity and, despite educational achievements, French speakers appeared to be in a preponderance of low-paid and relatively unskilled jobs. Priests meanwhile spoke against unionism, thus negating the one organization that could have led the fight against discrimination in the workplace.

KEY TERM

Separatism Desire for self-government.

Conscription Compulsory enlistment in the armed forces.

In Quebec again, there were the stirrings of **separatism** with the growth of the journal *Action française* and the *Ligue des droits du français* movement. Already these had been involved in a bitter dispute during the war about the introduction of **conscription**. Now they sought to maintain French identity and rewrite Canadian history in which the British were seen as constant oppressors of French Canadians.

Uneven growth

The economic growth was uneven. In the eastern provinces growth seemed uncertain while the Pacific coast and Vancouver saw huge expansion. The fastest growing staple industry, for example, was in pulp and paper, which began to rival wheat as Canada's main export. After the USA abolished its tariffs on imported newsprint in 1913, Canadian output grew from 402,000 tons in 1913 to almost 3,000,000 by 1930, when it supplied almost 60 per cent of all the newsprint consumed in the USA.

However, one should not take the point about the unevenness of prosperity too far. While, as we have seen, the prairies faced continuing problems, we should nevertheless note that the years 1925–9 saw 24 million hectares under cultivation and 400 million bushels produced annually, supplying 40 per cent of the world's export market. Moreover, wheat pools were set up in which farmers sold to a common pool rather than risking their individual produce in the **Winnipeg Grain Exchange**.

Economic dependence on the USA

More significant was the increasing economic dependence on the USA. Most of the investment in the newsprint industry came from the USA. Its firms also controlled Canadian motor vehicle production. Industries in the south-east of Canada increasingly bought their coal from the USA; Canadian coal prices fell by 40–50 per cent during the 1920s. These indicators may not have alarmed those enjoying the prosperity. However, they indicated a vulnerability should economic problems occur.

Many historians agree that in the event of a depression, Canada would be particularly exposed and, as we shall see, its prosperity lay on even more fragile foundations than that of the USA.

KEY TERM

Winnepeg Grain Exchange A Canadian market for selling wheat, barley and oats.

Successes	Problems
Political • Greater autonomy from UK	**Political** • Tension between federal and provincial governments • Resentment of Americanization of culture • Determination to promote French identity in Quebec
Economic • Consumer boom period	**Economic** • Short post-war recession • Uneven economic growth • Over-reliance on US trade and investment

SUMMARY DIAGRAM

Canada in the 1920s

The causes and effects of the Depression in Canada

> ▶ **Key question:** What were the causes and effects of the Great
> Depression in Canada?

The causes of the Great Depression

How far was the onset of the Great Depression based on weaknesses in the Canadian economy?

Canadian prosperity in the 1920s, while real at the time for those who enjoyed its benefits, was based on weak foundations. There was an over-reliance on staple exports such as wheat, industries began to overproduce and supply exceeded demand. In addition, the stock markets were involved in the same unstable practices as in the USA and the effects of the Wall Street Crash soon spread over the border, leading into depression. In this section we will consider the underlying causes of the Great Depression:

- over-reliance on staples for export
- overproduction
- stock market collapse.

Over-reliance on staples for export

KEY TERM

Staple exports Exports of primary products such as wheat and timber.

Canada depended on a reasonable price level and active demand for **staple exports**. In the 1920s, 25 per cent of Canadian gross national product (GNP) was derived from exports. The collapse in the price of and demand for wheat, for example, hit Canada hard. Already it was facing increased competition from Australia and Argentina at a time when global demand was falling due to on-going economic problems resulting from the First World War. As a result, the global surplus was 12,000 million bushels in 1934, a rise of more than 50 per cent since 1925. Moreover, attempts in fascist countries such as Italy to develop self-sufficiency in food production also drove the value of Canadian exports down. The reduction in demand was compounded by the prohibitive Hawley–Smoot Tariff in the USA in 1930 (see page 65). As countries looked to protect their own economies, countries such as Canada that relied heavily on exports were particularly badly affected.

Wheat production in Canada had peaked at 567 million bushels in 1928; by 1934 it was down to 276 million bushels. Prices meanwhile fell from $1.66 per bushel in 1929 to 33 cents in 1932. Many farm incomes fell by 75 per cent. As we will see (page 152) this was compounded by a series of natural disasters such as the Dustbowl, drought and crop failures.

Indeed, part of the wheat crop of 1928 had been stored rather than sold in the hope that prices would rise. The ploy failed: all this meant in effect was that buyers bought wheat from other countries such as Argentina.

Overproduction

Canada suffered from the same overproduction problems as the USA (see page 35). Studies show that increasingly the working classes could not afford to meet the demand for the volume of goods being produced as incomes lagged far behind the availability of new goods. This meant that firms had to cut production and lay off workers, thereby adding to unemployment and exacerbating the problem.

Stock market collapse

Canada had suffered from the same issues in the stock market as the USA – such as buying on the margin and bull pools (see pages 32 and 41). The collapse of the US stock market quickly spread to that of Toronto. The Toronto market had been volatile for months: on 4 October 1929, for example, it recorded losses of $200 million. On 24 October 1929, mass selling began at 11a.m. and six minutes later the market had collapsed. Canadian **bluechip stocks** lost $5 billion. The smaller exchange at Montreal which usually saw 25,000 shares changing hands saw 400,000 transactions that day. During the course of 1929, Canadian stocks lost $5 billion. By mid-1930, the value of the stocks in the leading 50 companies had fallen by a further 50 per cent.

KEY TERM

Bluechip stocks Shares in the biggest companies.

The effects of the Depression

Canada was particularly hard hit by the Depression because it relied so much on the exports and trade, which diminished rapidly. The Depression led to significant fall in demand. By the early 1930s, automobile sales, for example, had fallen to 25 per cent of the 1929 levels. This collapse in overall demand led to millions losing their jobs: unemployment rose to 27 per cent by 1932. The two main railroad companies alone laid off 65,000 employees. In terms of overall figures this meant an increase from 116,000 unemployed persons in 1929 to 826,000 by 1933. These statistics, however, did not include farmers or fishermen who were classed as self-employed, or their families – although food producers may have been able to feed themselves. They also omit those underemployed on short-time working and those engaged in menial jobs below their qualifications and skills.

How serious was the impact of the Depression in Canada?

Fall in the value of the Canadian dollar

By September 1931 the value of the Canadian dollar had fallen to such an extent that the New York financial markets refused to make any more Canadian loans and indeed began to call in existing ones. The result was the collapse of three major Montreal financial concerns, and the Sun Life Insurance Company found itself on the verge of bankruptcy. So many companies were technically bankrupt that the federal government and even competitors agreed to accept the theoretical value of their assets, even though in reality they were actually worth far less, in order to stave off their collapse.

Fall in demand

The collapse in demand for wheat had significant knock-on effects: the income from railroads for example fell by 50 per cent and the annual deficit in the Canadian National Railway rose to $560 million. This was largely for two reasons:

- The collapse in demand for wheat meant railways were not carrying so much freight.
- Increasing poverty in the prairie states meant there was less demand for goods so less for the railroads to carry out to consumers.

Demand for consumer goods plummeted because of increasing poverty and unemployment. By 1932 industrial production fell to 58 per cent of that of 1929. Unemployment stood at 33 per cent; in 1929 it had been three per cent. Worse, when Canada was a developing nation during the nineteenth century, if people were thrown out of work in the cities during cycles of economic downturn, they could return to their rural roots in the hope of finding employment; with depression throughout all sectors in the 1930s, this was no longer possible.

? Rewrite Woodsworth's statement in Source A in your own words.

SOURCE A

Extract from a speech by the radical MP J.S. Woodsworth in the House of Commons. Woodsworth was commenting on the hopelessness engendered by the Depression.

In the old days we could send people from the cities to the country. If they went out today, they would meet another army of unemployed coming back from the country to the city; that outlet is closed. What can these people do? They have been driven from our streets; they have been driven from our buildings; and in this city [Ontario] they actually took refuge on the garbage heaps.

The human cost of the Depression

The effects of the Depression were far reaching and touched both rural and urban populations. By 1935, 10 per cent of both the rural and urban populations were on some form of relief. In the western province of Saskatchewan this rose to 66 per cent.

Farmers

In the 1930s farmers were effectively crippled by the combination of two factors: the collapse in wheat prices and crop failures. Wheat exports dropped by 75 per cent and the prairies became a barren, windswept landscape. The drought had begun in the 1920s; much of the soil was already fine and dry. As in the USA (see page 115), the Dustbowl struck: high winds blew the topsoil away, leaving many farmers destitute. The problem was compounded by an epidemic of grasshoppers for which the hot, dry conditions made ideal breeding conditions. There are tales of poor families living off gophers; the provincial government even offered bounties on gopher tails to offer children some small incentive whereby they could augment the family income.

The period from 1931 to 1941 saw 250,000 people migrate from the prairies to cities such as Alberta, Regina and Calgary or to more fertile areas to the north. Saskatchewan was particularly badly hit. Between 1928 and 1933, its income from farming fell from $363 million to $11 million; relief costs exceeded £62 million, far beyond the ability of the provincial government to pay. The 1930s saw boy-scout and girl-guide groups in Winnepeg organizing clothing parcels to the victims of the Depression in Saskatchewan and the federal government running 100 railway cars filled with relief food supplies including cod, cheese and fruit.

The need for relief

Even with 10 per cent of the population needing some degree of relief, there was little organized welfare in Canada. Although Mackenzie King had introduced old-age pensions in 1926, welfare provision was mainly the responsibility of provinces, **municipalities** or private charity. Clearly these lacked the resources to tackle the extent of the problem. Moreover, relief would not right the economy.

Most urban workers depended on wages, and without wages they lacked the resources to buy the goods whose sale might set the wheels turning again. So relief might prevent starvation, but it would not increase demand for manufactured goods.

Many politicians, moreover, lacked any sense of co-operation to deal with the crisis. In a studied piece of partisan politics, on 3 April 1930, Mackenzie King made a speech which has become notorious (see Source B and page 156).

SOURCE B

An excerpt from Mackenzie King's speech in Parliament, 3 April 1930.

Every winter in this country, ever since there was a winter in Canada, there has been unemployment and there always will be … we have no right to say there is any national unemployment problem in this country … I might be prepared to go to certain lengths possibly in meeting one or two western provinces that have progressive premiers at the head of governments. With respect to giving moneys out of the federal treasury to any Tory government in this country for these alleged unemployment purposes, with these governments situated as they are today with policies diametrically opposed to those of this government, I would not give them a five cent piece.

KEY TERM

Municipalities Smaller areas within provinces, for example towns and their hinterlands.

What can you infer from Source B about Mackenzie King's attitude towards:

a) the Depression in Canada?

b) the possibility of federal relief programmes?

c) co-operation with other political parties?

The provinces initially tried new forms of taxation such as a tax on company profits. By 1940, every provincial government did this and four had introduced the income tax. Provincial taxes on petrol rose by 50 per cent.

However, it was insufficient to meet the demand for relief. In effect, therefore, the provinces passed on the burden of welfare to the municipalities. Their tax revenues had fallen because of unemployment but they were expected to find more from diminishing returns to give relief to the growing numbers of unemployed. As a result, they faced financial problems: the municipality in Burnaby, British Columbia was facing tax arrears of 72 per cent of taxes levied, while North Vancouver District overspent by 144 per cent. By 1933 one and a half million Canadians were dependent on some form of direct relief.

In Newfoundland, semi-independent from Canada, it was even worse. In 1933, bankrupt and with a government that was hardly functioning, it had to submit to an emergency commission administered by Britain as the colonial power.

As a result there were thousands of homeless, unemployed people.

SOURCE C

? What are the advantages and disadvantages of the kind of oral histories as seen in Source C?

Extracts from two accounts of life in Vancouver in the 1930s, from _The Chuck Davis History of Metropolitan Vancouver_ by Chuck Davis published in 2011 (see also www.vancouverhistory.ca). This book contains primary sources from every year in the history of Vancouver.

About 1,000 homeless people occupied four east-end hobo jungles. One jungle bordered Prior Street, close to Campbell Avenue and the Canadian National Railway yards. Another existed under the Georgia Street viaduct, a third was located on the harbour at the end of Dunlevy Avenue, and the fourth was situated at the Great Northern Railway sidings. Shacks were built from boxes, boards and old cars.

The Great Depression had settled like a sodden shroud on the city. Thousands of us were on relief (34,000 at the peak), and hundreds more were riding the roads into town on every freight train. (The author's father was one of them.) The Sun's Alan Morley counted 1,250 men in the breadline at First United Church. The city's relief cost for the 1931–1932 year was over $1.3 million. A symbol of the economic downturn: the unfinished form of the Hotel Vancouver.

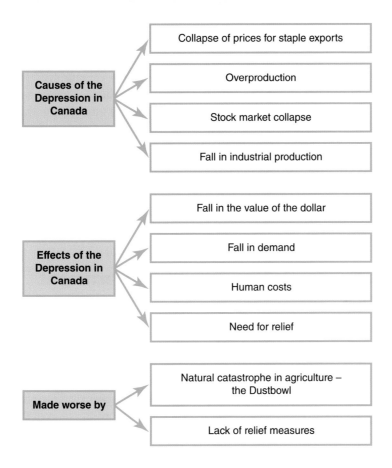

Causes of the Depression in Canada
- Collapse of prices for staple exports
- Overproduction
- Stock market collapse
- Fall in industrial production

Effects of the Depression in Canada
- Fall in the value of the dollar
- Fall in demand
- Human costs
- Need for relief

Made worse by
- Natural catastrophe in agriculture – the Dustbowl
- Lack of relief measures

SUMMARY DIAGRAM

The causes and effects of the Depression in Canada

Federal government responses to the Depression 1929–34

> ▶ Key question: How effectively did federal governments respond to the Depression?

Federal governments were slow to respond to the crises occasioned by the Depression. In this section we consider the policies adopted by Mackenzie King's Liberal regime (1925–30) and R.B. Bennett's Conservative government (1930–5).

Mackenzie King's government 1925–30

How effective was King's initial response to the Depression?

Mackenzie King felt it was best for the federal government to do nothing; essentially a believer in *laissez-faire*, he believed the economy would right itself if left alone. As a politician, King believed vehemently in balancing the budget and a limited government role. He was at times reluctant even to admit there was a depression in Canada (see Source B, page 153). King believed that his cautious economic policies had facilitated the prosperity of the 1920s and the downturn had been caused largely by unwise speculations on the part of the business community and an adverse climatic cycle which had led to drought and the Dustbowl. He felt, almost like US bankers such as Andrew Mellon (see page 11), that any government intervention would only make matters worse.

King thought that the Depression would right itself by a resurgence of international trade. He was therefore opposed to any policies that would raise tariffs and thereby restrict trade. As we have seen (Source B), he refused to give any money for relief to 'Tory' or Conservative-run provinces, adding for good measure, 'I would not give them a five cent piece'.

Not surprisingly, King's party lost the 1930 election.

How effective were Bennett's policies of relief and imperial preference?

R.B. Bennett's Conservative government 1930–5

The Conservatives, led by R.B. Bennett, were returned with a majority of 31 seats. Bennett had replaced Arthur Meighon, who had lost his seat in 1927. A successful businessman, Bennett had an overpowering personality and great charisma but could be overbearing and indifferent to the views of others. He had said during the election campaign, 'Mackenzie King promises you conferences; I promise you action. He promises consideration of the problem of unemployment; I promise to end unemployment. Which plan do you like best?'

Despite the rhetoric, however, his policies were traditional and based on relief and higher tariffs. However, the effects of the one tended to negate the other. High tariffs may have stabilized Canadian prices by excluding foreign competition, but they meant that those on relief could afford to buy even less because the high price of imports maintained domestic prices.

Relief

Although believing in *laissez-faire* economics, the government adopted the wartime precedents of **public loans**. The National Service Loan was set up to borrow $150 million. In the event in a burst of patriotic fervour it was oversubscribed to the tune of $72 million and the federal government was able to meet its financial commitments to keep operating. This was more than could be said for provincial governments, which could often no longer afford basic functions let alone public works schemes and ambitious relief programmes.

The Unemployed and Farm Relief Act 1931

The federal government allocated $20 million for emergency relief to be administered by the provinces and municipalities. In other words, echoing

KEY TERM

Public loans Loans to the federal government, similar to war bonds.

the policies of Hoover in the USA, there was no direct federal government action. It meant less than $20 for every unemployed person. However, Bennett was to commit over $28 million in subsequent measures to offer relief and public works, and was to create jobs in every year of his premiership.

Public Works Construction Act 1934

This introduced a federal building programme of $40 million to create jobs. Much work was undertaken for example in National Parks and historic sites; one project was to build a replica Port Royal Habitation, reconstructing the seventeenth-century buildings of the former French colony, at its historic site in Nova Scotia. The federal government provided the funds using local labour who otherwise may have been unemployed.

Farmers' Credit Arrangement Act 1934

This allowed farmers to remain in their farms rather than face eviction through foreclosure. Farmers could make agreements or compromises about delaying repayment of their debts with their creditors under the supervision of a government board. If two-thirds of the creditors agreed to the compromise, the Board could then impose the agreement on the rest of the farmer's creditors. This arrangement generally benefited farmers more than their creditors. By 1938 36,000 cases had been handled, with $550 million of money owed and $4 million of interest on the debts being removed from the total indebtedness figure of $159 million.

Relief camps

This is the measure for which Bennett's government has faced the most criticism. With as many of 70,000 hoboes trekking around Canada in search of work, the idea was to set up work camps, possibly along the lines of the CCC in the USA (see page 92). However, unlike the CCC, they were run by the Canadian Department of National Defence along military lines with the intention of instilling military-style discipline into the participants. While they did offer food, clothing and work to the homeless, single and unemployed, they only paid 20 cents per day, which was 10 per cent of what the most lowly paid labourer could expect to earn. Conditions were at best spartan. Moreover, many of the jobs on which the participants laboured were pointless, like constructing roads that led nowhere.

The camps began with 2000 workers in eastern Canada clearing landing fields for Trans-Canada Airways and expanded to every Canadian province except Prince Edward Island. They tended to be in remote locations, which appears logical given the nature of the work which involved conservation and building projects to facilitate the development of communications across Canada. However, others complained that the scheme was a means of removing discontented men from urban locations where they could cause trouble or join radical political organizations such as the Communist Party. Certainly, while joining the camps was not compulsory, those who refused

? Describe the conditions in the hut in Source D. What can you infer from this picture about a relief worker's life?

were commonly arrested for vagrancy. The intention was to employ as many as possible for as long as possible as cheaply as possible, which meant often doing dangerous, back-breaking construction and conservation work by hand. Accidents were common. As we shall see (page 169), the camps became hotbeds of protest.

SOURCE D

Workers inside their hut on Relief Project No. 27 in Ottawa, March 1933.

KEY TERM

Mounties Nickname given to the Royal Canadian Mounted Police (RCMP), Canada's national police force.

Repression

Bennett has been accused of repressive measures against those hit by the Depression. Police dispersed marches of the unemployed, the press was censored and government spies infiltrated labour meetings. Some even said that Canada was becoming a police state. In 1932, for example, a march of 3000 unemployed workers to Ottawa was met by local police, **Mounties** and armoured cars. Even the conservative newspaper the *Ottawa Journal* wrote that 'the scene smacks more of fascism than of Canadian constitutional authority'.

Tariffs and trade

Increased tariffs

Tariffs were increased to protect Canadian production. Bennett had spoken of 'blasting his way into world markets', but the effect was to limit trade even more.

The increased tariffs were in part a response to the prohibitive Hawley–Smoot Tariff (see page 65). They were designed to exclude from Canada not only articles similar to those already produced there but any articles that might be produced in Canada in the future. While the measures may have saved some firms from bankruptcy, they did little to help exports because of the fall in international demand, and Canada clearly needed to continue to export its goods. Many producers of staples in particular were burdened with surplus products. In Manitoba, it was estimated that the overall cost of the tariffs in lost revenues was $100 per farm.

Imperial Preference

Bennett supported the idea of **Imperial Preference**. The Imperial Conference in London in 1931 focused on economic issues. While Bennett spoke of 'Canada First' he also offered Britain and the **Commonwealth** preferential rates for trading in Canada if these would be reciprocated. Interestingly, he included again not only goods which Canada sold at present but also those it may sell at some point in the future. Bennett took a lead in these negotiations; Britain was responsive because Imperial Preference was seen as a way of keeping the Commonwealth together, both through the current economic crisis and for the unseen international problems of the future.

The Ottawa Conference 1932

It was Bennett, however, who suggested that the ensuing conference to formalize the Imperial Preference arrangements should be in Canada, which allowed him, as chairman, to drive discussions through the preparation of the agenda. Clearly, Bennett sought to place Canadian interests first. Nevertheless, the smallness of the Canadian civil service and his determination to take personal control (possibly when he was personally preoccupied with his love affair with Hazel Colville) meant that the agendas arrived late and there was an aura of inefficiency that boded ill for what Bennett hoped would be a major international agreement to combat the Depression. In the words of British Chancellor of the Exchequer Neville Chamberlain, the reason for 'Bennett's difficulties is really inadequate preparation on his side. He has no civil service and no minister whom he trusts.'

Not surprisingly, perhaps, the Ottawa Conference of 1932 achieved comparatively little. There were no decisions as to monetary policies, for example. Nevertheless, tariffs were reformed. There was a gradual reduction

 **KEY TERM**

Imperial Preference
Favourable trading arrangements within the British Empire.

Commonwealth Countries of the former British Empire still closely associated with Britain, for example Canada and Australia.

on tariffs for those in the Commonwealth. In effect, Bennett agreed to concessions on only those goods not in need of protection, particularly metal products and textiles. Britain agreed to a duty on imported wheat which would be removed only when the price in Britain exceeded world prices, allowing Canadian wheat to enter at preferential rates. The agreements also referred to primary commodities such as timber, dairy and meat products and apples.

As a result of the Imperial Preference agreements, Canadian exports to Britain rose by 60 per cent while those from Britain to Canada rose by only five per cent. In this sense Canada clearly benefited, but overall volumes remained low and the Depression continued.

Trade with the USA

While there were high protective tariffs in the USA as a result of Hawley–Smoot, relations with the USA did grow closer. In July 1932, for example, President Hoover agreed to build the St Lawrence waterway, which would have gone through both countries, but the US Senate vetoed the proposal. President Roosevelt later invited Bennett to Washington to discuss developments in trade between the two countries. However, while Bennett saw US trade as desirable, little was achieved. The reality was that Canada needed the USA more than the USA needed Canada.

Growth in federal government responsibilities

Bennett's government was responsible for the setting up of the National Radio Broadcasting Service and the Central Bank. While these were important developments in themselves, they showed that he preferred British models rather than American ones where private competition was favoured. Given that the Canadian Supreme Court allowed their creation, they also set a precedent for the growth in federal government responsibilities to come later in the decade.

Radio

There was considerable concern that Canadians were overinfluenced by US values as a result of listening to American radio. In 1928, Mackenzie King had set up the Aird Commission to report on radio provision and make recommendations. Its report was very succinct – nine pages only – and said that, while Canadian radio should reflect the interests of both the Anglo and French communities, it should be above all Canadian, that is, free from US influences. King sat on the report, citing constitutional issues as to which level of government was responsible for regulating radio. Quebec was definite that it was the provinces.

In June 1931, the Canadian Supreme Court decided that it was in fact the responsibility of federal government. Quebec appealed to the authorities in Britain but the decision was upheld. On 9 May 1932 a Special Commission recommended that a Canadian Radio Broadcasting Commission should be set up to regulate programmes. In a speech on 18 May, Bennett argued persuasively that only public ownership could ensure impartiality and private ownership could leave it open to exploitation. In this sense he clearly favoured the British Broadcasting Corporation's (BBC) arrangement over the American free-enterprise model – and the Canadian Radio Broadcasting Commission was set up.

Bank of Canada

The Canadian banks were in a much healthier position than their US counterparts; in fact, there had not been a bank failure in Canada since 1923, when Home Bank, with 70 branches, collapsed. Even then the government responded by appointing an Inspector General of Banks to try to prevent future collapses and paid $3 million in compensation to depositors. Nevertheless, with different banks issuing their own banknotes, Bennett felt there needed to be a centralized system like the Bank of England. A Royal Commission was set up in March 1933 which recommended the setting up of a centralized bank. Interestingly, the only members of the Commission who demurred were bankers.

The Bank of Canada was set up in 1934. Banks were no longer allowed to issue their own banknotes and had to transfer their gold reserves. They charged a high price for this but Bennett thought it was worth it. He always felt the creation of the Bank of Canada was his greatest achievement. There is little doubt that a stable banking system prevented the effects of the Depression from becoming even worse; it also helped the economic recovery in the later years of the decade.

Conclusions

Overall, Bennett's initial responses to the Depression might seem timid, but the extent of the crisis was something neither Canada nor any other developed nation had experienced. He said himself, 'We are subject to the play of forces which we did not create and which we cannot either regulate or control … any action at all at this time except to maintain the ship of state on an even keel … involves possible consequences about which I hesitate to think.'

Many Canadians agreed. There seemed a helplessness exacerbated by the absence of hope. They seemed to realize that, unlike in the past, the Depression would not right itself with a little encouragement and renewed confidence.

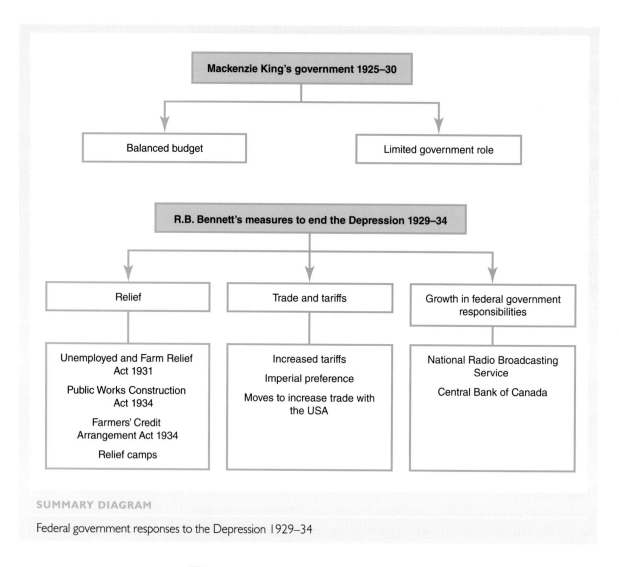

```
                    ┌──────────────────────────────────────┐
                    │   Mackenzie King's government 1925–30  │
                    └──────────────────────────────────────┘
                         │                          │
                         ▼                          ▼
              ┌──────────────────┐      ┌──────────────────────────┐
              │  Balanced budget │      │  Limited government role │
              └──────────────────┘      └──────────────────────────┘


          ┌──────────────────────────────────────────────────────────┐
          │  R.B. Bennett's measures to end the Depression 1929–34    │
          └──────────────────────────────────────────────────────────┘
                 │                    │                    │
                 ▼                    ▼                    ▼
        ┌────────────┐      ┌──────────────────┐   ┌──────────────────────────┐
        │   Relief   │      │ Trade and tariffs │   │ Growth in federal        │
        └────────────┘      └──────────────────┘   │ government responsibilities│
                                                    └──────────────────────────┘
```

Relief	Trade and tariffs	Growth in federal government responsibilities
Unemployed and Farm Relief Act 1931	Increased tariffs	National Radio Broadcasting Service
Public Works Construction Act 1934	Imperial preference	Central Bank of Canada
Farmers' Credit Arrangement Act 1934	Moves to increase trade with the USA	
Relief camps		

SUMMARY DIAGRAM

Federal government responses to the Depression 1929–34

 # Bennett's proposed 'New Deal' and the 1935 election

▶ *Key question: Why did Bennett change his view on the extent of government intervention?*

Although both King and Bennett affected belief in minimal government interference beyond agreements to extend trade, both changed their views as a result of the Depression. Bennett went so far as to propose a Canadian version of the New Deal. As we will see below, historians have been much concerned with his motives. As in the USA, the Depression changed the extent of involvement of the Canadian federal government forever.

Bennett's realization that the economy would not solve its own problems is why, unexpectedly, he offered a completely different solution. In January 1935, with his policies clearly not working and an election looming, Bennett astounded Canadians with the proposed introduction of a Roosevelt-type New Deal. In a series of radio broadcasts he announced that the capitalist system lay in ruins and proposed a series of radical measures to restore prosperity and change Canada forever.

SOURCE E

Extract from Bennett's radio address, January 1935.

I am for reform. And, in my mind, reform means government intervention. It means government control and regulation … I nail the flag of progress to the masthead. I summon the power of the state to its support.

How far does the statement in Source E mark a break in Bennett's previous policies?

Reasons for Bennett's conversion

Why did Bennett change his mind about the need for direct government intervention?

While Bennett clearly could be accused of simple electioneering, his conversion appears to have been genuine. Apparently his cabinet colleagues were as surprised as the general public; he had not discussed his conversion with any of them. He was, however, influenced by William Kerridge, his brother-in-law who, as Ambassador to the USA, was hugely impressed by Roosevelt's New Deal. Indeed, possibly before Roosevelt, who still hoped in 1935 that wholesale federal government involvement in the economy was temporary, Bennett seems to have believed that capitalism could only be saved by direct government intervention. He gave an example from horticulture: 'A good deal of pruning is sometimes necessary to save a tree and it will be well for us in Canada to remember that there is considerable pruning to be done if we are to preserve the fabric of the capitalist system.'

Others, even in the business community, had come to believe the same ideas. Many felt that only the federal government had the power to stabilize the economy to prevent social unrest. Others felt that cut-throat competition which led to companies minimizing their profits could be abolished by price controls. These groups admired the work in particular of the NRA (see page 89).

New Deal measures

How far reaching were the New Deal proposals?

Bennett's New Deal proposals were ambitious and far reaching. Had they been fully implemented they might have extended the role of federal government along the lines of the US New Deal.

Measures
- The cornerstone of the Canadian New Deal was to be an Employment and Social Insurance Act that offered comprehensive unemployment insurance and allied benefits.

Farm credits System to make federal loans to farmers.

Federal by-elections Mid-term elections for vacant seats due to, for example, the death of an MP.

Horse-drawn Fords Ford motor vehicles with no fuel, pulled along by horses.

- Other proposals included the creation of a National Products Marketing Board, minimum wages, a maximum eight-hour working day and 48-hour week, federally supported **farm credits** and the development of centralized economic planning.
- A Prairie Farm Rehabilitation Act was added to help 100,000 farmers in south Saskatchewan restore the fertility of their lands after the Dustbowl and drought by helping them to use more efficient farming technology and better methods of cultivation.
- A Canadian Wheat Marketing Board was set up in July 1935 to regulate the sale of wheat to protect farmers hit by the Depression.
- In 1934, Bennett had set up a commission under his Minister of Trade and Commerce, H.H. Stevens, to investigate mass purchase by big business and the difference between the price they offered to producers and that charged to consumers. As a result a Dominion Trade and Industry Commission was set up to regulate business activities.

However, barely had these measures been passed than Bennett was out of office. The Committee of the Privy Council in Britain declared many of them unconstitutional in 1937. The federal government did not have the authority to adopt such wide-ranging measures.

The 1935 election

Bennett knew his party was in trouble as the 1935 election loomed.

- In 1934 the Conservatives had lost provincial elections in Ontario and Saskatchewan and four out of five **federal by-elections**.
- Bennett had hoped that if he could introduce the New Deal legislation quickly, the Liberals would denounce it and he could call a quick election. While the Conservatives appeared to be solving the Depression, the Liberals, with no coherent policies of their own, would lose votes for appearing to attack popular measures to address the problem. However, this strategy did not work, not least because King showed restraint in criticizing the measures, but mainly because Bennett was taken ill and lost control of events.
- Perhaps unsurprisingly, if not fairly, Bennett was blamed for the Depression, like Hoover in the USA. **Horse-drawn Fords** were called 'Bennett buggies', and shantytowns where transient and unemployed workers lived became 'Bennettburghs'.
- When Bennett failed to act on the recommendations of the commission investigating business practices referred to above, Stevens resigned from the government and formed the Reconstruction Party. This advocated greater government intervention and made Stevens very popular. Bennett should perhaps have made more of an effort to appease him.

The election results

In the event, while the Conservatives gained 30 per cent of the popular vote, they were almost wiped out in the House of Commons. The Liberals won

173 seats to their 40. The Reconstruction Party won only one seat, but did attain almost nine per cent of the vote, which hurt the Conservatives. The *Toronto Evening Telegraph* reflected that 'a great statesman was defeated by a poor politician', meaning Bennett defeated himself through poor tactics. However, it was the Depression which defeated him; as in the USA in 1932, it would have been difficult for any incumbent party to win.

King meanwhile had fought the election under the slogan 'King or Chaos'. Many more conservative elements agreed because, as in the USA, there were increasingly more radical alternatives which were gaining strong support.

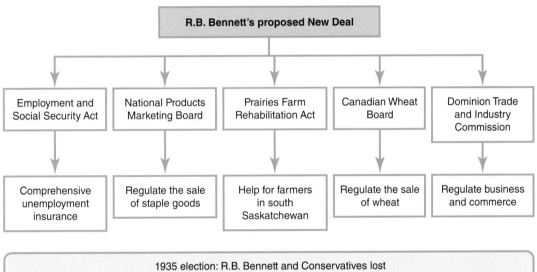

SUMMARY DIAGRAM

Bennett's proposed 'New Deal' and the 1935 election

Alternative responses to the Depression

▶ **Key question:** *What alternative approaches were promoted to address Canada's problems?*

In Canada there were several significant alternative approaches on how to tackle the Depression. Most of these originated in the provinces and could therefore be seen as a threat to the influence and leadership of the federal government. Some supporters actually gained power in the provinces, although, as in the case of social credit, the impracticality of their chosen schemes led to their influence being diluted.

Social credit

How influential was the social credit movement?

The idea of social credit was first propounded by an Englishman, Major C.H. Douglas, in the late 1920s, although there were similarities to Huey Long's 'Share our Wealth' scheme in the USA (see page 96). Douglas believed the Depression was caused by a lack of purchasing power on the part of the consumer because not enough money was in circulation. He advocated the distribution of money in the form of social credit so that people could buy what they needed. This in turn would stimulate the production capacity of the economy.

🔑 **KEY TERM**

Social Credit Party
A political party supporting the idea of social credit.

This idea found support especially in the predominantly agricultural province of Alberta, which had fared particularly badly in the 1920s. As in many of the rural states of the USA, there was noticeable hostility to banks and mortgage companies and people were responsive to movements which attacked these. The United Farmers of Canada had, for example, run the provincial government from 1921 to 1935 with a policy to control credit to forestall farm foreclosure. William Alberhart, a Christian evangelist with a popular radio show, became the leader of the **Social Credit Party**, speaking directly to farmers and those hard pressed to make mortgage repayments.

Alberhart felt there was a surplus of products in Alberta, just not enough money with which to buy them. He therefore proposed to improve purchasing power by means of paper credit by which everyone in Alberta would be given $25 per month. The Social Credit Party won the 1935 election in Alberta with 54 per cent of the popular vote and was to remain in power in that province until the 1970s. However, when it tried to implement its proposal the courts intervened to say that provincial governments did not have the authority to print their own money because this was the responsibility of federal government. Alberhart could therefore blame the federal government in Ottawa for the failures of the social credit scheme.

The Antigonish movement in Nova Scotia and the maritime provinces

How widespread was support for the Antigonish movement?

Nova Scotia was comprised mainly of farmers, fishermen and small-scale producers who relied on others for marketing and distribution of their products and subsequently felt a loss of control as the Depression developed. Two Catholic priests, Jimmy Tompkins and Moses Coady, based at St Xavier University in Antigonish began the Antigonish movement. It was essentially born out of a desire to enable small producers to regain their power of economic ownership through controlling the economic processes themselves. It advocated the setting up of co-operatives, banks, marketing agencies and stores to sell their goods. It looked back to a pre-industrialized age that clearly spoke to the small-scale producers of Nova Scotia and other

semi-rural environments but was not appropriate for a wider audience. At best, then, the movement raised awareness of what was wrong with capitalism but offered no serious remedies.

However, it was very influential in its emphasis on adult education and community cohesion. It was felt that it was necessary to educate the participants in the principles of self-help and co-operation before progress could be made. By 1932, there were 179 study clubs with 1500 members in Nova Scotia alone. By 1938, the number rose to 1110 with 10,000 participants. In particular it advocated **credit unions**, which gave people access to credit that the banks and finance houses would not offer. The movement spread beyond Nova Scotia to other maritime provinces and out into the prairies. By 1939, every Canadian province had a credit union.

Co-operative Commonwealth Federation

The Co-operative Commonwealth Federation (CCF) was founded in Calgary in 1932 by a coalition of socialist, intellectual and labour groups. The idea was the elimination of capitalism and the establishment of socialist planning, which is why many saw this as a Communist organization. However, it was more properly a successor to the progressive movement (see page 145), with support in the impoverished provinces of British Columbia and Saskatchewan. It had close ties with the **League of Social Reconstruction** (LSR), founded in 1931, and F.R. Underhill, a founder of the LSR, was important in preparing the statement of CCF principles which became known as the Regina Manifesto.

The Regina Manifesto
- All industries should be nationalized with compensation for owners.
- Welfare measures such as hospital treatment and old-age pensions.
- Federally organized social planning.

The new party attracted 300,000 votes in British Columbia but did not acquire a national following and tended to wither away as prosperity returned.

Communist Party of Canada

The Communist Party was founded in 1924 and was the only national party of protest. However, its support was poor and it faced government repression. Its ideas of international revolution were seen as irrelevant in Canada. As with many other Communist movements at this time, it was split over what appeared to be contradictory orders from Moscow and became immersed in technical and obscure matters of procedure. The federal government led by R.B. Bennett seemed particularly enthusiastic in its methods of repression, citing Section 98 of the Criminal Code introduced after the Winnipeg strikes of 1919 (see page 145), which disallowed any presumption of innocence on the part of those falling foul of it. This meant

KEY TERM

Credit unions Financial co-operatives, operating like local banks, providing loans and credit to participants.

League of Social Reconstruction Group of Socialists proposing radical reforms and greater political education.

What ideas did the CCF believe in?

How widespread a threat was the Communist Party of Canada?

that anyone supporting an organization that advocated violent overthrow of the state could be arrested; they only had to attend meetings or distribute literature. In 1931, for example, eight Communist leaders were arrested, including the Communist leader Tom Buck, who was subsequently found guilty of sedition and sentenced to two years' hard labour.

While in Kingston penitentiary, Buck remained in his cell while other prisoners rioted. It was alleged that eight bullets were fired into his cell and a play written about it, 'Eight Men Speak', suggested this constituted an assassination attempt by the authorities. In a subsequent **sedition trial** resulting from this play, the Minister of Justice admitted an attempt to scare Buck. The subsequent scandal led to the eight Communists being released early as champions of the cause of civil liberties.

KEY TERM

Sedition trial Trial for those accused of trying to overthrow the government.

How repressive was the Union Nationale?

Union Nationale in Quebec

We have already seen (page 148) that there was resentment in many French-speaking areas that the largest employers were English. Maurice Duplessis united the remnants of the former Quebec Conservative Party with reforming elements in the Liberals to form a new separatist party called Union Nationale. In particular, he embraced the ideas of Action Liberale Nationale (ALN), which suggested that Quebec was effectively subject to colonial oppression, as it was run by Anglos, and non-French Canadian-owned businesses there should be nationalized.

The Union Nationale advocated:

- legislation to promote small-scale businesses by destroying the power of big business
- regulation of banks and financial institutions.

Union Nationale won 58 per cent of the vote in Quebec in 1936. However, as Prime Minister of the Province, Duplessis abandoned the reformist agenda of the ALN and purged its leadership. As it became more right-wing and authoritarian, Union Nationale argued that radicals and federal powers were in fact the cause of Quebec's problems and allied with the clergy against what it considered radical ideas. The Union Nationale was accused by detractors of being fascistic in character. The Quebec government passed the notorious Padlock Law which permitted the seizure of any premises suspected of being used to spread Communist ideas, but was in fact used against any organization Duplessis felt a threat. Union Nationale remained in power in Quebec until the 1960s, often using patronage and bribery to maintain its support.

How far did people in relief camps become politicized?

Organized protest

Regina riots and the On-to-Ottawa trek

The period saw the development of organized protest, much of which turned violent. The notorious 'Regina riots' were part of the 'On-to-Ottawa trek', a protest organized by men from the relief camps. As we have seen, Bennett had established work camps for the unemployed where conditions were harsh and the labour was hard for little remuneration. Public works projects such as road building were undertaken, often in dangerous conditions. There had already been a strike at a camp at Vancouver in 1935 when workers began to demand first-aid equipment and compensation in the event of accidents. In fact, they only requested that the Workmen's Compensation Act, which was valid for those in regular employment, be extended to them. As a result, the Communist-inspired Relief Camp Workers' Union gained considerable influence in the camps.

SOURCE F

An extract from a written account of life in the camps from Ron Liversedge, a worker in a relief camp, found on www.cbc.ca/history/.

In those bunkhouses there were more men reading Marx, Lenin and Stalin than there were reading girlie magazines.

Explain what can be inferred from Source F.

With widespread support, leaders organized the On-to-Ottawa trek in June 1935. Over 1000 men from the camps left Vancouver with the intention of arriving at Ottawa to demand wages and work. The freight trains in which they travelled refused to go any further east than the city of Regina. The police isolated the participants in a stadium there while only eight leaders were allowed to proceed to Ottawa. While a meeting was organized with Bennett, it was only so he could berate them as radicals and revolutionaries. When they returned to Regina to announce their failure, the mood turned ugly and led to serious clashes with the police and military in which two protesters were killed.

Violence in industrial disputes

Relief camps were abolished when King was returned to office, but most of the people in them returned to homelessness and unemployment. Indeed, violence continued. In April 1937, for example, 4000 employees of the General Motors Plant in Oshawa, Ontario, went on strike for better working conditions including the introduction of an eight-hour day (which had been part of Bennett's 'New Deal') and recognition of the United Automobile Workers' trade union. Provincial Prime Minister Mitchell Hepburn sided with General Motors and brought in police and volunteers to intimidate strikers, but Mackenzie King would not call out the Mounties. General Motors gave in to most of the strikers' demands because of the impact of the strike on their production.

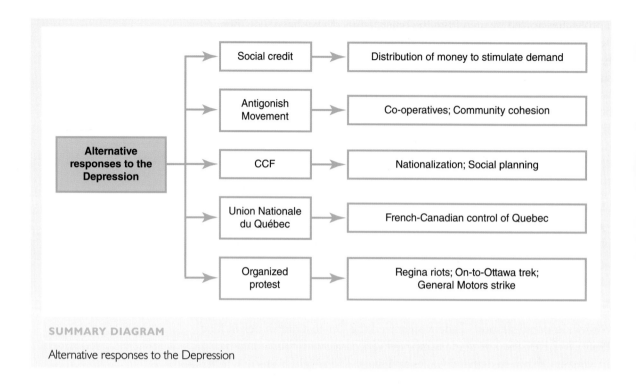

Alternative responses to the Depression

6 Mackenzie King's government 1935–48

▶ *Key question: What were the main features of Mackenzie King's domestic policies to 1939?*

Mackenzie King returned as prime minister having disparaged Bennett's proposed New Deal and still wedded to traditional economic policies such as the extension of trading agreements. However, he may already have realized the economy would not right itself without federal support and, by 1937, a short recession returned and he gave up on the idea of a balanced budget.

How did Mackenzie King's government deal with the Depression?

→ The economy

As we have seen, in the late 1920s Mackenzie King had been cautious in his economic policies and felt the economy was best left alone. However, he had also been responsive to the need to win electoral support by making his policies as vague as possible to appeal to as wide a consensus as possible. As early as 1929, he had said, 'The supreme effort of my leadership of the party has been to keep its aims and purposes so broad that it might be possible to unite at times of crisis under one banner those parties which for one reason or another have come to be separated from the Liberal Party.'

By 1934, however, King may have accepted that the economy would not right itself and direct action by federal government was necessary. He had an idea to create a central bank with more authority than the Bank of Canada to control the money supply, although he did not pursue the plan very far. Mainly, however, he sought to restore international trade.

Trade agreements with the USA

Mackenzie King first made an agreement with the USA in November 1935 that reduced the high tariffs between the countries. Then, in 1937, US President Roosevelt, with whom he got along very well, asked him to use the next imperial conference to negotiate a deal between the USA and Britain. Mackenzie King had to tread carefully here because arrangements between the USA and Britain could negate the Imperial Preference agreements that benefited Canada, on timber for example. Eventually, a complex triangular agreement was signed in 1938, the effects of which became largely subsumed by the impact of the Second World War.

Government spending

Mackenzie King had originally wanted a balanced budget, but as the Depression worsened in 1937 – with the prairies, facing the driest summer on record, particularly suffering – he agreed to deficit spending in 1938 and 1939 to pay for job creation schemes. By this time, however, King's focus had turned to international developments.

Recovery

Recovery from the worst of the Depression began slowly in 1934, but by 1937, as in the USA, the economy saw a downturn. In 1938, unemployment was still at 11 per cent. However, some areas of the economy rebounded more quickly than others. In terms of manufacture, automobiles and radios recovered. Cinema did well, as did oil and gas. It is also important to remember that those people who kept their jobs tended to do well during the Depression years because the prices of many goods fell. There was a boom in gold mining fuelled by the price increase from $20 to $35 an ounce during the Depression. Both Ontario and British Columbia experienced **gold rushes** during the 1930s.

 **KEY TERM**

Gold rush Rapid movement of people to find gold in a particular area.

One of the real success stories was the discovery of the mineral pitchblende near Bear Lake. Pitchblende contained radium, increasingly used in the treatment of cancer, and uranium, hitherto seen as useless, but subsequently used in the development of nuclear power.

It was war that eventually brought Canada out of the Depression. By 1943, unemployment was down to two per cent and federal spending rose from 3.4 per cent of GNP in 1939 to 37.6 per cent in 1944. GNP itself rose from $5.6 billion in 1939 to $11.6 billion in 1945.

'A Place to Sleep for a Price'. A homeless man sleeping on a cot provided by the Canadian government, 1930

? What point is being made on the written notices in Source G? How valuable in this image of the Depression in Canada.

How did federal government grow under King?

→ Growth in federal government

Problems raised by the Depression

The Depression had shown that the municipalities and provinces were not equipped to deal with welfare on the scale that the downturn had required. Most Canadians were looking to the federal government rather than the provinces for relief because they realized only the federal government had the necessary resources. As we have seen, the federal government had placed funding at the disposal of the provinces; between 1932 and 1935 the western provinces had received almost $178 million. To help finance this, the federal government had raised income taxes by almost 50 per cent and **sales tax** from one to eight per cent. Nevertheless, the Depression had shown that the Canadian system could not cope and needed to be reformed.

At a conference of provincial prime ministers in 1935, they had complained that they needed more federal grants and loans to meet the increasing costs of welfare at a time when their tax revenues were falling due to growing

 **KEY TERM**

Sales tax Tax on purchased goods.

unemployment. While King offered to increase federal funding until spring 1936, he also said there might need to be some constitutional adjustments as to whose responsibility welfare was. The objective was for all levels of government to pay for their programmes out of their own revenues. Clearly at present this was not possible. King set up a National Employment Commission in 1938, which recommended measures such as unemployment insurance provided by the federal government – in other words a shift responsibilities. As we have seen, while the Depression saw the demise of weaker companies and the success of stronger ones, most Canadians were shocked by the human cost and had come to believe that government intervention was necessary to avoid mass unemployment in the future.

Rowell–Sirois report

King appointed a Royal Commission in 1937 to investigate federal and provincial relationships. It was chaired first by Newton Rowell of Ontario and then by Joseph Sirois of Quebec, but did not report until May 1940, by which time Canada was at war.

It recommended that the federal government take over those functions that provincial governments could not afford, such as welfare provision. It further stated that the federal government should receive most of the income derived from taxation. A commission set up to study the proposals effectively shelved them for the duration of the war. Its provisions, which were gradually implemented after the Second World War, gave Canada a much stronger federal arm with wider responsibilities.

Mackenzie King 1930	*Laissez-faire*
R.B. Bennett 1930–5	Relief – Unemployment Farm Relief Act Trade – Imperial Preference Repression Proposed Canadian New Deal 1935
Mackenzie King 1935 onwards	Increased trade with USA Increased federal government spending Rowell–Sirois Commission

SUMMARY DIAGRAM

Government attempts to end the Depression

The impact of the war on Canada

> ▶ *Key question: How far did Canada become a planned economy during the Second World War?*

During the Second World War, Canada significantly developed its armaments industry, but the economy expanded dramatically in all sectors as it supplied *matériel* of all kinds to its Allies. Canada emerged from the war one of the wealthiest countries on earth, with negligible unemployment and unprecedented living standards. Like the USA, it maintained these for many decades to come.

→ Federal government control

How did federal government grow in influence?

We have already seen a growth in federal government as the Depression showed the inadequacies of the existing systems. King's government built on this growth to effectively centralize planning and production during the war years. The federal government achieved the war economy without excessive borrowing; it was funded in the main by increased taxation and the sale of War Bonds.

Department of Munitions and Supply

The Department of Munitions and Supply was set up in September 1939, and given the ambitious tasks of expanding existing industries, creating new ones where needs arose, and focusing resources almost totally on the prosecution of the war. King's former Minister of Transport, Clarence Decatur Howe, was appointed director in April 1940. He decided, with the support of his cabinet colleagues, that central government, rather than private industry, should assume responsibility for production although private concerns would be able to tender for contracts.

🔑 KEY TERM

Crown Corporations
Organizations set up by the Canadian government to produce goods and services the private sector was unable to provide.

Howe set up 28 '**Crown Corporations**' to oversee production of everything to do with the war effort, from aircraft to the complex machine tools which were essential for the production of armaments. He appointed successful businessmen as aides, who, seconded by their companies, worked for a token 'dollar a year'. Howe said that Canadians could produce anything: whatever was needed to win the war.

Wartime Prices and Trade Board

The Wartime Prices and Trade Board employed officials whose job it was to ensure supply was maintained, if necessary by cutting through 'red tape' or easing logjams in production. They were also responsible for rationing supplies so resources went to those who needed them most for the war effort.

Social security

In 1940, the federal government introduced unemployment insurance schemes, although by the time they came into effect they were largely unnecessary because of war production. In 1944 **family allowances** began. The precedents were set for welfare provision in the future.

Economic growth

Clearly, the prosecution of the war saw a dramatic growth in those employed by government and its cost. The number of civil servants rose from 46,000 in 1939 to 116,000 in 1944. Its industrial production was the fourth highest among the Allies. By 1945, Canada had produced over 16,000 aircraft, 850,000 vehicles and 600 ships; over 50 per cent was destined for the Allies.

The labour force

As in the USA, Canada went from having high unemployment to a labour shortage within a few years; in its case from 500,000 jobless in 1939 to technically nil by 1941.

Women

With so many men in the armed forces, from 1942 there was active recruitment of women into war work. At first only single females between the ages of 20 and 24 were targeted; by 1943 all women, whatever their marital status. As a result the numbers of women in paid employment rose from 638,000 in 1939 to over one million by 1944 when 255,000 were engaged in war production, although they did not achieve equal pay.

> In what ways did the economy grow during the war?

> How did the labour force change as a result of the war?

> 🗝 KEY TERM
>
> **Family allowances**
> Government money to parents to help with the cost of raising children.

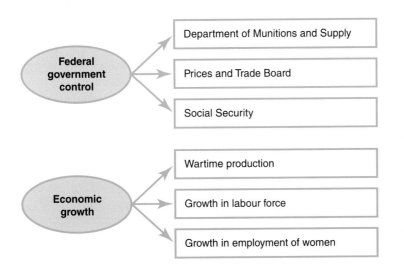

SUMMARY DIAGRAM

The impact of the Second World War on Canada

8 Key debate

▶ *Key question: How far did the Great Depression lead to the growth of the role of federal government?*

Historians tend to agree that, as in the USA, the Depression showed that the systems in place in Canada to address it were wholly inadequate. Welfare was the responsibility of provincial governments or charities, neither of which had anywhere near enough funds. The Depression saw a growth in federal government but politicians and historians disagree as to the extent and impact of this. The Second World War followed the Depression, so many of the effects of the latter on federal government were concealed by the effects of the war.

R.B. Bennett and Mackenzie King

Bennett, a Conservative who had supported a balanced budget and was opposed to any welfare system, shocked many Canadians with his apparent conversion to policies based on the New Deal which he announced in January 1935. He said, perhaps more forcefully than Roosevelt, that the capitalist system would not survive without massive government intervention. Many historians including John Boyko in his 2010 biography agreed that Bennett's conversion was genuine, although Boyko went on to argue that his change of heart had not come quickly enough. King appeared to disagree with the idea of federal government expansion. He accused Bennett of behaving like a dictator and argued that the proposals were beyond the powers of federal government.

The Keynsian experiment

J.M. Keynes, the eminent economist, writing in the early 1930s, had favoured a growth in government spending to stimulate demand supply, thereby expanding the economy. Writing in the 1970s, historian J.L. Findlay argued that the ideas were taken up in Canada before Bennett's apparent conversion. He gave the examples of the $20 million allocated for relief in 1931, the development of the relief camps, and the setting up of the Wheat Marketing Board in 1934. All of these were precedents pre-dating the announcement of the Canadian New Deal. Even King agreed to deficit spending (see page 171) in the 1938 budget.

Lessons of the Great Depression

Finkel, Conrad and Strong-Boag, writing in the 1990s, agreed that the Depression hit Canada particularly badly and required extensive measures. The Depression may not have dislodged capitalism, but its lessons were harsh. The strongest firms survived but weaker ones collapsed, with attendant economic and social costs. Their point here is that most Canadians did not believe survival of the fittest was a suitable tenet for a modern democracy. The government should provide the means of survival for all. This led both to the development and growth of social security and to the Rowell–Sirois Commission, set up to examine federal–provincial relations, which was to recommend a shift in funding and powers (see page 173). Historian J.M. Bumstead agreed, adding that many even in the business community favoured a growth in government.

Impact of war

Some mid-twentieth-century historians, for example John Francis Bannon and J.M. Careless writing in the 1950s, emphasize the impact of war in solving the Depression and argue that Bennett and King did relatively little. Careless goes on to add that King sidestepped difficult decisions about the growth in government responsibility by referring it to the Rowell–Sirois Commission. Bannon examines how King pursued traditional liberal policies, for example reciprocal trade arrangements.

Although in his 1990 study of the human cost of the Depression, Pierre Berton is very scathing about the limited nature of government intervention, most historians agree that the Depression did lead to a growth in federal government, although clearly it is difficult to discern how much precisely because the growth was subsumed into the impact of the Second World War. However, Finkel, Conrad and Strong-Boag do emphasize that it was in part the precedents set in greater government involvement during the 1930s that allowed the centralized economic system during the Second World War to run so comparatively smoothly.

The Great Depression in Canada

While Canada experienced economic prosperity in the 1920s there were significant social, economic and political issues, for example the over-reliance on staples for export and relations between federal and provincial governments. These meant, in part, that Canada entered the 1930s ill equipped to deal with the Depression both economically and in terms of its political structure. It was still largely dependent on primary trade products such as wheat and timber. The downturn in world trade affected Canada particularly badly. It had no real infrastructure to deal with the provision of welfare on the scale that was necessary. The provinces, whose role it was to provide welfare, were inadequately resourced to do so while the federal government, with the ability to tax to provide the necessary finance, was constitutionally unable to offer relief measures. As in the USA, the Depression showed that the role of the federal government must be enhanced. However, neither Bennett nor King was, at least not initially, a radical innovator in the mould of US President Roosevelt.

While politicians of both major parties were slow to appreciate the depth of the problem, they did develop policies which at least did not make things worse and sometimes did improve the situation, for example the creation of public works programmes. The creation of the Bank of Canada was impressive because it meant that unlike the USA, Canada had a stable banking system. Bennett's transformation into an advocate of direct government intervention was genuine and his policies, based on those of Roosevelt's New Deal, would have had a real impact. However, it was the declaring of them as unconstitutional that in part led Bennett's successor, Mackenzie King, to set up the Rowell–Sirois Commission to investigate the relationship between the federal and provincial governments. While this was shelved during the Second World War it nevertheless later laid down the basis for federal–provincial arrangements and suggested a structure that would be appropriate to a post-war world. As with the USA, however, it was the impact of war that finally restored prosperity to Canada and, in so doing, created a more modern and confident country.

 Examination advice

How to answer 'evaluate' questions

Questions that ask you to evaluate want you to make judgements that you can support with evidence, reasons and explanations. It is important for you to demonstrate why your own assessment is better than alternative ones.

Example

> Evaluate the success of Canadian policies to solve the economic problems caused by the Great Depression.

1 For this question you must first identify what the economic problems were in Canada and then discuss specific Canadian policies to overcome these. Be sure to separate your answers into the different administrations

(Mackenzie King: 1925–30; R.B. Bennett: 1930–5; Mackenzie King: 1935–48). Finally, you need to judge how effective these policies were in solving the problems.

2 First, take at least five minutes to write a short outline. In this outline, you could make a chart that illustrates the problems, the government's policies and the results. It might include the following information.

Problems	Policies	Results
Exports and trade collapsed	King did little in his first term. Bennett's efforts ran counter to his original beliefs but he slowly introduced federal measures	Problems continued until the onset of the Second World War
High unemployment	Unemployed and Farm Relief Act, 1931	Money allocated was to be administered by provinces not the federal government. Too little money
	Public Works Construction Act, 1934	Federal building programme to create jobs. Many found work. Nonetheless, unemployment remained high until the Second World War
Farmers' distress: foreclosures due to drought and collapse of wheat prices	Farmers' Credit Act, 1934	Many farmers were allowed to remain on their farms rather than face eviction
Need for relief	National Service Loan	Public bought these and government was able to meet its financial commitments. Provincial governments could not take care of the needy
High tariffs	Tariffs increased to protect Canadian production	Trade was limited further
	1935 Trade agreement with USA	King and Roosevelt agreed to reduce high tariffs between the two nations
Troubled banks	Bank of Canada set up in 1934	Banks could no longer issue their own banknotes and had to transfer their gold reserves to the Bank of Canada. Created a stable banking system

3 Your introduction should discuss briefly the problems Canada faced after 1929 and how King, Bennett and King again tried to ameliorate the situation. Be sure to include a thesis statement that might say something such as: 'While the Canadian governments were not prepared for an economic disaster on the scale of the Great Depression, Bennett and King did try to improve the Canadian economy. However, the measures they took were not great to deal with the scale of the economic downturn. It was not until the onset of the Second World War that Canada's economy was finally out of its darkest economic chapter.'

4 In the body of your essay, try to explain how the Canadian government tried to solve the serious problems of the Great Depression. One way would be to devote a paragraph to each problem and specifically what the government did to address the problem. You also need to discuss the results of the government's policies and to what extent they failed or succeeded.

5 In the conclusion, you should tie together the ideas you have explored and come to a judgement about how successful the government's policies were on solving the economic problems caused by the Great Depression.

6 Now try writing an answer to the question following the advice above.

 # Examination practice

Below are two exam-style questions for you to practise on this topic.

1 'Successive Canadian governments failed to solve the problems that arose from the Great Depression.' To what extent do you agree with this assessment?
(For guidance on how to answer 'to what extent' questions, see page 44.)

2 Discuss the success of alternative responses to the Depression.
(For guidance on how to answer 'analyse' questions, see page 228.)

CHAPTER 6

The Great Depression in Latin America

This chapter examines political and economic developments in Latin America during the 1920s and 1930s. It starts with a general consideration of the economic factors, leading into the causes of the Great Depression. It then examines political, social and economic conditions inside Argentina and Brazil, focusing on how each fared during the Depression years, and the impact of the Second World War. Developments in arts and literature in Argentina are also covered.

You need to consider the following questions throughout this chapter:

* ✪ How healthy were the economies of Latin American countries during the 1920s?
* ✪ What strategies did the governments in Argentina use to deal with the issues arising from political, economic and social conditions in the 1920s?
* ✪ How effectively did the governments in Argentina cope with the Depression?
* ✪ How far did the arts and literature in Argentina reflect a mood of pessimism?
* ✪ To what extent did the governments in Brazil deal with the political and economic problems faced by Brazil in the 1920s?
* ✪ How effectively did Vargas confront the Great Depression?
* ✪ What were the characteristics of the *Estado Novo*?

① Latin America in the 1920s

▶ *Key question: How healthy were the economies of Latin American countries during the 1920s?*

The countries of Latin America relied heavily on the export of raw materials. Few, apart possibly from Argentina, had seen sustained industrial development by the 1920s. Many were largely dependent on the production and sale of one product or monoculture, for example coffee in Brazil. This was to lead to considerable problems as economic conditions changed.

Economic developments in Latin America

The countries of Latin America relied heavily on the USA and Western European countries, particularly Britain, for foreign trade and investment. Some had likened this to **neo-colonialism** in which the developed nations effectively controlled the economies of Latin American countries by buying their imports and selling them manufactured goods, which hampered their own industrial development. Conditions that would lead to an oversupply of

 **KEY TERM**

Neo-colonialism Where developed countries controlled aspects of other countries almost as if they were part of their empire.

← How far were countries in Latin America capable of independent economic development?

Central and South America in the 1920s

primary products such as coffee and cotton were already underway and the markets remained volatile throughout the 1920s. This dependence was to exacerbate the seriousness of the Depression when it came.

However, while the decade saw the end of this export-led growth and the beginnings of industrial development, we should beware of generalizing too much. Latin America is a vast area covering many disparate countries which developed at different times, at differing rates of change and in differing ways.

The signals that change was necessary were weakened in the 1920s due to various factors:

- The high levels of investment from the USA (see below) stimulated economic activity.
- The volatility of international pricing behaviour concealed the long-term trends. During the First World War, for example, import prices rose while the commensurate rise in export prices was concealed due to their non-availability.

In the 1920s, moreover, few countries had coherent policies for industrial development. There was, in addition, little investment in the skills training for employees or technological developments that would be necessary for industrial development to take off. As a result in Brazil and Chile, industrial growth actually fell; in the latter country from nine per cent per year from 1913 to 1918 to less than two per cent between 1919 and 1929.

Reasons for dependence on foreign trade and investment

There were several reasons for the dependence on foreign trade and investment:

- Often geographical factors such as mountain ranges, jungles and deserts made it difficult for Latin American countries to trade significantly with each other.
- Most of the populations remained comparatively poor and could not afford manufactured goods despite the apparent wealth of the country. By the 1920s, for example, Venezuela was the second largest oil producer in the world but comparatively few people saw any material benefits. Three-quarters of the population of Mexico were peasant farmers, but until the reforms of the early twentieth century, all land was in the hands of five per cent of the population.
- Industrialized nations, such as Britain, demanded food imports and natural resources while seeking an outlet for their manufactured products. Countries of Latin America simply could not compete with the cheaply produced European and US manufactures and, therefore, made few sustained efforts to industrialize. Until the 1930s, most governments obtained the bulk of their revenues from tariffs rather than **direct taxes**. This meant that as markets decreased, they received less income. This led to retrenchment and opposition from those public employees who lost

KEY TERM

Primary products
Products that have not been manufactured, for example food products such as wheat and coffee.

Direct taxes Taxes taken directly from income, for example income tax.

their jobs. In Argentina this was a major factor in the overthrow of the government in 1930.

Growth of US investment

Traditionally, Britain had been a major investor, especially in Argentina where its capital had helped to tame the **Pampas**, build railways and develop the industry in beef. However, as a result of the First World War, Western European countries such as Britain and Germany became less significant as trading partners whereas the USA became far more important. US investment in Latin America grew from $1.5 billion in 1924 to $3 billion by 1929. Overall, between 1924 and 1928, the USA accounted for 44 per cent of new investment. Chilean mining concerns attracted more US investment than any others in the world. In Brazil, the USA became the primary source of new capital. Throughout the hemisphere, American companies dominated in the field of media: radio, cinema and newspapers. By 1930, they also controlled much of the electricity in 12 countries including Argentina, Brazil and Uruguay. While the US State Department encouraged investment only in sound ventures, the trend was general, even in Mexico where there was severe political unrest for much of the decade.

Many feared the influence of their northern neighbour and looked to Britain even more as an alternative. This was a reaction to 'dollar diplomacy'.

Argentina regarded itself as the leading country in Latin America and was particularly sensitive to the USA as a rival for influence: it saw itself as the 'colossus' of the southern continent. However, as Source A shows, the growth in US trade seemed incontrovertible.

SOURCE A

a) What conclusions can your draw from the statistics in Source A?

b) What are the advantages and disadvantages of using figures such as these as evidence?

US trade with Latin America as a percentage of total Latin American trade. From R. Thorp, 'Latin America and the international economy from the First World War to the world depression', in L. Bethell (editor), *The Cambridge History of Latin America*, published in 1986.

Countries of South America	1913	1918	1927
Imports from USA	16.2	25.9	26.8
Exports to USA	16.8	54.8	25.2
Countries of Central America	1913	1918	1927
Imports from USA	53.2	75.0	62.9
Exports to USA	71.5	73.4	58.4

Extent of US investment

Despite these figures, the USA was less interested in trade – it protected its own industries with prohibitive tariffs – than investment. US salesmen aggressively pressed loans on to Latin American governments which often overextended their ability to repay them. There were 61 branches of US banks in Latin America, and a Senate Committee found 29 representatives of US financial houses in Colombia alone. Often graft was involved in acquiring contracts. Juan Leguía, the son of the Peruvian president, for example, received $250,000 in commission in 1927 from J. & W. Seligman's, a New York investment banking house, as payment for helping them to win two large foreign loan contracts.

Political developments

From the late nineteenth century many Latin American countries, notably Argentina, Brazil, Uruguay, Chile and Costa Rica, developed some notion of democracy; although as we shall see it was often tenuous and found it difficult to survive the onset of the Great Depression.

While other Latin American were often governed by some colourful characters – Juan Gómez, dictator of Venezuela, for example, allegedly fathered over 100 children and presided over a huge oil boom – even in the ostensible democracies, effective power largely still lay with powerful landowners, and most people were ill educated with few prospects.

Growth of politicized working classes

There had been considerable industrial unrest during the years 1917–20, much of which had resulted in successful strikes. However, as the 1920s developed, many governments developed forces of repression. The period also saw the growth of political parties aimed at the working classes, notably the Communists.

Organized labour

The industrial unrest over 1917–20 informed developments during the 1920s. There were various reasons for this unrest. It is important to remember that conditions varied from area to area.

- The disruption in trade resulting from the First World War had led to high levels of unemployment and increased living costs.
- Often, the shortage of imported manufactures did lead to the development of domestic industry in some places. But wages fell behind the increased cost of living almost everywhere.
- International developments such as the **Russian Revolution** and the fall of the dictator Porfirio Díaz in Mexico stimulated militant activity.

The extent of industrial unrest often caught governments by surprise. In Brazil, for example, 45,000 stopped work in São Paulo in July 1917. The workers' success in securing wage increases of up to 20 per cent spurred unionists elsewhere, for example in Rio de Janeiro. In Argentina over 100,000 workers struck in each of the three years between 1917 and 1919, culminating in Tragic Week, January 1919 (see page 189). Chile meanwhile saw 229 strikes in the cities of Santiago and Valparaíso between the years of 1917 and 1921. However, the 1919 uprising in Puerto Natales was brutally crushed by the army as a forerunner of repression elsewhere.

 **KEY TERM**

Russian Revolution
Communist revolution in Russia in 1917.

Reactions

When governments regained their confidence they often turned to the military or right-wing vigilante groups to put down strikes. Their violent and intimidating tactics were usually successful. In Chile, for example, striking nitrate workers were killed in San Gregorio in 1921 and at La Coruña four years later.

Governments, while generally opposed to trade unions, increasingly supported state-sponsored ones which they could control. Also, many governments initiated social reforms to minimize industrial unrest, for example restrictions on the hours of the working day and regulations concerning the employment of children.

Growth of Communist parties

Communist parties in Latin America were all influenced by the Russian Revolution and followed instructions from Moscow. They remained small, but did succeed in unionizing some previously non-organized groups such as peasants in Mexico, Peru and Chile, and white-collar workers in Argentina. Moscow in fact attached little importance to Latin America because it felt the hemisphere was not ready for the revolution. This was because it had not sufficiently gone through the industrial and urbanization process necessary for the development of a situation in which a revolution could take place. However, Moscow did insist that Communist parties should not co-operate with any other groups, which clearly limited their effectiveness.

What were the causes of the Depression in Latin America? → # The onset of the Depression in Latin America

Various factors meant that the great Depression would hit the countries of Latin America hard as they were not well equipped to deal with it.

- In the regimes we have considered, democracy was partial and tenuous. This meant the same powerful groups effectively remained in control. Countries could not adjust to changing economic conditions.
- International demand for the primary products supplied by Latin American countries was largely in decline, in part because countries in Europe were struggling economically after the First World War.
- There was a growth in foreign ownership and investment, particularly from the USA, in many Latin American countries. This meant that profits from trade often went outside that country.

Overall, the reliance on primary products for export and the continuation in power of traditional élites prevented the modernization and diversification of economies that could have meant countries would not be hit so badly by the Depression.

As a result, it seemed that they were all very ill prepared to address the severe downturn in economic conditions. In the following sections we shall see how true this statement was for Argentina and Brazil.

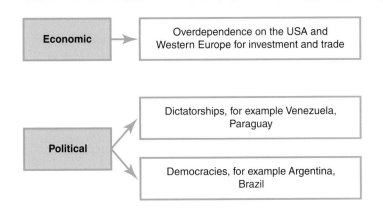

SUMMARY DIAGRAM

Latin America in the 1920s

 # Argentina in the 1920s

> ▶ **Key question:** *What strategies did the governments in Argentina use to deal with the issues arising from political, economic and social conditions in the 1920s?*

Argentina had great potential for development. In the first two decades of the twentieth century it had achieved annual growth rates on a par with the USA of five per cent. Between 1870 and 1914 it had absorbed six million immigrants, mainly from Spain and Italy. However, it was still dominated by primary production, notably of wheat and beef, and the same groups, particularly landowners and owners of meat-packing factories, dominated politically. There was tension between the emerging middle classes, who felt excluded from the political processes, and these élites.

Buenos Aires

The growth of Argentina in the early decades of the century can be exemplified by the development of Buenos Aires, whose population had grown from 200,000 in 1870 to over a million by 1914. The city had developed primarily as a port, eventually handling not only the majority of Argentina's import and export trade but also that of Bolivia and Paraguay. It was the hub of the railway system; British architects had based its great terminals on those of London and Liverpool.

> **How did Buenos Aires grow in the early twentieth century?**

Social structure
Buenos Aires was divided into zones; the wealthy lived in the north, the middle classes in the central areas and the west, with the working classes crowded in the industrial centres in the south.

The city

Buenos Aires regarded itself as the 'Paris of the South'. With wide boulevards – the Avenida 9 de Julio was the widest street in the world – and grand buildings in centres such as the Plaza de Mayo, it certainly looked impressive. The shops in Florida Street were regarded as stylish as anywhere in the world. However, there were severe housing shortages as immigrants moved into the working-class areas. Shanty-towns, known as *villas miserias*, began to appear, with accompanying fears of growing crime and immorality. As in the country as a whole, Buenos Aires looked good on the surface, but when one began to investigate further, serious problems soon emerged.

Political developments

From 1916 to the military coup of 1930 Argentine politics was dominated by the personality of Hipólito Yrigoyen, leader of the Radical Party and president from 1916 to 1922 and from 1928 to 1930, when he was overthrown by the military. He was the first leader to be elected by popular vote as a result of the Sáenz Peña political reforms of 1912, which introduced male suffrage, representation in Congress for minority groups such as **Amerindians** and supposedly an end to corruption in elections. The Radical Party was committed to openness and fair dealing in politics.

As we shall see, however, through extensive **patronage**, Yrigoyen continued the tradition of political corruption of his **Conservative** politician predecessors.

Problems for Yrigoyen's government 1916–22

Politically, the battles between Radicals and Conservatives had been going on since the 1890s. Conflicts had been worsened by cycles of depression which affected people very unevenly across the country, and wartime inflation which distorted the relative wealth of different classes. Yrigoyen's government was handicapped above all by the fact that the Conservatives controlled Congress, which in turn controlled the revenues and feared he would use expensive policies to build up his own base of support, and so vetoed most of what he proposed. Legislation to introduce an income tax, for example, was rejected in 1919, as was the creation of a state bank to fund agricultural improvements. Even timid reform measures such as subsidies for farmers hurt by drought were defeated in the Congress, which decided that Yrigoyen could be controlled effectively by cutting his revenues to a minimum and ensuring his government achieved little.

Having said this, Yrigoyen genuinely sought improvements in Argentine life:

- He opened three new universities offering more opportunities to the middle classes.
- He supported strikers, for example, the port workers in Buenos Aires, thus weakening their traditional alliances with the Socialists.

How effectively did Yrigoyen address Argentina's political problems?

Yrigoyen nonetheless alienated conservative forces with his policies and unwittingly unleashed **vigilante groups** which threatened the stability of the country.

Tragic Week, January 1919, and the growth of political violence

Trade unions in Argentina had been dominated by **anarcho-syndicalist groups**. These were often made up of emigrants from southern Europe who were used to direct methods such as calling strikes to achieve their goals. When metallurgical workers went on strike in Buenos Aires there was an upsurge of violence which saw the death of a policeman. The police responded with violence of their own and in one demonstration five onlookers were killed. The city erupted, with police and vigilante groups joining together to target those whom they perceived as enemies, notably Russian Jews who were accused of organizing a Communist revolution. General Luis Dellepiane and his armed forces restored order. These events became known, because of the violence and bloodshed, as 'Tragic Week'.

When the violence came to an end, right-wing groups organized themselves into the Argentine Patriotic League, which continued to threaten and intimidate those it perceived as opponents throughout the decade. Yrigoyen was powerless to stop them – it is difficult to marshal the law enforcement agencies against violence when they themselves are the perpetrators of it. In Patagonia in 1921–2, for example, strikes by shepherds and rural workers resulted in massacres; possibly as many as 1500 were killed.

KEY TERM

Vigilante groups Groups who take the law into their own hands.

Anarcho-syndicalist groups Groups who sought direct action, for example strikes and political violence, to achieve their aim of the overthrow of capitalist society.

SOURCE B

Strikers burning motor vehicles in Buenos Aires during Tragic Week, January 1919.

What does Source B suggest about political violence in Argentina?

Labour conflicts and apparent government support therefore led to the entry of the military into politics.

To counter this, Yrigoyen turned to populist policies such as increased government spending and the growth of government bureaucracy to facilitate patronage, thus tying members of the middle classes particularly to his regime, to which they owed their livelihood.

How successfully were economic concerns dealt with?

Economic problems

Yrigoyen's successor after his first term of office in 1922 was Marcelo T. de Alvear, a wealthy landowner who may have been expected to enjoy happier relations with the élites. However, he was faced with three on-going problems, none of which he could solve:

- a crisis in the beef industry
- tariffs and debt
- oil.

Crisis in the beef industry

The pre-war chilled-beef trade which dominated exports was generally geared to middle-class tastes wanting high-quality beef. Unfortunately, with the onset of the First World War, demand fell while demand for cheap beef products to feed the troops grew vastly. Many ranches met this shift, investing in inferior stock and opening new processing plants in Zárate near Buenos Aires, Concordia in Entre Ríos and La Plata.

However, after the war this demand collapsed. The number of cattle slaughtered for export in 1921 was less than 50 per cent of 1918 figures and prices had fallen by half. While all sectors of industry suffered, those higher up the chain – processors for example – protected their own profit margins by lowering prices to ranchers. Ranchers meanwhile gained control of the influential **Rural Society** to try to pressurize the government. Nothing, however, was achieved.

Tariffs and debt

The 1923 tariff extended protection to various raw materials such as cotton in an attempt to diversify the agricultural sector, but it had no greater effect than to restore duties to 1914 levels. In the meantime, the national debt had increased significantly, as a result in part in the growth of the bureaucracy. While between 1921 and 1922 government revenue fell from 481 to 461 million **paper pesos**, expenditures increased from 503 to 614 million paper pesos. This meant Argentina's debt grew from 682 to 893 million paper pesos. Needing to retrench, Alvear sought to cut back the bureaucracy, which alienated those people whose support Yrigoyen had won through patronage. In 1924, the Radicals split into those who wanted Yrigoyen back and those conservative elements who did not – the so-called **Antipersonalist Radical Party**. Alvear, trying to remain neutral, won the support of neither group.

 KEY TERM

Rural Society Alliance of powerful conservative cattle ranchers.

Paper pesos Pesos in paper banknotes as opposed to gold pesos (pesos valued in gold had a greater value).

Antipersonalist Radical Party More conservative elements of the Radicals who were opposed to Yrigoyen.

Oil

Oil had been discovered in 1907 in Patagonia and the government, fearing foreign involvement, had created a 5000-hectare reserve in Comodoro Rivadavia from which all foreign firms were excluded. However, Congress had been unwilling to give sufficient funding for the proper development of an Argentine oil industry and as time went on foreign interests grew in other fields, from three per cent in 1916 to 20 per cent by 1922. This was partly because the Argentine industry could not develop to meet increased demand. Although oil output trebled between 1922 and 1928, domestic oilfields still supplied only half of domestic consumption while the amount of imported oil doubled.

Alvear set up a new managerial and supervisory board for the state oil industry, *Yacimientos Petrolíferos Fiscales* (YPF), under the leadership of General Enrique Mosconi. Its aim was to develop the oil industry and exclude foreigners as far as possible. However, British and American investment in particular was too developed for it to succeed in this goal. Despite energetic efforts to open a new refinery at La Plata and a retailing network, foreign involvement continued to grow: by 1928 it was 38 per cent. US-owned Standard Oil, in particular, had interests in every aspect of the Argentine oil industry, from drilling to refining to distribution. Argentina could not compete. When Standard Oil won concessions to drill in the poverty-stricken border province of Salta, the issue moved into a new dimension. The intention was to link up with fields in neighbouring Bolivia, so the fields would effectively be **supranational** and placed output outside Argentinian control.

In 1927 supporters of Yrigoyen introduced legislation for the **nationalization** of the oil industry; this passed the Chamber of Deputies but was defeated in the Senate. In 1929 Shell was granted the right to develop an oil refinery in Buenos Aires so long as it agreed to train students from the newly established Petroleum Institute at the University of Buenos Aires. In this way Argentines began to develop the technical skills to compete with the foreign companies.

In 1930 the oil issue therefore remained unresolved.

USA and trade

Argentina suffered as a result of the Fordney–McCumber Tariff (see page 11). It tried to counter this by restoring its European trade. In 1926, for example, when US President Coolidge banned the import of dressed beef on the grounds that it might be infected with foot-and-mouth disease, Argentina countered with embargoes against Standard Oil, while not extending these to Royal Dutch Shell. In 1928, US Commerce Secretary and President-elect Herbert Hoover met with an unfriendly reception and a foiled assassination attempt on his trade mission to Argentina. In the following year, a British

 **KEY TERM**

Supranational Involving more than one country. In this context, the Salta oilfield straddled the borders of Argentina and Bolivia.

Nationalization State ownership of an industry.

What developments took place in trading policies?

> What problems did Yrigoyen face as a result of the onset of the Great Depression?

trade ambassador, Lord D'Abernon, was welcomed and promised concessions. The Rural Society promoted trade with Britain with the slogan, 'Buy from those who buy from us'.

Indeed, while trade with the USA had grown, with the value of North American exports at 516 million gold pesos, 85 per cent of Argentine exports were still to Western Europe in 1929.

Re-election of Yrigoyen

In 1928, Yrigoyen was re-elected president with 57 per cent of the popular vote. However, he knew he needed to win the support of conservative forces. By 1930, as the Great Depression devastated the Argentine economy, the **budget deficit** was 350 million paper pesos. Yrigoyen had to cut public spending, so many of his supporters lost their jobs. The cabinet disintegrated into warring factions. The conditions seemed ripe for a coup.

As we shall see, similar conditions prevailed in Brazil.

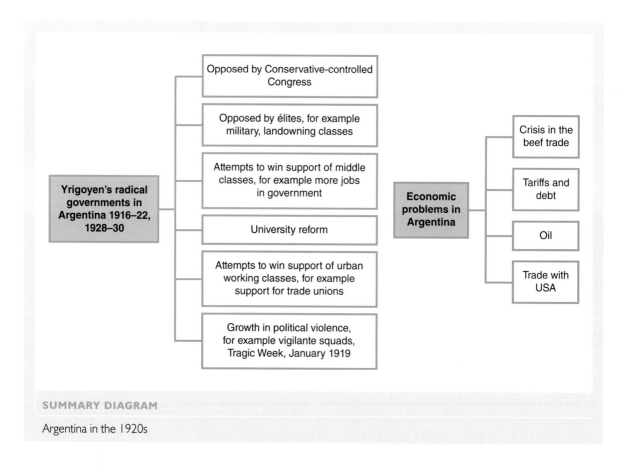

SUMMARY DIAGRAM

Argentina in the 1920s

Argentina in the 1930s

> ▶ **Key question:** *How effectively did the governments in Argentina cope with the Depression?*

The 'Infamous Decade'

The 1930s is often known as the **'Infamous Decade'** because of the corruption and intimidation. Effectively, it was period of military dictatorship although the leaders governed as civilians. Potential opponents could be persecuted. In 1931, for example, three anarchists, known as the 'prisoners of Bragado', were tortured and given a **show trial** in which they were accused of plotting to assassinate members of the family of the conservative politician José M. Blanch. A 'Special Section' was formed within the police to investigate opponents. However, the onset of Depression tended to quieten industrial unrest and either fear or indifference weakened overt political opposition.

Despite their reputation for corruption, politicians introduced substantial reforms to move Argentina out of depression and these largely worked. While GNP fell 14 per cent between 1929 and 1932, by 1939 it was 15 per cent higher than in 1929 and 33 per cent higher than in 1932. Clearly this shows significant progress, and it is inadequate to dismiss the rulers as corrupt dictators. The period saw more direct government intervention in the economy and greater diversification. While the élites were little changed, the period also saw the introduction of the urban middle classes into the power-sharing process.

The 1930 coup

In September 1930, Argentina's first military coup saw the appointment of José Félix Uriburu as president. The coup was led by junior officers who took control of Government House, *La Casa Rosada*. Uriburu became president and promoted the paramilitary *Legión Cívica Argentina*. He appointed supporters to key positions and purged known radical sympathizers from government positions in the guise of cutting expenditures. In December he attacked Irigoyen's pro-labour legislation and demanded that the traditional élites – by which he meant largely landowners, the Church and army – replace those who had participated in government since the onset of democracy in 1916. He went on to close the legislature, and arranged for an election to be held in November 1931 to ensure the traditional élites were returned to power. This would involve bribery, corruption and brutality.

However, General Agustín Justo, commander-in-chief of the army, and other more moderate conservatives were secretly plotting, if not to return Argentina to democracy, then at least not to open it up to fascism. Uriburu,

How fair is it to term this period the 'Infamous Decade'?

'Infamous Decade' Name given to the 1930s because it seemed characterized by political corruption.

Show trial Unfair trial of government opponents. Its purpose is to warn others of what might happen if they joined in any protest.

Legión Cívica Argentina Militia made up of nationalists and supporters of fascism.

increasingly ill with the cancer that would kill him the following year, made two errors of judgement:

- In April 1931, he agreed for a trial election in Buenos Aires province to elect a new governor; the Radical candidate won.
- In July, a rebellion in Corrientes orchestrated by left-wing members of the military led to both Uriburu temporarily exiling Alvear, the Radical leader, and the annulment of the April elections in Buenos Aires.

This, coupled with a failure to deal with the Depression, led him to lose face and military support. Uriburu retired, to be replaced as the conservative National Democratic Party candidate by Justo.

? What alternative caption could you suggest for the photograph in Source C?

SOURCE C

Demonstrators appearing to support the arrival of troops to the National Congress during the military coup of September 1930.

The 1931 elections

In 1931, as a protest against corruption and intimidation, and in particular the exile of Alvear and annulment of the election for governor of Buenos Aires, the Radicals decided to boycott the November 1931 presidential elections. During the campaign, the police had confiscated the ballot tickets of known Radical supporters and in the port city of Avellaneda, conservative leaders had arrested many of them and switched ballot boxes to ensure a conservative majority. Justo 'won' a large majority; and the Radicals did not officially fight elections again until 1935. This effectively returned to power all the old élites: the landowners from the Pampas, the cattle interest, the Church and the army.

Concordancia

The conservative regime of the 1930s was known as *Concordancia*. It had three main components:

- Old-style conservatives who referred to themselves as 'National Democrats'; these were probably the majority. They opposed extremism of any sort and were opposed to political corruption; their leader was Justo.
- The Independent Socialist Party, a small conservative group who broke away from the Socialists in 1927.
- Nationalists formerly led by Uriburu who had often been associated with the right-wing paramilitary movements of the 1920s and were increasingly influenced by European dictators such as Mussolini in Italy and Primo de Rivera in Spain.

While the *Concordanica* was never really popular – after all, it ruled with the backing of the military – there was no real effective opposition. Indeed, the biggest demonstrations in Buenos Aires in the 1930s were those at the funerals of Yrigoyen in 1934 and the much-beloved tango dancer Carlos Gardel two years later.

The main influence as the decade progressed was General Agustín Justo, who took over as president in 1932. A former minister of war, Justo believed in conservative policies with constitutional limitations; in other words, his government was not far short of dictatorship.

Justo was no architect of repression, however. He released political prisoners including Yrigoyen, reinstituted university professors who had been dismissed for radical views, curbed the activities of paramilitary groups such as *Legión Cívica Argentina* and used conciliation to settle labour disputes. Having said this, his government would openly allow fraud in election, such as helping the fascist sympathizer Manuel Fresco to win the governorship of Buenos Aires province in 1936. Finance Minister Federico Pinedo (see page 202) produced a manifesto of the right in which he warned against the rise of the working classes and justified the use of fraudulent practices to get government supporters elected.

Clearly the biggest problem to face was the Depression.

Argentina during the Depression

Effects of the Depression in Argentina

The Depression affected Argentina severely. Aggregate production fell by 14 per cent between 1929 and 1932. The exchange value of the peso fell by 20 per cent. In 1930, there was a fall of 34 per cent of exports on the previous year and their value fell in the first six months of 1930 by 188 million gold pesos. While the government's account at the *Banco de la Nación* was overdrawn by over 140 million paper pesos, customs revenue fell by 30 million pesos and inland revenues by six million pesos. The cost of bankruptcies and company liabilities soared to 105 million paper pesos. Clearly the priority of any government would be to combat the effects of such a Depression.

Government response to the Depression

At first, the government's response was orthodox, in trying to reduce debts, cut government spending, boost trade and maintain key industries.

Reduce debts

With the devaluation of the US dollar in 1933 (see page 83), Argentina began to repay its loans to the USA on favourable terms. In 1933, meanwhile, Justo devalued the peso, which made Argentine goods cheaper, and in so doing was able to reduce its foreign debts.

Spending cuts

Uriburu sought to save government expenditures by savage spending cuts, for example, dismissing 20,000 government employees in Buenos Aires. National government expenditure fell from 934 million paper pesos in 1929 to 702 million by 1934.

Trade

Justo saw the solution to the Depression in increased trade, particularly with Argentina's old partner, Britain. This was threatened by the introduction of Imperial Preference (see page 159) in which Britain had agreed to cut imports of Argentine beef by five per cent. Vice-President Julio Roca Jr was sent to London in 1932 to try to negotiate a trade agreement. This resulted in the Roca–Runciman Agreements.

Roca–Runciman Agreements 1932

This treaty between Argentina and Britain, secured for three years, guaranteed Argentina a fixed share in British markets for meat and ruled out tariffs on British cereal imports.

- Britain agreed to two concessions: to admit in future years the same quantity of Argentine beef as it did 1932, and to agree that Argentine meat-packing plants could supply 15 per cent of British beef imports.
- In return, Argentina agreed to reduce tariffs on 350 British goods to the 1930 rates, currency exchanges favourable to Britain, and the preservation of British commercial interests in Argentina such as the railways.

- Currency exchanges were particularly contentious. Any payments to Britain deferred because of the weakness of the paper peso were to be automatically taken from Argentine earnings from exports in sterling. In other words, Britain deducted any monies owing from payments before paying for Argentine imports. Moreover, any blocked funds not released in this way were to be regarded as an interest-bearing loan.
- All trade between Britain and Argentina was to be carried in British ships.

It also meant that Justo gave in to British demands in other areas, in order to protect the agreements. For example, the street-railway system in Buenos Aires was British owned, and in a generally decrepit condition for which the British owners blamed high taxes and uneconomic fares. Shareholders complained of poor dividends while **Porteños** moaned about the quality of the service. The revenue from the tramways fell from 43 million paper pesos in 1929 to 27 million in 1943. Voting with their feet, Porteños had begun to patronize privately owned buses. The British then demanded a new charter for a new monopoly, with tax exemptions, guaranteed returns of seven per cent to investors and the elimination of the competition. Justo, fearful the Britain might pull out of the Roca–Runciman Agreements, gave in and in 1935 a new British-owned *Corporación de Transportes* was introduced. However, the government ignored its agreements and allowed the privately owned buses to flourish.

KEY TERM

Porteños Inhabitants of Buenos Aires, literally people of the port.

Bilateral agreements Agreements between two countries.

The Eden–Malbrán Treaty

In 1936, when the original treaty ran out, it was renewed by the Eden–Malbrán Treaty, which favoured Britain even more. Britain was allowed to impose taxes on Argentine meat imports and more favourable terms for British-owned railways in Argentina.

> **Argentine railways**
>
> The Argentine railways were British owned and in poor repair. During the 1930s, the volume of freight transport fell by 25 per cent and railway profits by 50 per cent. The British owners were reluctant in these circumstances to invest in new stock. As a result, by 1940, 50 per cent of the locomotives were over 50 years old and poorly maintained. Nevertheless, the railway interests campaigned against the government building new roads to compete. They asked for tax exemptions and for fare increases. Not surprisingly, the government was unsympathetic. The answer to the problems of transport was not, it was felt, to subsidize inefficient foreign-owned railways but to develop road transport. Although Justo did double the amount of roads (see page 200), many felt this was not enough.

In the 1930s, Argentina made more of these **bilateral agreements** so that by 1940, 60 per cent of its imports came through them. However, the USA refused to open its markets to Argentine beef and cereals in order to protect its own agricultural interests.

Maintaining key industries

The example of the oil industry illustrates how the issue of foreign involvement was shelved in order to ensure the supply of oil, while that of the meat packers shows how corruption was tolerated to ensure the continuation of a key industry.

Oil

The controversy over foreign involvement in the Argentine oil industry (see page 191) became less significant during the 1930s. The government gave up on the idea of a state oil monopoly and allowed foreign interests free rein. As a result, Argentine oil production trebled between 1930 and 1946; the YPF share of the market meanwhile fell to one-third. More importantly, Argentine oil production in total grew by enough to significantly reduce foreign imports; in 1930 Argentina imported 58 per cent of its oil and in 1940, 37 per cent. In 1932, a law exempted from customs duties equipment imported by YPF; in return it contributed 10 per cent of its profits to the national exchequer.

This is not to suggest there was no controversy. In 1934, just after YPF had invested in the expansion of its marketing processes in Buenos Aires, the foreign companies announced price cuts. In 1936, Justo resolved the price war between YPF and foreign competitors by establishing market quotas.

The government had decreed that YPF would control oil importation as it saw fit. However, as it was felt this might upset Britain, on whose trade Argentina relied heavily, the decree was soon rescinded. A market-sharing agreement was reached by which the foreign companies conceded half the Buenos Aires market to YPF.

The point was that Argentina needed significant amounts of oil for its industrial development. Overall production rose from 0.5 million cubic metres in 1922 to 3.3 by 1940. The issue of who supplied it became less important than its availability.

Meat packers and fraudulent practices

As in the 1920s (see page 190), in the early 1930s meat packers formed a pool to force ranchers to bear the brunt of the falling prices. Between 1929 and 1933, the amount paid to ranchers for live steers halved from 34 to 17 centavos. At the same time packers' profits soared.

In 1935, Congress recognized that a pool was operating and a leading Senator Lisandro de la Torre widened the criticism to denounce packers for income tax evasion and other fraudulent practices. One of his supporters was assassinated on the floor of the Senate. A congressional investigation found evidence of widespread corruption. British-owned meat-packing firms already enjoyed generous tax rebates and favourable exchange rates due to the Roca–Runciman Agreements. They also falsified their account books to avoid taxation. The ranch-owning minister of agriculture appeared to turn a blind eye, possibly because British buyers paid 10 times more for his cattle than for those of his competitors.

Justo complained meanwhile that his room for manoeuvre was limited. The government could not afford to upset those groups whose activities just might help pull Argentina out of the Depression. This cut little ice with others who pointed to the fact that chilled beef accounted for only 16 per cent of total imports of Argentine beef by Britain. They argued that the real purpose of the Roca–Runciman Agreements, as with many other government initiatives, was to protect the meat-packing interest to the exclusion of everyone else.

This dissatisfaction with government responses, and particularly with the Roca–Runciman Agreements, led to the growth of nationalism in Argentina.

Political developments

The 1930s saw a growth of nationalistic fervour in Argentina, particularly aimed against foreign, especially British, involvement. Many people thought that Argentina had the potential to be as wealthy as the USA but had not met its potential because of mismanagement and economic exploitation in the past.

Growth of nationalism

The nationalist movement developed specifically from the paramilitary groups of the 1920s, but had wider origins.

- A general feeling of **Argentine Exceptionalism**, that Argentina was potentially a superpower but had underperformed.
- The dislike of foreign, particularly British, involvement in the economy. It was felt that British gains far outweighed any advantages Argentina gained from the close relationship. Oil, meanwhile, was the only sector where efforts had been made to exclude foreign investment and, as we have seen, even these were now weakened.
- The Radical youth movement FORJA (*Fuerza de Orientación Radical de la Juventud*) supported nationalist ideas and attacked foreign involvement. They said, 'We are a colony. We want a free Argentina.'

Nationalism tended to be dominated by right-wing authoritarian groups. There were impediments to working-class nationalism; for example, any working-class urban dwellers tended to be immigrants and their adoption of Argentine identity was slow.

Growth of unionism

As economic conditions improved there was a growth in labour unions. By 1939, the largest union, the railroad workers' union Ferroviara, had over 100,000 members and 50,000 construction workers were unionized.

In October 1935 the latter held a 90-day strike in Buenos Aires, while in January 1936 the umbrella union organization the General Confederation of

> How significant were the nationalist movements that developed in the 1930s?

 **KEY TERM**

Argentine Exceptionalism Belief that Argentina was destined to become the wealthiest and most influential state in Latin America.

Labour (CGT) called for a two-day general strike. While the government attacked unionism – a Residency Law for example allowed them to deport unionists of Italian origin – unions nevertheless won some concessions such as:

- Railroad workers gained security of employment, although their pay was cut.
- Office workers gained sick pay and severance pay in the event of dismissal.
- Working hours were gradually reduced and some retirement schemes came into operation.

Some fascist supporters such as Manuel Fresco were sympathetic to unions, hoping they could be developed on corporate lines as in Fascist Italy and Brazil (see page 214) where employers and unionists would agree on issues, with government guidance (or control). A National Department of Labour was formed to promote collective bargaining and state arbitration where necessary.

Desire for greater social mobility

There was a frustration that the social mobility which Yrigoyen had promoted was now restricted and the old élites were again firmly in control. However, there was significant migration into the cities from the countryside as industry developed which would have political effects as the 1940s developed, such as the support for popular leaders like Juan Perón.

→ # Economic developments

How effective were economic developments in terms of combating the depression?

The notion of **Import Substitution Industrialization** (ISI) was to be very important across Latin America in the middle years of the twentieth century but, as we have seen, its origins pre-dated the Depression.

The idea was to develop industry so economies were not so dependent on primary products. In Argentina, for example, firms such as Tornquist and Bunge y Born began to diversify their activities and invest in products aimed at local markets. In the 1930s, the giant firm SIAM, created by Torcuato di Tella, an Italian immigrant, manufactured a wide range of electrical products such as refrigerators and washing machines. Much of their success was based on copying equipment under US licences. By 1940 SIAM had branches in Brazil, Uruguay and Chile. In 1943, for the first time, the value of manufactures exceeded that of agriculture; 35 per cent of those paying the highest taxes meanwhile were industrialists, compared with 10 per cent of ranchers.

 **KEY TERM**

Import Substitution Industrialization
The development of domestic industry to avoid over-reliance on imported industrial goods.

Government was directly involved also. In 1932, for example, the government levied petrol taxes to finance a highways bureau and the construction of 30,000 km of roads by 1938. Government spending increased by 27 per cent between 1932 and 1937. The government was keen that industrial development should be harnessed to military defence. In 1941, the

Dirección General de Fabricaciones was created to provide military supplies and equipment. It was run by the military itself; hence the army administration organized activities as diverse as a factory producing pig iron, and aircraft manufacture, while the navy took responsibility for shipbuilding and explosives manufactures.

Industries grew too. Between the years 1927 and 1943, the manufacturing sector grew by 3.4 per cent annually, compared with the agricultural sector figure of 1.5 per cent and GNP of 1.8 per cent. Imports of manufactured goods fell from 40 per cent of the total in 1930 to 25 per cent by the late 1940s. Argentina, it seemed was *en route* to prosperity.

SOURCE D

Growth of GDP in Argentina 1930–45.

Year	Gross domestic product (millions of pesos)	Manufacturing sector (millions of pesos)
1930	8,206	1,198
1935	8,976	1,319
1940	10,257	1,620
1945	11,642	2,037

Study the figures in Source D carefully. What can you learn from them?

Despite the development of ISI in heavy industry, industrial companies tended to remain small scale. In 1939, 60 per cent of firms had fewer than 10 employees and of the rest, 75 per cent had fewer than 50. The large-scale employers tended to be the meat packers. There were very few medium-sized firms, traditionally the ones with resources for investment. Also, the vast majority of industrial concerns – 60 per cent or more – were based in Buenos Aires, rather than spread evenly throughout the country.

The main industrial growth in Argentina came in the fields of textiles and more modern goods such as electrical appliances. SIAM notwithstanding, these were often produced by subsidiaries of US firms who had located to Argentina. Firestone, Goodyear and the electrical firm Philco had opened operations in Argentina.

Textiles

The textile industry had grown even during the Depression. Between 1929 and 1932 the number of textile factories in Buenos Aires grew from 12 to 20. In 1930, domestic manufactures provided nine per cent of Argentine total consumption; by 1940, this had risen to 46.9 per cent and by 1943, 82 per cent. Imports meanwhile fell from 25 per cent in the late 1930s to 14 per cent by the 1940s. During the 1930s and 1940s, textile production grew annually by 11 per cent and its workforce increased from 83,000 to 194,000. Clearly, the **dislocation of supplies** due to the Second World War was largely responsible, but domestic production was stimulated to meet the shortfall.

 **KEY TERM**

Dislocation of supplies
Where supplies of goods stop or become unreliable due to war conditions, for example.

Reasons for the growth in textile production

- During the interwar period the price of raw cotton fell by 50 per cent, thus stimulating domestic use as it could not be sold profitably on foreign markets.
- The amount of land devoted to cotton cultivation more than doubled from 101,000 hectares in 1931 to 225,000 by 1936.
- The junta for cotton production controlled production and sales, making the industry as a whole run on more efficient lines.
- Textiles was an **inelastic market** which pushed up the profits for producers.
- The textile industry was protected. It benefited from bilateral trade agreements which pushed out cheaper foreign suppliers such as the Japanese.

KEY TERM

Inelastic market A market where demand for the product would remain despite price rises; usually involves staple and essential products such as bread.

Federico Pinedo

Federico Pinedo was appointed minister of the treasury in 1933 and imposed emergency measures to address the deficits in revenues caused by the shortfalls in foreign trade.

Introduction of income tax

Income tax meant that tariff duties formed a smaller proportion of total government revenues, from 80 per cent in the 1920s to 50 per cent by 1940.

Central bank

The centrepiece of Pinedo's reforms was the creation of a central bank in 1934. Previously, the privately run banking system made it impossible to control the monetary supply and manage the economy at large. During the 1920s, the Gold Standard had operated but this was rigid and inflexible. Now the central bank could regulate interest rates and the monetary supply, to uphold the peso at attractive rates, while avoiding deflation if the value of the gold reserves fell. Effectively the central bank became the financial agent of the government.

Creation of juntas for products

Juntas were organizations created to manage the production and marketing of specific products to guarantee quality and control supply. They would buy surplus products to maintain price.

What was the impact of the Second World War on Argentina?

The end of the *Concordancia*

Argentina recovered relatively quickly from the Depression. However, it had changed rapidly during the 1930s. There was significant migration to the cities, creating a new urban working class. There was significant industrial development. There was less reliance on primary goods for export, and the Second World War severely disrupted trade, stimulating domestic production. In fact, the onset of war closed European markets to Argentine grain and reduced the availability of imports of every type. Coal imports for example fell by 66 per cent between 1939 and 1941; for much of the war railways relied on grain to provide one-third of their fuel.

In 1940 Pinedo launched his 'Economic Reactivation Plan' which favoured industrial expansion and the development of domestic markets in the face of disruption of trade caused by the Second World War. Part of the plan was to stimulate the construction sector by providing funding for cheap housing schemes which, it was hoped, would create 200,000 jobs. However, Radical opponents in Congress voted against the plan, citing the cost, but in reality hoping to bring down the government.

In 1941, the USA undertook to supply arms to the various Latin American nations which supported the Allies to help cement the friendship. Argentina, which professed neutrality, was excluded. This in part prompted the creation of its own *Dirección General de Fabricaciones* to produce military supplies. With Brazil receiving US weaponry, there was briefly tension between the two countries.

In June 1943, the civilian politicians were overthrown in a military coup. The scene was set for a new direction in the dictatorship of Juan Perón, whose efficacy (or disaster) still attracts great controversy.

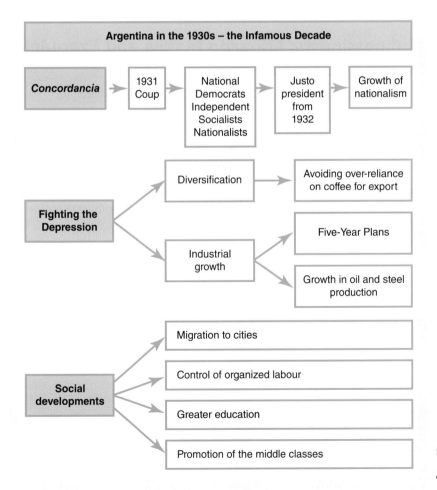

Literature and the arts in Argentina

> ▶ *Key question: How far did the arts and literature in Argentina reflect a mood of pessimism?*

Argentina's intellectuals and exponents of popular culture exerted considerable energies in trying to explain what had gone wrong in Argentine society. There was a feeling of malaise beyond the fact of the Depression; that the earlier potential had not been achieved, that society was out of kilter. This was reflected both in the ferment of ideas that permeated the 1930s and in the very popular cinema which spoke mainly to the working classes. However, the pessimism and despair became most iconic in the national dance of Argentina: the tango.

First we need to consider how the malaise in Argentine society was explained in the realm of intellectual writing.

What did the pessimists argue?

The pessimists: Eduardo Mallea and Ezequiel Martínez Estrada

In his novel *La Bahía del Silencio* (*The Bay of Silence*, 1940), and more importantly the essay *Historia de Una Pasión Argentino* (*History of an Argentine Passion*, 1937), Mallea (1903–82) argued that there was no solution to Argentina's problems. He felt that the scramble for materialism reflected the demoralization and lack of achievable goals that were worthwhile.

Martínez Estrada (1895–1964), in his essay *Radiografia de la Pampa* (*An X-ray of the Pampas*, 1933), believed Argentina had been damned from the start; the Argentine people inherited the worst characteristics of their Spanish forebears. He argued more specifically:

● that Argentina was a victim of its geographical isolation
● that Argentina lacked any avenues for meaningful values
● that Argentina was a victim of circumstance in that independence had solved none of its problems, particularly those of the huge peasant population
● that by the 1930s, Argentina had grown to maturity dependent on monoculture and economically dominated by Britain. There was, he agreed with Mallea, no solution.

While Estrada catalogued an exhaustive set of problems, some felt his analysis offered excuses to the élites who argued that he had proved that Argentina's problems were beyond anyone's control and therefore not their fault.

The solutions

What solutions were proposed to society's problems?

Other writers suggested solutions to these problems.

Attacking decadence: Manuel Gálvez
In his novel *Hombres en Soledad* (*Men in Solitude*, 1938), Gálvez (1882–1968) argued that Argentina's problems resulted from the decadent lifestyles of the élites. He depicted the fictional Toledo family as being characterized by all he considered wrong with Argentina, such as unearned wealth, vulgarity and ready acceptance of British economic colonialism.

Anti-Semitism: Gustavo Martínez Zuviría
Going by the pen-name Hugo Wast, Zuviría (1883–1962) wrote a series of extremely popular novels which blamed the Jews for Argentina's problems. Heavily influenced by anti-Semitic literature, he argued that Argentina was a victim of some international Jewish conspiracy. While this was clearly fanciful, his novels sold 53,000 copies between 1935 and 1942 and went through nine editions.

Corrupt politicians: Alejandro Bunge and Benjamin Villafane
Bunge, who edited the well-respected magazine *Revista de Economica*, and Villafane, a Senator, both blamed corrupt Radical Party politicians for encouraging labour leaders to call strikes and campaign for better pay and working conditions, which they believed undermined the economy.

The overwhelming response to the problems highlighted by literature was nationalism. As a typical example, in *La Grande Argentina* (*The Great Argentina*, 1930), Leopoldo Lugones called for authoritarian government, strict control of foreign investment and state exploitation of national resources. Elsewhere there was a fatalism, that Argentina's problems were in fact insurmountable. In the words of Senator Antonio Santamarina in 1940, 'We are sitting on top of a volcano.'

Popular culture

What was the significance of the tango and the development of the cinema?

In Argentina, the tango developed a significance far beyond its simply being an erotically charged dance, while its cinema industry became, until the mid-1940s, the most successful in Latin America.

The tango
The tango, a dance originally confined to ports and some of the roughest areas, had developed by the 1920s into a powerful reflection of people's frustrations and demoralization. Many of the lyrics were pessimistic and cynical in the extreme. One of the most famous examples was *Cambalache* (see Source E).

Tango became extremely popular and Carlos Gardel, its leading exponent, became a superstar. His funeral following his death in an air crash in 1935 saw scenes of mass hysteria.

SOURCE E

Lyrics to *Cambalache* (*Junkshop*), written in 1935 by Enrique Santos Discépolo, translated by John Kraniauskas.

That the world's always been rotten
Don't remind me, it always will be
In the year 506 and 2000 too!
There've always been crooks
Me and those who pretend to be,
The content, the sad,
Pickpockets and Machiavellis
But this twentieth century
Has put insolent evil on show, and that,
No-one can deny.
Floundering in the mess
We're rolling in the mud
Manhandled all.

Cinema

Argentina came to dominate Latin American cinema during the 1930s and early part of the 1940s. Historians divide its development into two periods.

1933–7

When cinema first developed, it focused on 'tango melodramas' and comedies. For much of this period the middle classes eschewed the cinema as vulgar and so the films concentrated on pleasing working-class audiences and the stories overwhelmingly featured the poor triumphing against the odds.

Tango melodramas were developed by José Ferreyra; the stories usually involved a hero living in urban slums and dogged by misfortune until redemption came in the guise of families or friends. The tango offered musical interludes to reflect the plot. Often, for example, when Carlos Gardel was the star, the hero would be a tango dancer.

Comedies, often directed by Manuel Romero, followed **Chaplinesque** themes, in which an underdog found himself at odds with society but came through in the end.

1938–43

Argentine films became very popular throughout Latin America and even the USA. As they developed from 1938 to 1943, they became more lavish, featuring epic stories and **social realism**.

- Mario Soffici developed social realism with themes such as opposition to British imperialism, medical care, corrupt politicians and the exploitation of plantation workers.
- These themes were continued by directors such as Francisco Mújica, whose 1941 film *El Mejor Papá del Mundo* (*The World's Best Dad*) showed how international concerns could destroy the aspirations of independent farmers.

- The most influential film, however, was probably *La Guerra Gaucha* (*The Gaucho War*) based on novels by Leopoldo Luganes, which charted the liberation struggles of the **gauchos** in the north of Argentina against the Spanish.

KEY TERM

Gauchos Workers on ranches, often cowboys.

Post-1943

After 1943, Argentine cinema fell into decline. Various reasons have been offered:

- The USA disliked the success of the Argentine film industry and began to limit the amount of raw film stock it was prepared to sell.
- The USA invested in Mexican cinema, which eclipsed that of Argentina. In 1943, for example, 70 movies were produced in Mexico, the most for any Latin American country, and some of its major stars such as Dolores del Rio were also gaining Hollywood fame.
- The Argentine film industry was run inefficiently.
- It began to concentrate on pallid copies of American romantic comedies to appeal to the middle classes, but the US and Mexican versions were far superior.

Eventually, Argentine cinema, which had achieved so much, went into a decline. This became a metaphor for the country itself.

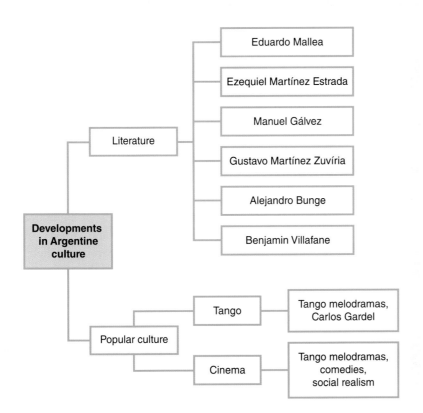

SUMMARY DIAGRAM

Literature and the arts in Argentina

5 Brazil in the 1920s

> ▶ **Key question:** To what extent did the governments in Brazil deal with the political and economic problems faced by Brazil in the 1920s?

The 1920s in Brazil saw the final decade of the '**Old Republic**', which was ended, as it had begun, by a military coup.

What were the underlying economic problems faced by Brazil?

Economic problems

Brazil faced severe economic problems during the 1920s.

KEY TERM

Old Republic Name given to the constitutional system of government that operated in Brazil from 1890 to 1930.

Valorization Scheme first introduced in 1906 whereby the government would buy coffee and hold stocks until the international price rose.

- The Brazilian economy was dominated by coffee production and coffee magnates controlled huge swathes of national life. In 1920, the government reintroduced **valorization** whereby if coffee prices fell below a certain level, the government would buy coffee beans and store them until the market price rose again.
- Earlier mass production of rubber had declined because of more efficient South-East Asian producers entering the international markets.
- Sugar production was similarly in decline.
- Like Argentina, Brazil had concentrated on the production of primary products and had to import most of its manufactured goods and 80 per cent of its grain. It was wholly dependent on trade with developed countries like Britain.

There was also a shift away from European trade and towards that with the USA. By 1927, the USA was Brazil's major trading partner and owned 35 per cent of Brazilian national debt. Brazil also saw significant immigration – 500,000 people in 1911–12 – mainly from southern Europe, bringing new ideas and ambitions.

How far were the political problems of the 1920s addressed?

Political problems

Ostensibly, Brazil was a democracy with a central government and 20 states. In effect, elections were rigged and the office of the presidency alternated between the dominant south-eastern states of São Paulo and Minas Gerais. This process was called *café com leite* or coffee with milk because of their respective main agricultural products. Only five per cent of the adult population met the literacy qualifications for voting while the percentage of voters who participated in presidential elections was less than three per cent. For many, life was poor; average life expectancy in 1928 was only 28.

However, the latter years of the Old Republic saw two significant developments. The growing urban middle and working classes demanded a greater say in the running of the country, particularly in terms of modernization. The army meanwhile was the one national institution which combined a growing involvement in politics with the same desire for modernization. There could therefore be common ground between the urban classes and the military against the old élites, who still dominated Brazilian politics but seemed to be holding back progress.

Political role of the military

Until the 1920s, the military was generally content to allow the civilian politicians to rule as long as they granted them generous budgets. However, this changed after the First World War for various reasons:

- President Epitácio Pessoa vetoed a bill to increase military spending and placed civilians to head the ministries of the army and navy; traditionally these posts were given to military personnel.
- In 1921, a charismatic general, Hermes da Fonseca, returned from service in Europe. He had the ability to unite the different military factions and was elected to be head of the influential Military Club of Rio de Janeiro. Ominously he said, 'The political situations change but the army remains.'
- A series of economic problems beset the country such as the fall in coffee prices.
- The two dominant provinces fell out when Artur Silva Bernardes was selected for president. He was from Minas Gerais and was out of sequence; the political élites in São Paulo felt it was their turn. This led to their forming the Republican Reaction movement with members of other states such as Rio Grande do Sul and Rio de Janeiro. Increasingly, they appealed to the military for support.
- In a dispute over whether the government had the right to place army groups at the disposal of its favoured candidate for the governorship of Pernambuco, General Fonseca was arrested and the Military Club was closed down for six months.
- However, it was junior officers – the so-called *tenentes* – who took direct action in a series of rebellions independent of their senior officers. They sought modernization and reform; effective government was preferable to democracy, which did not feature high on their agenda.

 **KEY TERM**

Tenentes Junior officers who wanted modernization and effective government in Brazil.

Army rebellions

During the 1920s the army was involved in a series of abortive rebellions.

- July 1922 – rebellion at the fort on Copacabana beach. While order was quickly restored, it set the tone and precedent for future rebellions.
- July 1924 – revolt at São Paulo in which the officers made common ground with members of the working classes. They held the city for 22 days before order was restored. This rebellion spread to Aracaju, Manaus, Belém and Rio Grande do Sul, where there was almost civil war.
- The 'Prestes Column' – rebels from Rio Grande do Sul under Captain Luís Carlos Prestes joined forces with those escaping São Paulo and marched over the course of three years through inhospitable jungle terrain to sanctuary in Bolivia.

Discontent

The government downplayed the significance of the rebellions, especially after 1925 when the price of coffee rose again. They looked to the fact that the young officers had not won the support of peasants, who were still controlled by powerful landowners or the urban workers.

However, there was considerable discontent. Many looked back to the period of empire before 1890 when they felt Brazil was on the verge of becoming a major power. Others disliked the continuing power of the coffee magnates with the concomitant political corruption. Moreover, there was widespread sympathy with the young officers that Brazil was in desperate need of modernization. The Communist Party meanwhile was founded in 1922, offering a national organization and clear policies for **egalitarian revolution**. The Catholic Church began to concern itself with the appalling social conditions in which many members of the working classes were forced to live and became critical of the political classes and governments for not doing anything to alleviate them.

Improved conditions

In 1926, Washington Luís won the presidency with 98 per cent of the 700,000 votes cast. He was fortunate to preside over an improvement in economic conditions. He was able to balance the budget, control public finances and also set up a Stabilization Office which issued a new paper currency backed by gold. The Coffee Institute of São Paulo moreover gained control of coffee marketing and distribution nationally, limiting production as necessary and storing the produce for sale when international prices rose.

However, there were still problems, particularly with the amount of national debt. In 1926 this stood at $900 million, with annual interest payments of $175 million; by 1930 it had risen to $1.18 billion and $200 million, respectively.

What events led to the military coup of 1930?

→ The military coup of 1930

At the end of his four-year term of office, Washington Luís wanted to hand over power to the governor of São Paulo, Júlio Prestes. This annoyed most other political groups; those from Minas Gerais because they felt it was their turn and those from the other states because they felt ignored again. This political crisis was exacerbated by the onset of the Great Depression.

In the years 1929–32 the price of coffee beans fell from 22.5 to 8 cents a pound and the volume of trade with Britain by 37 per cent. By 1930, Brazil's gold reserves were exhausted. The warehouses meanwhile were full of unsold coffee – as many as 26 million sacks.

Opponents of Júlio Prestes formed the Liberal Alliance, nominating Getúlio Vargas as their candidate. In a non-violent election, Prestes won one million of the 1.9 million votes cast. This was unsurprising as no official candidate had ever lost a presidential election. All went peacefully until Vargas's erstwhile Vice-President, João Pessoa, was assassinated while waiting for his girlfriend in an ice-cream parlour in the city of Recife. The opposition accused the outgoing President Washington Luís of organizing this crime. A military-led rebellion resulted in the appointment of Vargas as the new president and the scene was set for a new type of regime which many argued was influenced by European fascism.

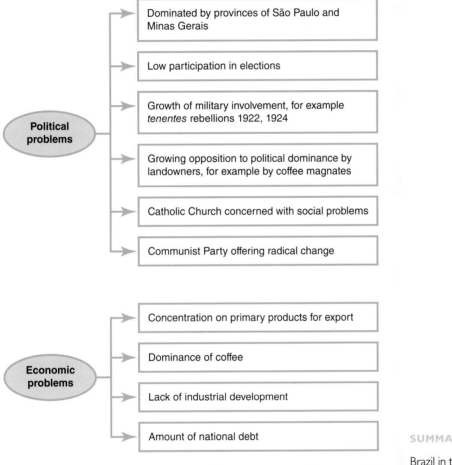

SUMMARY DIAGRAM

Brazil in the 1920s

Brazil in the 1930s

> ▶ **Key question:** *How effectively did Vargas confront the Great Depression?*

After 1930, Brazil was dominated by the leadership of Getúlio Vargas, who was president from 1930 to 1945 and later from 1951 to 1954. In the 1930s, Brazil, like the rest of Latin America, was faced with Depression. Vargas's aims were to modernize and industrialize Brazil, and above all perhaps, end its over-reliance on coffee for export. He was a radical in that his vision was to transform Brazil and in so doing shift power away from the traditional élites to more forward-looking groups including an urban middle class.

How did Vargas gain control of Brazil during the years 1930–4?

Head of the Provisional Government 1930–4

Vargas became head of government in 1930 following a military coup. His first government was termed 'provisional' because it took place while a new constitution was being drawn up. In February 1932, a new electoral code was passed which:

- gave the vote to all literate adults over the age of 18 and to working women
- introduced the secret ballot
- created the organization Election Justice to organize and supervise elections. The intention was to stabilize elections and reduce fraud. A Constituent Assembly was elected by this new procedure in March 1933 to draw up a new Constitution.

Relationship with the *tenentes*

The *tenentes*, the former revolutionaries in the military (see page 209), wished to strengthen central government and modernize Brazil at the expense of what they perceived to be the old, corrupt political élites. While Vargas agreed with their ideas to some extent, he was naturally cautious and while seeking change, did not wish to alienate the old élites. He did seek a stronger central government and intervened in states far more than his predecessors, but his measures were not radical enough for many of the *tenentes*.

Clube 3 de Outubro *(3 October Club)*

Disaffected *tenentes* formed the *Clube 3 de Outubro* in February 1931. They advocated ideas such as:

- a stronger presidency
- a legislature indirectly elected by delegates appointed by others
- state-directed plebiscites to promote national unity
- land reform

- more equal distribution of income
- the importance of the group over the individual.

Overall, many of these ideas replicated those of fascist parties in Europe. In particular, they advocated nationalization and modernization. Vargas certainly found them useful allies and sent some *tenentes* out as **state interventors** and appointed others as advisers.

However, within a few years the influence of the *tenentes* was removed. This was because:

- they lacked unity and many held conflicting ideas
- rebellion in São Paulo (see below) required them to return to military duties
- their ideas were incompatible with the liberal reforms and moves towards greater democracy favoured by the middle classes whose support Vargas also sought.

Political problems

Many of the old élites, particularly in São Paulo, opposed Vargas. In November 1930, in assuming all executive and legislative powers, he dissolved the Congress and State assemblies. In August 1931, an Interventors' Code was drawn up in which the autonomy of states was limited and subordinated to central authority. In particular, in an attempt to ward off any future rebellions, states could not spend more than 10 per cent of their budget on militias or police and could not supply them with artillery, aircraft or firearms in excess of what the national army possessed.

Paulista War 1932

Vargas sent General Isidoro Dias Lopes, the leader of the *tenentes'* 1924 revolt, to command the military in São Paulo and former *tenente* João Alberto as interventor. Alberto immediately decreed a five per cent wage increase for workers and began to distribute land among army veterans. **Paulistas** accused him of communism. When Vargas listened to their complaints and replaced Alberto with a civilian, Pedro de Toledo, the Paulistas saw this as a sign of weakness and, in June 1932, rebelled.

This insurrection appeared popular among most groups in São Paulo; a 'Gold to help São Paulo' movement saw thousands donate jewellery and other valuables to the war treasury and envoys dispatched to the USA to buy weapons. No other state joined in, however, and São Paulo was left isolated.

Although the rebellion collapsed after a three-month siege of São Paulo, Vargas chose leniency and agreed to the instillation of a constitution. While this may have annoyed the military, Vargas was reassured that neither the middle classes nor the workers had joined the rebellion so he felt his position was secure. He realized, however, that he could not ignore the powerful São Paulo élites, whose wealth had been based on coffee exports, and began to appease them:

 **KEY TERM**

State interventors Officials appointed by Vargas to run Brazilian states after the state governments were suspended.

Paulistas People from the state of São Paulo.

- on a personal level by passing, in August 1932, an Economic Readjustment Act which reduced the debts of those planters badly affected by the Depression
- on a state level by appointing a Paulista civilian, Armando de Sales Oliveira, as the new interventor.

The 1934 constitution

While maintaining the federal system, the 1934 constitution strengthened the power of the presidency. The president was elected by both houses of the Congress for a period of four years and could not serve more than one consecutive term. The Chamber of Deputies was made up of representatives of 50 corporations on Mussolini's fascist economic model, plus 250 deputies representing areas and the population as a whole. Clearly the intention was to reduce the power of the old élites.

What political threats did Vargas face between the years 1934 and 1937?

Constitutional Government 1934–7

The period of the Constitutional Government saw an increase in political extremism from left and right.

Left: the Communist Party

The Communist Party had been formed in 1922 but gained in support as the depression intensified.

National Liberation Alliance

The National Liberation Alliance (NLA) emerged in 1935 from within the Communist Party. With a slogan of 'Bread, Land and Liberty' it called for the nationalization of foreign enterprises, redistribution of land among the rural working classes, cancellation of foreign debts and full democracy. Its membership grew to as many as 100,000. Many of its supporters embraced nationalism rather than socialist ideas, however; none of its principal ideas related to workers' rights.

Its leader was the Radical *tenente* Luís Carlos Prestes. When he called for the defeat of Vargas and the establishment of a provisional revolutionary government, the NLA was banned under the National Security Act of March 1935, which designated all left-wing groups as subversive.

Further separate military uprisings in November 1935 gave the government the excuse to have known Communists and their sympathizers arrested. Two institutions of repression were created:

- Bureaux for Repression were introduced in January 1936, such as the National Commission for Stopping Communism, specifically to investigate any civil servants and others participating in activities against the state.
- A National Security Tribunal was set up in October 1936 to try such people, who were invariably found guilty and sentenced to various periods of imprisonment, often in grim conditions. The extent of the

repression was enough to defeat any Communist threat for the period covered by this book.

Right: the Integralist Party

The Integralist Party (*Ação Integralista Brasileira*, AIB) was set up by Plínio Salgado, a writer, in October 1932. It openly copied European fascists, specifically in Mussolini's Italy and Salazar's Portugal. Its main aim was to enhance national consciousness above everything. With their **sigma symbol** and green-shirted uniform, it emphasized ideas such as hierarchy and obedience and had slogans like 'God, Fatherland and Family'. Membership grew to between 100,000 and 200,000 by 1937, mainly recruited from the urban middle classes. They attacked Jews, Freemasons and Communists. While they had no official links to the government or Catholic Church, many members of those institutions supported them.

Vargas's responses to political extremism

Vargas believed political parties of any description weakened national purpose because they highlighted ideological differences. In September 1937, he announced the discovery of the 'Cohen Plan'. Originally 'discovered' by the **Integralists** and now known to be a convenient forgery, this purported to be a blueprint for widespread Communist insurrection. Details included plans for wholesale massacre, rape, pillage and the burning of churches. Vargas used it as an excuse to ban all political parties, cancel the planned presidential elections, dismiss Congress and assume all political power for himself. This was effectively a coup by the president.

Estado Novo 1937–45

The *Estado Novo* ('New State') was the name given to the regime of Vargas's personal rule. He ruled by decree, set up a special police force which used torture and other means of repression, abolished personal freedoms, introduced strict press censorship and to all intents and purposes introduced a fascist-style dictatorship.

The reality was far more complex, however.

Reactions

- Those supporting democracy were outraged but impotent in the face of government forces.
- The working classes appeared indifferent to whoever was in power.
- Most nationalists supported Vargas.
- Most importantly, perhaps, he had the support of the military. In 1932, after first assuming power, Vargas had purged the army of politically unreliable senior officers. By 1933, 36 out of the 40 serving generals had been promoted by, and owed their allegiance to, the new government. Many of his policies were to their advantage. He increased military salaries and the armed forces were doubled in size from 38,000 in 1927 to 750,000 in 1937. Regional commands absorbed state militias, which strengthened central

 **KEY TERM**

Sigma symbol The Greek letter (Σ) used as a symbol by the AIB.

Integralists Members of the AIB.

← **What were the characteristics of the *Estado Novo*?**

authority and weakened the states further. The two senior officers, Góis Monteiro, who served as chief of staff from 1937 to 1943, and Eurico Gaspar Dutra, minister of war from 1937 to 1945, remained fiercely loyal.

● When the Integralists learned that the ban on political parties included them too, they rebelled, attacking the presidential palace on 10 May 1938. Vargas, trapped inside, was relieved by troops arriving via a network of secret tunnels connecting the palace with a football stadium. The revolt collapsed. This is significant because it shows that a president accused of a fascist-style dictatorship had actually banned the fascists who might have been expected to support him.

Relationship of *Estado Novo* to fascism

On the surface, certain components of a fascist regime were indeed in place. There were corporations, repression, and an emphasis of the nation over the individual. Vargas himself said, 'The *Estado Novo* does not recognize the rights of the individual against the collective. Individuals do not have rights; they have duties. Rights belong to the collective.'

However, Vargas never created a political movement like the fascists in Italy, nor a paramilitary organization like the **SA** in Nazi Germany nor even a political party. As we have seen, Vargas believed all political parties were divisive. He always insisted his regime was non-political. Although he did create a Department of Press and Propaganda in 1939 there was little attempt to indoctrinate people or regiment them into organizations like the Italian **Dopolavoro**. It may be more accurate to view him as a dictator who sought modernization above all and nationalism to some extent but had no real political ideology. He repressed opponents but he did not force people to believe in any specific ideologies.

On the other hand, the media had to toe the official line. Given the mass illiteracy in Brazil, Vargas understood the importance of radio and film. He often gave 'fireside chats' on the radio, and most film-shows included government-sponsored newsreels. Newspapers could be controlled through the government control of newsprint. They might be punished for articles critical of the government by insufficient supplies to bring out a full edition, but if they were perceived to present a threat they would actually be closed down. In this way, for example, Vargas shut the influential *O Estado de São Paulo* (*The State of São Paulo*) and then reopened it as a government mouthpiece.

Vargas's support base

While Vargas encouraged the support of the middle classes and the military, he also tried to broaden his political base through winning the allegiance of the growing urban working classes. He referred to himself as 'Father of the People' and encouraged state-controlled trade unions which did win real concessions for workers such as the introduction of social security through the introduction of a Labour Code in 1943.

Economic policies

← **How effectively did Vargas's economic policies address the problems caused by the Depression?**

The period of the *Estado Novo* saw a more cohesive economic policy in terms of state promotion of, and involvement in, industrial development. However, policies to this end had been evident since the 1930s. Some historians see 1930 as the pivotal point, when the onset of Depression brought home the vulnerability of having to rely so much on imports.

Coffee

Coffee was central to the Brazilian economy. In the 1920s, it accounted for 75 per cent of all Brazilian exports. As the Depression developed the fall in coffee prices was spectacular: from an average of 21.7 cents per pound in 1929 to 9.8 cents between 1931 and 1937. In the 1930s, Brazil exported 337 million pounds of coffee compared to 806 million in the 1920s. Clearly these figures show the problems with relying so heavily on one commodity.

National Coffee Council

Vargas set up the National Coffee Council in 1931 to control the production and marketing of coffee. In 1933 it changed its name to the National Department of Coffee. Its main response was to order cutbacks in the planting of coffee trees: 3 billion were planted in 1933, 2.5 billion in 1939 and 2.3 billion by 1942. It also encouraged coffee burning whereby the department would buy up surplus produce with the proceeds of export receipts, and destroy it. By 1939, 60 million bags of coffee had been destroyed, a policy which only stopped in 1944 when Brazil was more prosperous as a result of its involvement in the Second World War and there was less need to support the coffee producers.

Diversification

Vargas tried to encourage the agricultural sector to diversify. In this context the biggest expansion was in livestock raising and cotton production. The Depression signalled the end of coffee domination.

Industrial developments

Many Brazilians saw industrialization as the means by which Brazil would develop as a modern power. Industrialization and economic development were allied in many minds with nationalism. As early as the second decade of the twentieth century the influential Brazilian economist Alberto Torres was writing that any nation could only develop when it controlled its own commerce and resources. Like many other Latin American countries, it was argued that Brazil had entrusted its economic development to foreign countries like Britain, which had exploited it. The coming of the Depression was a harsh lesson in the dangers of this reliance on foreigners.

As in other Latin American countries, economic nationalists such as Roberto Simonsen argued that the answer lay in Import Substitution Industrialization (ISI) (see page 200). Others still felt that Brazil lacked the resources and infrastructure to develop its industry and should aim to continue to buy manufactured goods at the cheapest price. Vargas had no time for such timidity. He was determined to drive the economy through planning. His would be an interventionist government. Vargas supported industrial development and would place the resources of the state to help make it happen.

Industrial growth

The Depression saw a reduction in the amount of imports, if only because Brazil could no longer afford them. Between 1929 and 1932 imports fell by 75 per cent from $416 million to $108 million. This led to favourable trade balances which could be invested in industry and domestic production increased as imports fell. As a percentage of GDP, the industrial sector more than doubled from 21 per cent in 1920 to 43 per cent by 1940. Production in specific areas such as metallurgy and electrical equipment also doubled.

Reasons for industrial growth

- Domestic prices had not fallen as much as international ones so it was more profitable to produce goods for domestic consumption than for export.
- Brazil had ample productive capacity: textile production could increase, for example, without the need to expand facilities.
- Vargas's economic policies protected Brazilian industry. He imposed import controls and duties to protect new industries, with important exemptions on the importation of machinery to facilitate their development. In addition, his government gave long-term loans with low interest rates to new industries.
- Brazil had lots of hitherto undeveloped natural resources such as diamonds, quartz, lead, zinc and copper.
- Since the 1920s, there had been limitations on foreign exploitation of national resources. All the constitutions included articles that banned the sale of land with mining resources to foreigners. For example, in 1937, a law banned foreign interests from the exploitation of minerals and waterfalls. In 1939, only banks with Brazilian shareholders could operate in Brazil. However, there was a period of grace whereby foreign firms could convert themselves into Brazilian ones.
- In 1942, the government established the *Companhia Vale do Rio Doce* (River Valley Company) to exploit the wealth of the iron ore at Itabira. By 1951, production of Brazilian iron ore had quintupled in volume.

The Five-Year Plan

In January 1940, a Five-Year Plan was introduced with a focus on expansion of the railway network and steamships and the development of hydroelectric power. In 1939, the National Council for Hydraulic and Electric Energy had been created in part to harness the power of the rivers. However, the big story was the development of Brazilian industrial production in oil and steel.

SOURCE F

Inside the Ehrle metal works, Caxias do Sul 1941.

Oil

Many Brazilians resented the fact that foreign companies controlled much of the Brazilian electricity supply. Vargas initiated a search for oil to facilitate an alternative source of power. Until 1939, the Brazilian petroleum industry had been limited to refineries. The search for oil became a national obsession. In 1938, the National Petroleum Company (CNP) was formed; in January 1939, oil was discovered just outside Salvador da Bahia. While the amounts were modest, there was a determination that no foreigners would get involved. Vargas said, 'Whoever hands over petroleum to foreigners threatens our own independence.' Later, in 1953, the state monopoly on all petroleum-related activities was established through the creation of Petrobras, leading to the cry from Brazilian people, 'The oil is ours!'

What impression is given by the photograph in Source F?

The National Steel Company

The National Steel Company was organized in 1941 to control steel production and work began on a new plant at Volta Redonda. The military wanted steel production to be exclusively Brazilian controlled but Vargas, pragmatic as ever, was willing to accept foreign investment. Protracted negotiations with US Steel went on throughout 1939; eventually funding came both from the US Import and Export Bank and Britain; at one point Vargas had threatened to go cap in hand to Nazi Germany. By 1955, Volta Redonda produced 646,000 tons of steel annually.

Other industries

While oil and steel may have been Vargas's biggest success stories, other industries also grew. From 1924 to 1939, including the years of Depression, annual industrial growth averaged six per cent, while in the five years after 1933 the value of industrial production rose by 44 per cent. During the 1930s, three times more plants were operational than in the previous decade. In 1940, **capital investment** in plant was $700 million. These were examples of real success.

In addition, the agricultural capacity was developed; swamplands in Rio de Janeiro state were drained to take land into production, for example.

New industrial developments took place in pharmaceuticals, printing and publishing, and chemicals. Most of what was produced was destined for domestic consumption. This trend was extended during the Second World War, for example in textiles where belligerents could not supply Brazilian markets. Brazil, in fact, developed considerable foreign exchange surpluses as a result of lower imports: from $71 million in 1939 to $708 million by 1945 when the second Five-Year Plan began.

Obstacles to industrialization

It was not entirely a one-sided picture, however. There were real obstacles to unimpeded industrial growth:

- Plants were still largely dependent on heavy machinery imported from abroad.
- The transport network was still relatively undeveloped. Most of the new roads were unpaved.
- Industrial development was uneven across the vast country.
- Most industrial development took place in the wealthy states of the south-east. São Paulo was the industrial powerhouse; it contained 15 per cent of the population but accounted in 1938 for 43 per cent of Brazilian manufactured goods; by 1943, this figure had risen to 54 per cent. The southern states employed 75 per cent of all industrial workers.
- Elsewhere, the economy was still dominated by agriculture, often using traditional methods such as **slash and burn**. With fertilizers in short supply, the land quickly became exhausted. Only one farm in 100 owned a tractor and only one in four a plough; half of these were in one state: Rio Grande do Sul. The *latitfundia*, or large estates, still predominated. The peasants who lived and worked under these conditions could not afford industrial goods. Indeed, the average monthly wage across all sectors was only $11.80. Most Brazilians had very little purchasing power.
- Much of Brazil was still undeveloped. Vargas spoke of the 'March to the West' and attempted to develop the state of Goias by giving 50-acre plots to settlers, but the policy had little impact because people were reluctant to move there.

Social developments

Internal migration

In the 1930s, there was considerable migration from rural areas into towns and cities. Often new arrivals found themselves in shanties or *favelas*. Vargas marketed himself as the 'Father of the Poor' and aimed to win the support of this constituency, although being illiterate in the main, few could vote. Nevertheless, he adopted a paternalistic approach.

Organized labour

Vargas sought the support of the working classes, but he feared independent trade unions, which he saw as dangerous. His solution was to control their activities. Therefore, in March 1931, a decree empowered the Ministry of Labour to organize workers into government-sponsored unions. By 1944, there were 800 of these with 500,000 members. While strikes were illegal, courts and codes of practice were set up which gave workers real gains. Bureaux of Reconciliation and Arbitration were set up, to be replaced by Labour Courts in 1939. In July 1940, a union tax of one day's pay was imposed on all workers whether they belonged to a union or not. Benefits achieved for workers included pension schemes, minimum wages (introduced in May 1940), health and safety regulations and a maximum 48-hour working week.

However, the benefits did not apply to the rural peasantry or those working in small-scale industry. Even such measures as were adopted such as the introduction of a minimum rural wage in 1943 were widely ignored by employers. Moreover, much of the union funding often found its way into government **slush funds**. Union bosses usually put the interests of the state before those of their members.

Education

Vargas attached great importance to education, speaking of it as 'a matter of life or death'. His first Minister of Education, Francisco Campos, reformed the system, building new schools and improving teacher training. Attendance at primary school became compulsory. New universities were opened in São Paulo in 1934 and Rio de Janeiro in 1938. The university population increased by 60 per cent between 1920 and 1940 from 13,200 to 21,200.

While the emphasis was on improving education for the middle classes, Vargas was aware that, with annual birth rates of three per cent, Brazil had a young population and education was the key to a new generation of technologists and managers as well as skilled workers who could drive industrial development.

However, funding for education was tight and resources were poor. There were only 12 free secondary schools in Brazil by the 1940s. Teachers were

> **How far did Brazilian society change during the period of Vargas's presidency?**

 **KEY TERM**

Slush funds Money used for bribery and other fraudulent purposes.

poorly paid. Illiteracy improved slightly, dropping from 69.9 per cent of 15 year olds in 1920 to 56.2 per cent in 1940. Despite being 'compulsory', attendance remained low at 21 per cent because of the need to contribute to the family income or help in the family fields. It was the case, as with many of the other reforms, that the poorer members of society were relatively unaffected.

Middle classes

Above all Vargas promoted the development of the middle classes whom he saw as his most important supporters and who would be those technologists and managers of the future. One significant development was the creation of the Administrative Department of the Civil Service (DASP) in 1938, which introduced competitive examinations based on merit rather than patronage to facilitate the professionalism of the civil service. However, patronage continued. Ministers' desks were piled with letters asking for favours.

How did Vargas fall from power?

→ Fall of Vargas 1945

During the late 1930s, Vargas had moved closer to Nazi Germany, particularly in terms of trade. Between 1935 and 1938 Germany doubled its imports from Brazil, becoming the biggest customer for Brazilian cotton; indeed 466,364 bales from Brazil as opposed to 200,182 from the USA. It was Brazil's second biggest market for coffee. Brazil only sold more cacao to the USA and Britain than to Germany. Germany bought lots of Brazilian tobacco.

In 1938, the German armaments giant Krupp agreed to supply the Brazilian military with artillery. With the Nazis applauding the creation of *Estado Novo* and these trade developments, it might be expected that Vargas would move easily into the **Axis** camp. Certainly, his government contained fascist sympathizers, particularly among the military leaders. At the same time, however, Vargas banned the Integralists and ordered the deportation of the German Ambassador when he was implicated in the setting up of Nazi groups in Rio Grande do Sul. This led to tension because the German government sought to encourage immigrants of German origin to maintain their German identity and embrace Nazi ideas, while Vargas preferred them to integrate as Brazilians.

By August 1942, Brazil had declared war on Germany because of the sinking of Brazilian cargo vessels *en route* to Allied ports. It participated in the war more actively than most other Latin American countries, sending 25,000 troops and an air force to the Italian theatre in 1944, and allowing the USA to establish air and naval bases in the north of the country to be used as an air-bridge to Africa.

Brazilians began to ask why they were fighting for democracy in Europe while experiencing dictatorship at home. It was actually the military who began to put pressure on Vargas to democratize Brazil, and he set a date for presidential and congressional elections for 2 December 1945. Many did not

KEY TERM

Axis The alliance of Germany, Italy, Japan and other countries during the Second World War.

trust him, however. In July 1945, his supporters called for political continuity. On 25 October, he appointed his brother chief of police in Rio de Janeiro. Many thought he was plotting another coup. Four days later the military ousted him in a fairly bloodless coup. Vargas retired, blaming foreign enemies angry at his policies of economic nationalism for his downfall. He would return as a democratically elected president between 1951 and 1954, when he was overthrown again and committed suicide.

Vargas's legacy

During Vargas's 15 years in office, Brazil was increasingly changing from a rural nation dominated by coffee interests to an urban, industrial one with a burgeoning middle class. Undoubtedly, his governments achieved much – for example the creation of national unity – not least through the development of industry, the promotion of the middle classes and wooing of the workers, all of which broadened the support for government.

The electoral reforms of 1932 introduced the secret ballot and gave the vote to women in paid work. The civil service was increasingly appointed on merit rather than patronage. All these developments weakened the powers of the old élites. So under Vargas, Brazil developed as a more modern country. However, it was at the cost of political repression and dictatorship.

In promoting industrial development, Vargas saw great strides in Brazilian economic growth. He realized that if Brazil was to become independent of foreign economic involvement, it needed to diversify its own economy and industrialize. New industries catered for domestic demand, thus reducing dependence on imports. Vargas realized too that the agricultural sector needed modernization, and encouraged greater mechanization and diversification here too, for example in the cattle and sugar sectors. However, while Brazil did move towards self-sufficiency, the growth was uneven. Moreover, the continuation of a poor rural peasantry and traditional methods of agriculture in the poorer states precluded the rate of development at which he may have hoped to see Brazil rise as a global economic power.

Nevertheless, the Vargas era saw substantial developments in industry such as oil, steel and textiles. He had steered Brazil out of the Depression, although as with all Latin American countries, it was the impact of the Second World War and the demand for their goods which eventually brought prosperity. Vargas, however, could go some way to claiming to have created the infrastructure which made industrial expansion possible. By 1938, industrial production was twice that of agriculture, being valued at over a billion dollars. By 1950, Brazil was the most industrialized country in Latin America.

Vargas promoted the economic nationalism that saw Brazil's economy grow and dependence on foreign imports reduced. He gave Brazilians pride in their country and its achievements.

←---- **What impact did Vargas have on Brazil?**

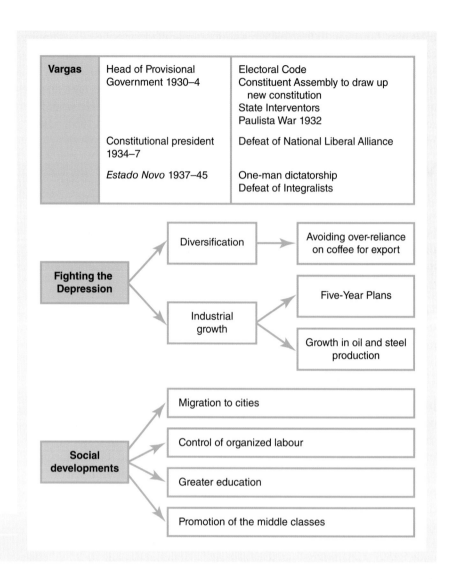

Vargas	Head of Provisional Government 1930–4	Electoral Code Constituent Assembly to draw up new constitution State Interventors Paulista War 1932
	Constitutional president 1934–7	Defeat of National Liberal Alliance
	Estado Novo 1937–45	One-man dictatorship Defeat of Integralists

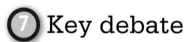

SUMMARY DIAGRAM

Brazil in the 1930s

⑦ Key debate

▶ *Key question: What were the characteristics of the Estado Novo?*

Clearly, the *Estado Novo* was an authoritarian regime with similarities to fascist groups in Europe. However, it also emphasized modernization and a break with the past. Historians have put different emphases on its different characteristics to explain its nature.

Getúlio Vargas

In his New Year's address to the Brazilian people in 1938, Vargas himself emphasized that the *Estado Novo* was a Brazilian solution to Brazilian problems. He argued that he had abolished political parties because they prevented direct lines of communication between government and people. However, the new regime was necessarily authoritarian.

SOURCE G

Extract from Vargas's New Year Address, 1938.

We will not permit that the struggle and patriotic determination of good Brazilians might come to endure turmoil and alarms originated by personalist ambitions or the ideological craziness of false prophets and vulgar demagogues.

Rewrite Vargas's statement in Source G in your own words.

?

Vargas emphasized elsewhere the need for modernization. Overall, the *Estado Novo* was an authoritarian, modernizing regime where the Brazilian people would be protected from subversive influences by necessary repression.

Oliveira Vianna

Vianna was a member of Vargas's close circle who believed individuals should be subservient to the needs of the state. He felt that the *Estado Novo* was about the needed restoration of central authority. 'The King reigns, governs and administers.' In this sense, Vargas was compared to an all-wise absolute monarch.

Bailey W. Diffie

Writing after a visit to Brazil in 1940, Diffie, a well-respected academic, emphasized the repressive nature of Vargas's regime. He compared the *Estado Novo* to fascist governments and found they had much in common, notably repression and fear. Even if Vargas was not personally a fascist, he felt he was surrounded by fascists in the highest echelons of power, so ultimately it did not make much difference. He concluded that 'if this isn't fascism we are being pretty squeamish about the meaning of words'.

José Maria Bello

Bello was a Brazilian historian who first wrote in the 1940s but whose work was much reprinted and updated. He felt that Vargas was an absolute dictator, whose main aim was to stay in power. Hence the pragmatism. The *Estado Novo* therefore could best be viewed as a government by one man to keep himself in power.

Boris Fausto

Writing in the 1990s, Brazilian historian Boris Fausto felt the *Estado Novo* was authoritarian in support of the state. In this way it differed significantly from fascism. Fascism placed party above all else, whereas the *Estado Novo* simply supported the state. There was no real attempt to mobilize people behind an idea. They were simply expected to obey the government as exemplified by Vargas and his ministers. This to a certain extent explains why the army supported it so tenaciously. The state knew best how to modernize, industrialize, centralize and the state was exemplified by the person of Vargas.

R.M. Levine and John J. Crocitti

In their introduction to the Vargas section of *The Brazil Reader* (1999), historians Levine and Crocitti argue that Vargas changed the face of Brazil forever. He advocated 'safe but bold change' but grafted new practices onto older ones; in other words, built on existing practice. They felt that pragmatism was the most important factor. Vargas more or less left the old élites, particularly the military, untouched. They would agree with Bello that his real aim was to hold on to power. They show, for example, how patronage continued, and despite advocating more independence, Brazil actually became more dependent on USA investment and influences, particularly during the period of the Second World War. Most Brazilians were aware that Vargas's propaganda had inflated his achievements, but industrialization and modernization had at least begun.

E. Bradford Burns

Bradford Burns, writing in the 1990s, believed that Vargas's main aims were to centralize and modernize. The *Estado Novo* was the most centralized and powerful government Brazil had experienced. Vargas had supreme power but exercised it reasonably. He listened to a variety of opinions and generally his policies were popular. He introduced new forces into government, noticeably the industrial and technologically inclined middle classes, and reduced the influence of the traditional élites. However, he did not go out of his way to make enemies and did not deliberately antagonize the traditional élites.

Conclusions

Overall, there appears a consensus, certainly among more contemporary historians that, despite appearances, the *Estado Novo* was not a fascist regime. It was certainly authoritarian and dismissed the rights of individuals if these clashed with what it considered to be the interests of the country. It could and did repress opponents, particularly Communists, but there was no secret police to spy on individuals. Its aims were industrialization and modernization. Vargas believed that he and his officials knew best how to achieve these. Undoubtedly, one of the prime methods was central direction and a reduction in the autonomy of the different states. Most historians agree that a prime characteristic of his rule was pragmatism; he would adapt to circumstances and was always prepared to be flexible. Clearly, the *Estado Novo* did not solve all Brazil's problems and did little for the poorest groups. However, it firmly set Brazil on the road to industrialization and modernization, which were its stated aims.

Country	Type of government	Political	Social	Economic
Argentina	1916–30: Democracy 1930–43: Authoritarian, supported by military	Political violence, for example Tragic Week 1919 University reform Some repression	Growth and development of middle classes Some movement of people into cities	Over-reliance on one product – beef Crisis in cattle industry Tariffs Debt Onset of Depression Debt reduction Spending cuts Trade agreements, for example Roca–Runciman Agreements ISI
Brazil	1890–1930: Democracy 1930–45: Authoritarian, supported by military	Development of dictatorship *Estado Novo*	Growth and development of the middle classes Movement of people into cities	Over-reliance on one product – coffee Onset of Depression Economic nationalism Industrialization ISI

SUMMARY DIAGRAM

Argentina and Brazil in the 1920s and 1930s

Chapter summary

The Great Depression in Latin America

Political tensions were evident in Latin American countries as the traditional élites, comprised mainly of landowners, tried to maintain their hold on power. However, changes were taking place, noticeably the emergence of an urban middle class. The result was an opposition to the growing modernization and industrial development which would have rendered countries more able to combat economic depression.

The Depression brought home the realization that countries of Latin America had over-relied on a limited number of primary products for export. Many used the 1930s as an opportunity to address this problem by developing their own industries. This process was known as Import Substitution Industrialization (ISI).

- Argentina saw the introduction of a military dictatorship known as the *Concordancia*. However, under Justo, while corruption was rife, it was not particularly brutal and did encourage economic progress particularly under Finance Minister Pinedo.
- The Roca–Runciman Agreements were criticized as being too favourable to Britain and encouraged the growth of nationalist sentiment.
- Developments in literature and the arts reflected a growing mood of pessimism in Argentina.
- Brazil was dominated by Getúlio Vargas, who later became dictator of the *Estado Novo*.
- Vargas suppressed opposition, but did encourage industrial development. The later 1930s saw some impressive progress, particularly in steel production.

Overall, many countries of Latin America recovered relatively quickly from the Depression. However, while modernization was promoted they remained relatively undeveloped and maintained a huge lower class with little access to education or any improvements in living standards.

 Examination advice

How to answer 'discuss' questions

When answering questions with the command term <u>discuss</u> you should try to identify the various arguments or factors and their relative importance.

Example

> <u>Discuss</u> the political impact of the Great Depression on one Latin American country.

1 The command term <u>discuss</u> suggests you investigate the political impact of the Great Depression by looking at various components or sides to the issue. Another key word on which to focus is <u>political</u>. The question does not ask you about the social or economic impact of the Great Depression. That said, social and economic issues often overlap with political ones. If you raise these, be sure to explain how they relate to the political impact. For a question such as this one, use a Latin American country as your example and not Canada or the USA. From this chapter, you could use either Argentina or Brazil. Choose the one for which you think you have the most supporting evidence.

2 Take at least five minutes to write a short outline. Focus on what the
   question is asking. An example of an outline using Argentina might be
   as follows.

- *Yrigoyen re-elected in 1928.*
- *Great Depression devastated Argentine economy. Public spending cut.*
- *September 1930 military coup. Uriburu appointed president. Infamous Decade began.*
- *1931 elections: Radicals boycotted the elections. Old élites (land-owners, Church and army) returned to power.*
- *Conservative regime known as the **Concordancia** took power. General Justo became president in 1932. He released political prisoners, used conciliation to settle labour disputes and curbed paramilitary groups. Yet he also permitted fraud so friends could win elections.*
- *Roca–Runciman Agreements signed in 1932. Justo saw improved trade with Britain as a means to weather economic storm. Porteños boycotted British-owned transport systems.*
- *Nationalist movements developed because of Roca–Runciman, loss of what Argentines considered their sovereignty. Radical youth movements grew.*
- *Growing unionism projected their political power. Railroad workers union and umbrella group, the Confederation of Labour, called for strikes. Government made some concessions.*
- *Another military coup in June 1943.*

3 In your introduction, set out your key points about the various ways in
   which the Great Depression made a political impact on Argentina. An
   example of a good introductory paragraph for this question is given below.

As in much of Latin America, the Great Depression caused severe political dislocations in Argentina. When it appeared that elected governments could not adequately deal with the scale and scope of the crisis, the military often took power. Hipólito Yrigoyen, a Radical, was re-elected president in 1928 in Argentina. He was overthrown in 1930 by a military coup. The political structure of the country would be altered dramatically for the next decade. Old élites began to exert their influence again and even if the military changed into civilian clothing, they remained the power behind the government. Elections were often fixed which led to the Conservatives having no real opposition. As many workers moved from the interior to the major cities, union activity grew. Finally, the Argentine government felt forced to sign a number of trade agreements with Great Britain. This led to an upsurge in nationalist activity.

4 For each of the key points you raise in your introduction, you should be able to write one or two long paragraphs. Here, you should provide your supporting evidence. Be sure to also state the connection between what you have written and the political impact of the Great Depression on Argentina. An example of how one of the key points could be expanded is given below.

Because of the severity of the Great Depression, Hipólito Yrigoyen, the Radical candidate who won re-election in 1928, was not able to remain president for very long. In order to plug the holes caused by huge budget deficits, Yrigoyen had to cut public spending. This meant that many of his supporters lost their jobs, and Yrigoyen their support. His cabinet did not show unity in these difficult times but rather broke into warring factions. In September 1930, the military removed Yrigoyen from power. The president and many of his supporters were jailed. The 1930s became known as the Infamous Decade because of the lack of political democracy and the way in which the Conservatives wielded power. This was one example of how the Depression shook up the political system in Argentina.

5 In the final paragraph, you should tie your essay together, stating your conclusions. Do not raise any new points here or make reference to Argentina under Juan Perón, as he did not come to power until several years after the Great Depression. An example of a good concluding paragraph is given below.

In conclusion, the Great Depression greatly altered the political system in Argentina. The Conservatives ruled throughout the 1930s, effectively shutting out their traditional opponents, the Radicals. The power behind the Conservatives was the military which was ready to intervene if they felt the Conservatives were not following their orders. At the same time, new nationalist forces were beginning to organize because they believed unfavourable trade agreements gave away too much to foreign interests, particularly Great Britain. While the political impact may have been severe and democracy throttled, the economic impact was certainly less severe and long lasting than in other countries in the region.

6 Now try writing a complete answer to the question following the advice above.

 # Examination practice

Below are three exam-style questions for you to practise on this topic.

1 To what extent did Getúlio Vargas institute an authoritarian regime in Brazil during the Great Depression?
(For guidance on how to answer 'to what extent' questions, see page 44.)

2 Evaluate the effectiveness of Vargas in tackling Brazil's economic problems during the Depression.
(For guidance on how to answer 'evaluate' questions, see page 178.)

3 Compare and contrast the economic policies undertaken by Argentina and Brazil during the Depression.
(For guidance on how to answer 'compare and contrast' questions, see page 140.)

Timeline

Argentina

1916 April	Hipólito Yrigoyen became President of Argentina after first democratic election
1919 January	Tragic Week
1922 April	Alvear became president
1928 April	Yrigoyen restored to presidency
1930 September	Military coup in Argentina; beginning of *Concordancia*
1933 June	Roca–Runciman Agreements
July	London Economic Conference
1935 May	Central bank of Argentina set up
1936 August	Eden–Malbran Agreements
1940 January	Pinedo's economic reactivation plan
1943 June	Military coup

Brazil

1917 July	45,000 on strike in São Paulo
1922 July	*Tenetes* rebellion at Copacabana
1924 June	*Tenetes* rebellion in São Paulo
1930 October	Military coup; beginning of presidency of Getúlio Vargas
November	Vargas dissolved Congress
1931 February	*Clube 3 de Outabro* formed
1932 June	Beginning of Paulista war
1934 July	New constitution
1935 May	National Liberal Alliance set up
1936 January	Bureau of Repression set up
October	National Security Tribunal set up
1937 September	'Discovery' of Cohen Plan
October	Beginning of *Estado Novo*
1938 May	Integralist revolt
August	Administrative Department of the Civil Service (DASP) created
1940 January	Introduction of Five-Year Plan
1942 August	Entry into Second World War
1945 October	Overthrow of Vargas

Canada

1919 May–June	Winnepeg strikes
1921 December	Federal elections introduced new political force, the Progressive Party
1924 August	Communist Party of Canada founded
1926 October	Imperial Conference
1930 April	Mackenzie King's 'five cent' speech
July	Canadian election; beginning of premiership of R.B. Bennett
1932 May	Foundation of Co-operative Commonwealth Federation; Canadian Radio Broadcasting Commission set up
July–August	Ottawa Conference – Imperial Preference
1934 July	Bank of Canada set up
1935 January	Bennett's proposed 'New Deal' announced
1938 May	US–Canada trade agreements
1939 September	Entry into Second World War
1940 May	Rowell–Sirois Commission reported

USA

1921 November	Federal Highways Act
1922 September	Fordney–McCumber Act
1924 August	Dawes Plan
1929 March	Beginning of presidency of Herbert Hoover Young Plan
October	Wall Street Crash
1930 June	Hawley–Smoot Tariff
1931 June	Moratorium on foreign debts
1932 January	Reconstruction Finance Corporation set up
June	Bonus Army march on Washington
November	Hoover defeated in the 1932 presidential election
1933 March	Beginning of presidency of Franklin Delano Roosevelt Beginning of the 100 days
March–June	Alphabet Agencies set up
1935 May	Black Monday
August	Social Security Act
November	Roosevelt elected for a second term
1937 February	Roosevelt's battle with the Supreme Court (Judiciary Reform Bill)
June onwards	Roosevelt Recession
1941 December	Entry into Second World War

Glossary

Agricultural businesses   Large-scale farms using machinery and techniques of mass production.

Allotment   Each Native American family was given a plot of 160 acres to farm. This went against the traditional idea of common land ownership.

Alphabet agencies   New government bodies set up to tackle problems. They were so called because they became known by their initials, for example AAA, CCC.

American dream   The belief that everyone can be successful through hard work and effort.

American Federation of Labor   An organization representing American workers' unions.

American Medical Association   US doctors' professional association, governing medical practices.

Amerindians   Indigenous peoples of Argentina.

Anarcho-syndicalist groups   Groups who sought direct action, for example strikes and political violence, to achieve their aim of the overthrow of capitalist society.

Antipersonalist Radical Party   More conservative elements of the Radicals who were opposed to Yrigoyen.

Anti-trust legislation   Laws to break down trusts.

Argentine Exceptionalism   Belief that Argentina was destined to become the wealthiest and most influential state in Latin America.

Assimilation   The idea that Native Americans should adopt American lifestyles and values; their traditional way of life should disappear.

Axis   The alliance of Germany, Italy, Japan and other countries during the Second World War.

Bankrupt   When firms or individuals have insufficient money to pay their debts.

Belligerent countries   Countries involved in war.

Bilateral agreements   Agreements between two countries.

Blacklegs   People who break strikes by going into work.

Bluechip stocks   Shares in the biggest companies.

Broker   A person who buys and sells stocks and shares.

Budget deficit   Where the government spends more than it receives.

Bull pools   Method by which unscrupulous brokers bought and sold stocks to and from each other to keep prices high.

Capital investment   Putting money into the means by which goods may be produced, for example heavy machinery and factories.

Cartel   Group of companies agreeing to fix output and prices, to reduce competition and maximize their profits.

Census   Survey undertaken every 10 years to enumerate everyone in the country.

Chain gangs   Groups of convicts chained together while working outside the prison, for example in digging roadside drainage ditches.

Chaplinesque   Comedies in the form of those made by Charlie Chaplin (1889–1977).

Civilian Conservation Corps   An alphabet agency that employed young people to work on agricultural and conservation projects.

Collective bargaining   Discussions between employers and employees (usually represented by trade unions) about working conditions and pay.

Commonwealth   Countries of the former British Empire still closely associated with Britain, for example Canada and Australia.

Communists   People who believed that the planning and organization of the economy should be controlled by the state so people are rewarded according to the value of their contribution.

Conscription   Compulsory enlistment in the armed forces.

Conservatives   During the 1920s right-wing parties such as *Concentración Nacional* supported the right of traditional élites to govern and opposed political reform.

Consumer durables   Goods that can last a long time, for example, motor cars and electrical appliances.

Contour ploughing   Ploughing across hillsides so that the crested grooves retained the soil. Prior to this farmers had often ploughed up and down. In heavy rain the soil could get washed away.

Credit squeeze   When it is difficult to obtain credit.

Credit unions   Financial co-operatives, operating like local banks providing loans and credit to participants.

Crown Corporations   Organizations set up by the Canadian government to produce goods and services the private sector was unable to provide.

Customs Union   Agreement to abolish trade barriers between participating countries and raise those for other countries.

Dawes Plan 1924   Offered Germany scaled-down reparations and provided it with a loan of $250 million to help stabilize its currency.

Direct taxes   Taxes taken directly from income, for example income tax.

Dislocation of supplies   Where supplies of goods stop or become unreliable due to war conditions, for example.

Dollar diplomacy   The growth of American influence in a country through the power of its investment and trade.

Dominion status   Semi-independent within the British Empire.

Dopolavoro   Political organization for workers in Fascist Italy.

Dow Jones Industrial Average   An index showing how shares in the top 30 large companies have traded on the Wall Street Stock Market.

Egalitarian revolution   Revolution to make people more equal.

European fascist dictators   Extreme right-wing, nationalist leaders such as Hitler in Germany and Mussolini in Italy, who seemed to offer a viable alternative to democracy, and whose countries at the time seemed to be tackling the problems of the 1930s more successfully than the USA.

Executive Office of the President   The president's staff.

Executive Order   An order by which the president could force through any decision he made despite Congressional opposition.

Family allowances   Government money to parents to help with the cost of raising children.

Farm credits   System to make federal loans to farmers.

Farm lobby   Politicians and interest groups who put forward the farmers' case to the federal government and Congress.

Farmers' Holiday Association   A pressure group set up to improve pay and conditions for farmers.

Fascist   European-based movements associated with policies of extreme nationalism and racism which were spreading to the Americas.

Federal by-elections   Mid-term elections for vacant seats due to, for example, the death of an MP.

Federal inheritance tax   Government tax on the estate of the deceased.

Federal Trade Commission   Body charged to ensure businesses were operating fairly.

Feminists   Those who sought to improve women's opportunities.

Five-Year Plan   Where the government plans the economy, setting targets to be achieved over a five-year period.

Free market   A system that allows the economy to run itself with minimal government interference.

Gauchos   Workers on ranches, often cowboys.

Gallup Poll   A survey of people's views made by the Gallup organization.

Gold rush   Rapid movement of people to find gold in a particular area.

Gold Standard   Where the value of money is based on the amount of gold in the nation's reserves.

Government deficit spending   When the government spends more than it receives in income.

Government securities   Bonds and bills issued by the government to raise revenue.

Greenbelt communities   New towns in rural areas based on careful planning with residential, commercial and industrial sectors separated.

Gross national product (GNP)   The total value of goods and services produced in a country.

Hoboes   People who wandered around the USA in search of work.

Holding companies Where one huge company would obtain a controlling interest in smaller companies to control the market.

Horse-drawn Fords Ford motor vehicles with no fuel, pulled along by horses.

Imperial Preference Favourable trading arrangements within the British Empire.

Import Substitution Industrialization The development of domestic industry to avoid over-reliance on imported industrial goods.

Inauguration The ceremony that begins the president's term of office.

Inelastic market A market where demand for the product would remain despite price rises; usually involves staple and essential products such as bread.

'Infamous Decade' Name given to the 1930s because it seemed characterized by political corruption.

Integralists Members of the AIB.

Inter-state commerce Trade between different states.

Ku Klux Klan Racist group advocating white supremacy. It adopted methods of terror to intimidate other groups such as African-Americans and Jews. During the 1920s it was particularly prevalent in the southern and midwestern states.

Laissez-faire An approach where the government deliberately avoids getting involved in economic planning, thus allowing the free market to operate.

Lame duck presidency The period between one president coming to the end of his term and his successor taking over.

League of Social Reconstruction Group of Socialists proposing radical reforms and greater political education.

Legión Cívica Argentina Militia made up of nationalists and supporters of fascism.

Lynchings Illegal hangings, often used by the Ku Klux Klan as a means of terror.

Management science The application of technological and scientific ideas to running a company successfully – such as time and motion, where the amount of time it should take to complete a process in manufacturing is timed and subsequently monitored. The aim is to use scientifically proven methods to run the company.

Mass production Making large numbers of the same item using machinery and conveyor belts.

Means-tested benefits Where the levels of welfare benefits are based on the recipient's income.

Monetarist Economic theory that governments can control the economy through regulation of the money supply.

Moratorium Term given to Hoover's offer to postpone debt repayment for 18 months.

Mounties Nickname given to the Royal Canadian Mounted Police (RCMP), Canada's national police force.

Municipalities Smaller areas within provinces, for example towns and their hinterlands.

National debt The amount of money owed by the government.

Nationalization State ownership of an industry.

Neo-colonialism Where developed countries controlled aspects of other countries almost as if they were part of their empire.

New Deal President Roosevelt's programme to end the Depression and restore prosperity.

New Frontier President Kennedy's reform programme 1961–3.

New Left School of historians critical of the New Deal for not adopting more radical changes.

Oil concessions Involvement in foreign oil industries on favourable terms.

Old Republic Name given to the constitutional system of government that operated in Brazil from 1890 to 1930.

Open-market operations Buying and selling of government securities on the open market to control the monetary supply.

Pampas Vast Argentine grasslands, the heartlands of cattle ranching and wheat production.

Paper pesos Pesos in paper banknotes as opposed to gold pesos (pesos valued in gold had a greater value).

Patronage Political control through giving favours, for example government jobs.

Paulistas People from the state of São Paulo.

Payroll taxes Taxes paid by employers for each of their employees.

Per capita income Income per head of the population.

Populism   Nineteenth-century political movement favouring greater government intervention and policies such as nationalization of the railroads.

Porteños   Inhabitants of Buenos Aires, literally people of the port.

Positive discrimination   Where members of one group are favoured over those of others.

Price fixing   Where companies agree to fix prices between them, thereby preventing fair competition.

Primary products   Products that have not been manufactured, for example food products such as wheat and coffee.

Privy Council   Council made up of members of the British government and charged with interpreting matters of government such as which body holds which responsibilities.

Progressivism   Late nineteenth- and early twentieth-century political movement to expand the role of government in dealing with social and economic problems and tackle corruption and abuses.

Prohibition   The banning of the manufacture, transportation and sale of alcohol for consumption.

Provinces   Different political regions of Canada, such as Quebec and Ontario.

Public loans   Loans to the federal government, similar to war bonds.

Pump priming   Expression used to suggest that government spending would lead to economic growth.

Real wages   The value of wages in terms of how much they will actually buy.

Recession   Downturn in the economy.

Rediscount rate   The interest rate at which banks borrow money from the federal reserve banks.

Reparations   Under the post-war settlements Germany had been required to pay compensation of $33 billion or 132 billion marks to the victorious countries.

Repudiation of war debts   Where countries ceased repaying their war debts.

Residence qualifications   People had to be resident in a certain area for a specified period of time to qualify for benefits there.

Revenue Act   States how the government aims to raise money that year.

Riot Act   Call for demonstrators to disperse before the authorities use force.

'Roosevelt Recession'   Downswing in the economy associated with Roosevelt's cutbacks in government spending in 1937.

Rural Society   Alliance of powerful conservative cattle ranchers.

Russian Revolution   Communist revolution in Russia in 1917.

SA   Brown-shirted paramilitary organization in Nazi Germany.

Sales tax   Tax on purchased goods.

Screwball comedies   Absurd but very funny comedies with richly comic characters and crazy situations.

Sedition trial   Trial for those accused of trying to overthrow the government.

Separatism   Desire for self-government.

Share-croppers   Farmers who rented land and were paid by the landowners a percentage of what they produced.

Short-time working   Where the hours of work are reduced.

Show trial   Unfair trial of government opponents. Its purpose is to warn others of what might happen if they join in any protest.

Sigma symbol   The Greek letter (Σ) used as a symbol by the AIB.

Slash and burn   Cutting down and burning forests to create land for use in agriculture.

Slush funds   Money used for bribery and other fraudulent purposes.

Soap operas   Romantic serials, so called because many of the sponsors were soap companies.

Social Credit Party   A political party supporting the idea of social credit.

Social realism   Stories based on real life featuring real-life problems.

Social security   Relief and benefits for those in need of government support, for example the old and sick.

Staple exports   Exports of primary products such as wheat and timber.

State interventors   Officials appointed by Vargas to run Brazilian states after the state governments were suspended.

Subsistence   Minimum income necessary for survival.

Suffragists   Those who sought the vote for women.

Supranational   Involving more than one country. In this context, the Salta oilfield straddled the borders of Argentina and Bolivia.

Tariffs   Import and export duties.

Tenant farmers   People who rented the land they farmed.

Tenentes   Junior officers who wanted modernization and effective government in Brazil.

Ticker   Ticker-tape on which stocks and shares transactions were recorded.

Trusts   Companies that collude to control manufacture, supplies and prices to ensure that other firms cannot compete, thus guaranteeing maximum profits for themselves.

US Chamber of Commerce   Non-governmental organization responsible for speaking for business in the USA.

Valorization   Scheme first introduced in 1906 whereby the government would buy coffee and hold stocks until the international price rose.

Veterans' Administration   An organization to help ex-servicemen.

Vigilante groups   Groups who take the law into their own hands.

Voluntarism   The notion that business and state government should solve the Great Depression through their own voluntary efforts.

Wage labourers   People who worked for wages.

Welfare dependency   Where people come to rely on state benefits.

Winnepeg Grain Exchange   A Canadian market for selling wheat, barley and oats.

Work ethic   The feeling that people should work hard and the unemployed should go out and find a job. It derived from the notion that how well one worked was a sign of one's worth, both personally and socially.

'Yellow dog' clauses   Where employees had to agree not to join a labour union.

Young Plan 1929   Offered further scaled-down reparations to 37 billion marks, with annual payments to be made for 59 years.

Further reading

Canada

General texts

P. Berton, *The Great Depression: 1929–1939*, Anchor Canada, 2001
Helpful year-by-year examination of the Depression in Canada

J.M. Bumstead, *Peoples of Canada; Post Confederation History*, Oxford
University Press, 1992
An easy to read and comprehensive account.

A. Finkel, M. Conrad, with V. Strong-Borg, *History of the Canadian People*,
vol. 2, Copp, Clark, Pitman, 1993
Very good on economic and social developments with lots of easy to understand
data.

J.L. Finlay and D.N. Sprague, *The Structure of Canadian History*, Prentice-Hall,
1979
Useful for a longitudinal approach to Canadian history.

K. McNaught, *The Penguin History of Canada*, Penguin, 1978
Thorough and informative account, good on social and economic background.

N. Story, *The Oxford Companion to Canadian History and Literature*, Oxford
University Press, 1967
Still indispensible for quick reference.

Biography

J. Boyko, *Bennett: The Rebel Who Challenged and Changed a Nation*, Key Porter
Books, 2010
Sympathetic, comprehensive biography.

A. Levine, *King: A Life Guided by the Hand of Destiny*, Douglas & MacIntyre,
2011
Quite critical of the man although acknowledges King's political genius.

Latin America

L. Bethel (ed.), *The Cambridge History of Latin America*, vols IV and V,
Cambridge University Press, 1987
These volumes deal with Latin America 1870–1930. The Argentina chapter is
written by Rock (see below).

L. Bethel (ed.), *The Cambridge History of Latin America*, vol. VIII, Cambridge
University Press, 1991

L. Bethel (ed.), *The Cambridge History of Latin America*, vol. IX, Cambridge
University Press, 2008
These volumes deal with Brazil and Argentina during the 1930s; again the
Argentina chapter is written by Rock.

V. Bulmer-Thomas, *The Economic History of Latin America Since Independence*, Cambridge University Press, 2014
Thorough and accessible economic analysis with data well explained.

T.H. Holloway (ed.), *A Companion to Latin American History*, Blackwell, 2008
Modern essays on aspects of Latin American history. The chapter by J. Wolfe 'Populism and developmentalism' is very useful.

J. King (ed.), *Cambridge Companion to Modern Latin American Culture*, Cambridge University Press, 2004
Essays on the impact of cultural developments.

A. Knight and P. Drinot, eds. *The Great Depression in Latin America*, Duke, 2014
Ten insightful essays on the impact of the Depression on specific Latin American countries, as well as helpful overviews.

T.A. Meade, *A History of Modern Latin America*, Wiley-Blackwell, 2010
Emphasizes the role of class, ethnicity and gender in defining Latin American history.

E. Williamson, *The Pelican History of Latin America*, Penguin, 1992
Considers the continent as a whole, then examines individual countries.

Argentina

J.C. Brown, *A Brief History of Argentina*, Facts on File, 2003
Very readable yet thorough, useful vignettes giving different perspectives, for example on the popularity of Carlos Gardel.

M. Falcoff and R.H. Dolkart (eds), *Prologue to Perón*, University of California Press, 1975
Useful essays to explain how aspects of Argentine history in the 1930s and 1940s paved the way for the coming to power of Perón.

C.M. Lewis, *Argentina: A Short History*, Oneworld, 2002
An analytical approach that focuses on why Argentina appears not to have met its potential for development.

G. Nouzeilles and G. Montaldo (eds), *The Argentina Reader*, Duke University Press, 2002
Lots of excellent primary sources and analysis about Argentine developments.

D. Rock, *Argentina 1516–1982: From Spanish Colonization to the Falklands War*, University of California Press, 1992
Almost the standard text in English, indispensable reading on Argentina.

L.A. Romero, *A History of Argentina in the Twentieth Century*, Pennsylvania State University Press, 2002
Readable analytical approach translated from Spanish.

Brazil

J.M. Bello, *History of Modern Brazil 1889–1964*, Stanford University Press, 1966
Popular, if dated, history.

E. Bradford Burns, *A History of Brazil*, third edition, Columbia University Press, 1993
Very readable and comprehensive text.

B. Fausto, *A Concise History of Brazil*, Cambridge Concise Histories, 1999
Translated from Portuguese, probably the best short introduction.

R.M. Levine, *The Vargas Regime: The Critical Years 1934–38*, Columbia University Press, 1970
Argues that the period 1934–8 witnessed the last struggles of the states to avoid the transition to one-man rule.

R.M. Levine and J.J. Crocitti (eds), *The Brazil Reader*, Duke University Press, 1999
Lots of excellent primary sources relating to Brazilian development.

T.A. Meade, *A Brief History of Brazil*, Facts on File, 2003
Readable, and focuses on issues not always covered on other texts such as the role of women, and racial aspects in Brazil.

USA

General texts

H. Evans, *The American Century*, Jonathan Cape, 1998
Introductory thematic analyses, then examines events separately.

P. Johnson, *A History of the American Peoples*, Weidenfield & Nicholson, 1997
Right-wing and celebratory in style, but a very good read, Johnson applauds American capitalism.

M. Parrish, *Anxious Decades*, W.W. Norton, 1992
Comprehensive and readable account of the interwar period in the USA.

The 1920s

F.L. Allen, *Only Yesterday*, Harper & Row, 1931
Still very readable and entertaining journalistic account of the 1920s in the USA.

L. Moore, *Anything Goes*, Atlantic, 2009
A popular and lively account of the 1920s.

The Wall Street Crash and the coming of the Depression

L. Ahamed, *Lords of Finance: The 1929 Great Depression and the Bankers who broke the World*, William Heinemann, 2009
A modern interpretation of the onset of the Great Depression.

J.K. Galbraith, *The Great Crash*, Penguin, 1975
Still probably the most useful short, but specialized, account for students.

H. Hoover, *Memoirs: The Great Depression*, Macmillan, 1952
The former president's view of the Depression.

C.P. Kindleberger, *The World in Depression 1929–1939*, University of California Press, 1986
Economic-based account of the world in depression.

R. Sobell, *The Great Bull Market*, W.W. Norton, 1968
Banking and finance-based focus on the stock market of the 1920s and its collapse.

Biography

C. Black, *Franklin Delano Roosevelt: Champion of Freedom*, Weidenfield & Nicholson, 2003
Very supportive of FDR who, it is argued, transformed not only the USA but the world.

M.L. Faushold, *The Presidency of Herbert C Hoover*, University Press of Kansas, 1985
Sympathetic account of Hoover's presidency.

T. Morgan, *FDR*, Simon & Schuster, 1985
A standard popular biography of FDR.

M. Simpson, *Franklin D Roosevelt*, Basil Blackwell, 1989
Short and concise biography.

R.N. Smith, *Uncommon Man: The Triumph of Herbert Hoover*, Simon & Schuster, 1984
Takes the wider perspective on Hoover; sees the Depression in the light of his efforts to overcome it and achievements elsewhere.

The Depression and New Deal

A.J. Badger, *The New Deal: The Depression Years 1933–40*, Palgrave Macmillan, 1989
Exhaustive analysis of the New Deal, considering different aspects in turn.

R.A. Biles, *New Deal for the American People*, Northern Illinois University Press, 1991
Assesses the impact of the New Deal on people.

P. Conkin, *The New Deal*, Routledge & Kegan Paul, 1970
Accessible analysis from a left-wing perspective, arguing that the New Deal was a wasted opportunity to introduce radical changes to the USA.

B. Folsom, *New Deal or Raw Deal?: How FDR's Economic Legacy Has Damaged America*, Simon & Schuster, 2009
Very critical account which argues that the New Deal both wasted money and failed to solve the Depression.

S.M. Hanes and R.C. Hanes, *Great Depression and New Deal; Almanac*, Thomson Gale, 2003

S.M. Hanes and R.C. Hanes, *Great Depression and New Deal; Biographies*, Thomson Gale, 2003

S.M. Hanes and R.C. Hanes, *Great Depression and New Deal; Primary Sources*, Thomson Gale, 2003

S.M. Hanes and R.C. Hanes, *Great Depression and New Deal; Index*, Thomson Gale, 2003
The four volumes make up a comprehensive account of the Depression and New Deal.

D. Kennedy, *Freedom From Fear*, Oxford University Press, 1999
Exhaustive and clear analysis, possibly the definitive history of the 1930s in the USA.

J. Powell, *FDR's Folly: How Roosevelt and His New Deal Prolonged the Depression*, Three Rivers Press, 2003
Argues that the New Deal both prolonged the Depression and led to costly and unnecessary expansion in government.

S. Turkel, *Hard Times*, Pantheon, 1970
Excellent collection of oral histories from all perspectives.

Internet resources

- Dictionary of Canadian Biography online. Excellent for biographies of the major (and minor) characters in Canadian history: www.biographi.ca/index-e.html
- Useful for short accounts and themes: www.canadahistory.com
- Links to the Canadian National Archives: canadaonline.about.com
- Homepage for the US Library of Congress which contains many primary sources: catalog.loc.gov/
- Home to some very good economic-based perspectives on the Depression years and the effectiveness of the New Deal: http://www.forbes.com/2009/04/30/1930s-innovation-America-business-1930s_land.html

Films

The 1930s, 2009
Comprehensive five-DVD set on the Great Depression from PBS.

Gold Diggers of 1933, 1933
An example of the inconsequential musicals that aimed to help people to forget their problems.

Modern Times, 1936
Charlie Chaplin's devastating (and very funny) attack on the inhumanity of methods of industrial production.

The Dust Bowl, 2012
Director Ken Burns brings his recognizable documentarian outlook to the grim days of the Dust Bowl.

The Grapes of Wrath, 1940
John Ford's tragic but uplifting film version of the novel.

Internal assessment

The internal assessment is a historical investigation on a historical topic. Below is a list of possible topics on the Great Depression that could warrant further investigation. They have been organized by chapter theme.

Chapter 1: The USA in the 1920s: prosperity?

1 How did the automobile change US society in the 1920s?
2 To what extent was Hollywood a reflection of the Roaring Twenties?

Chapter 2: The Wall Street Crash and the causes of the Great Depression in the USA

1 What was the cultural impact of the Harlem renaissance?
2 Explain how Charles Ponzi's financial schemes cheated thousands out of their savings.

Chapter 3: President Hoover and the Great Depression

1 Why did General Douglas MacArthur forcibly remove the Bonus Army from Anacostia Flats?
2 What accounted for the rise of the Ku Klux Klan in the 1920s?

Chapter 4: The USA 1933–45: New Deals and economic recovery

1 How successful was the Liberty League in opposing Franklin Roosevelt?
2 What did the Federal Writers' Project accomplish?

Chapter 5: The Great Depression in Canada

1 What economic impact did the gold rushes in Ontario and British Columbia have on Canada's economy?
2 To what extent was the Ottowa Conference in 1932 a failure?

Chapter 6: The Great Depression in Latin America

1 How successful were the 1932 Roca–Runciman Agreements?
2 Why did many Brazilians find Plínio Salgado's Integralist Party attractive?

Index